INDIA'S ONLY COMMUNALIST

INDIA'S ONLY COMMUNALIST

In Commemoration of Sita Ram Goel

edited by
KOENRAAD ELST

VOICE OF INDIA
New Delhi

First Published 2005
First Reprint 2020

ISBN 978-81-85990-78-1

Published by Voice of India, 2/18, Ansari Road, New Delhi – 110 002.
Printed at Replika Press Pvt. Ltd.

Contents

Editor's Note

On 3 December 2003, in his home in Delhi, 82-year-old historian and publisher Sita Ram Goel passed away. Because of his leadership role on the side of Hindu and human values during the central ideological struggles of the second half of the 20th century, his family and friends have considered it fitting to bring out this commemoration volume in his honour. It contains 18 contributions written independently of one another, which I have brought into a more or less uniform format. Some are purely testimonial or biographical, others set out to continue his work by taking on historical or ideological controversies. Ideologically too, they span a spectrum from pro-Sangh to anti-Sangh and from a focus on economic or political to one on cultural or religious issues. This corresponds realistically to Mr. Goel's actual spectrum of interests and involvements.

Delhi, 10 March 2005 Koenraad Elst

1. The sagely activist

(What follows are the relevant parts of the interview with Pradeep Goel, published in *Hinduism Today*, July-September 2004.)

1.1. Transition

"Ardent atheist turned born-again Hindu, Sita Ram Goel committed the better part of his 82 years on Earth to restoring Hindu dignity."

Sita Ram Goel will be remembered by Hindus in India and around the world for a long time. For most of the last half of the twentieth century, he and mentor-friend Ram Swarup produced hundreds of books, articles and pamphlets extolling the glories of Hinduism while warning of its most malicious foes. They were a bold and outspoken twosome who published their works through the Voice of India (VOI), a publication house they created just for this purpose. Although both Sita Ram Goel and Ram Swarup have now passed away, the VOI is still active — dedicated exclusively to the promotion of issues important to the modern-day Renaissance of Hinduism, a cause for which Sita Ram Goel gladly and courageously dedicated his life.

Born on October 16, 1921, Sita Ram Goel finished his formal education with an MA in History in 1944 from the University of Delhi. Yet he spent his entire life pursuing and sharing a broad spectrum of knowledge on a variety of subjects. He was well versed in several languages and came to be respected as a scholar of literature, philosophy, religion, and sociology. By his own account, he drew his primary inspiration on all these subjects from the *Mahabharata*, the *Suttapitaka*, Plato and Sri Aurobindo.

Although he developed a keen interest in communism during his college years, he turned against the ideology in 1949 when he came to understand the plight of people living in communist Russia. After 1950, he committed himself to informing the Indian people of the real theory and practice of communism in Stalin's Russia and Mao's China. His careful and tediously researched work during this time rightly earned him a reputation as a formidable activist.

Rivals both respected and feared his mighty insights, which were too often too true and well-articulated to easily refute. Sita Ram Goel chose to fight his battles so far above the common, war-torn terrain of human emotions that contenders not matching his wit were left to look like fools. Hence, direct challenges to his writings were few, if any. The most damaging effect upon his work came from rivals following a strategy of "strangling by silence", a crafty tactic of blocking the publication of his name and his works. Such a passive confinement, however, was not nearly enough to stop his intellectual assault on anti-Hindu forces. The writings of Sita Ram Goel are alive and well today.

On December 3, 2003, at the age of 82, Sita Ram Goel passed away peacefully in his sleep following a long illness. It was a quiet end to a humble yet dynamic life dedicated to the revitalization of Hinduism and the evolution of India. We at *Hinduism Today* were honoured to have maintained a fruitful association with him for more than 20 years and will long remember our visits with him in New Delhi at his home and during his one visit with us here in Hawaii. He is survived by his two sons, Saroj Kumar Goel and Pradeep Kumar Goel.

Today, Pradeep manages the Voice of India, which is supported both by donations and by VOI profits which are invested back into publications. *Hinduism Today* correspondent Rajiv Malik recently chatted with Pradeep in New Delhi about his father, the state of Hinduism today and the prospects for India tomorrow. Here are some excerpts.

1.2. Interview with Pradeep Goel

When did you first realize your father was a Hindu activist?

In 1952 my father brought us to New Delhi from Calcutta. I was just seven years old then and too young to understand the kind of work he was doing. In 1964 there was some talk of his being arrested, but even at that time I was not really aware of what was going on. All I knew was that he had written a book criticizing Nehru, following the war with China, and a lot of people were getting upset. As time went on, my father brought together some Hindu scholars interested in defending Hindu society. This group stimulated the creation of the Voice of India in 1980. It was only then that I began to read my father's articles with interest and finally understood his work as a Hindu activist. At that time I was 35 years of age. Now I am 54.

What inspired your father to become an activist?

He felt that the Hindu society was going through a crisis and that a Hindu renaissance was necessary. He wanted to do his part in bringing about change, but gained the confidence and guidance to do so from Ram Swarup, his close friend and advisor. Together, these two men wrote pamphlets that were forceful and strong, with titles like *Hindu Society Under Siege*, *Defence of Hinduism*, and *Perversion of India's Political Parlance*. Eventually they decided that, to do this kind of controversial work, they needed their own publication house.

What was your father's most important contribution to the Hindu renaissance?

We are proud that he brought forward new ideas in defence of Hindu society, and that they were well written. We can now see that people from all over the country and around the world were affected by this literature. Even the RSS (Rashtriya Swayamsevak Sangh) and the

BJP (Bharatiya Janata Party), both Hindu nationalist organizations, used his literature. Not having such material themselves, they used Voice of India publications to give their positions substance.

What was the core of your father's message?

In the good old days, my father used to run an organization called the *Society for Defence of Freedom in Asia*. Ram Swarup, who was also associated with this organization, helped to bring about its focus. He proclaimed that humanity had suffered three terrible tragedies: Christianity, Islam and communism. Christianity is not now as bad as it used to be. The cruelties once practiced in the name of that religion have been eliminated by reforms. Now the only threat from the Christians comes from their missionary work. Because of the collapse of Soviet Russia, communism has also suffered a setback and has been weakened. The biggest danger humanity faces today comes from militant Islam. Sooner or later, we must take care of this threat that comes from these people. My father was saying this years ago. As I review his works today, I realize that his assessment of so many things was absolutely correct. He was ahead of his time.

Did you ever feel that your father and your family were in danger because of his work? Were there ever any threats?

I could not say that we were really ever in danger. We may have thought so at the time. But, yes, there were some threats. My father would get postcards saying he was indulging in anti-Muslim activities and that one day his sons and grandsons would be converted to Islam. Also, the fact that father's friends were frequently coming to him and advising him to act cautiously had us all a little worried. But he used to say that he had fulfilled his duties and was ready to face whatever consequences might come. He definitely had some spiritual power backing him up. All these threats that we received affected our family only monetarily, and only for a short time.

Was there one single incident that alarmed you more than the rest?

Yes, one incident stands out. We were working on the Hindi edition of Ram Swarup's book, *Understanding Islam Through Hadis.* We had finished printing the book and had taken it to the bindery. This bindery was located in the Muslim area of Old Delhi. Although a Hindu owned it, some of the workers there were Muslim. One Muslim boy saw the word *Hadis* in the title of the book and took it to a Muslim priest, who declared the book anti-Islam. About a hundred people then gathered around the bindery in protest, and the binder called my father on the phone saying, "These people want to burn down my shop!" The police picked up the son of the shop owner and took him to the police station for questioning. Because my father was the publisher of the book, he was also picked up. As a result of all this, our Hindu friends and well-wishers also gathered at the police station. That was a night of turmoil. Our whole family was quite disturbed and worried that father might be tortured. The next day was Sunday. A special court was convened to listen to our case. Although my father was released, the case took a long time to settle. It was introduced in 1987 and was finally settled sometime in 2000. In the end, all that happened was we were asked to delete certain portions of the book. We complied. But the antagonism of the whole incident really wore us down.

Did your father have a support group during troubled times?

Most of my father's Muslim and Christian friends deserted him when they came to know that his writings spoke against their religious beliefs. Although father put across his views in a very polite and analytical manner, there was often strong reaction. He used to say that just because he criticized Christianity, that did not mean he did not like Christians. He even invited critics to speak up against Hinduism in his same spirit. However, he did emphatically declare that it was clearly not fair to condemn Hinduism, then convert people from it. Back in the eighties, my father aggressively defended Hinduism when there was a mass conversion of Hindus [to Islam] at Meenakshipuram in South India. That one event was an important signal to my father that Hinduism was facing a major crisis and that something should be done to meet the challenge.

Tell us about your father? What kind of person was he?

He was a very simple man with very few requirements. His food was simple. His life was simple. When we provided him with a car on behalf of our business, we asked him many times to engage a driver, but he never did. He said that a driver would just waste a lot of time waiting around for him. My father's general approach to life was always very humanitarian. He never wanted anyone else to get held up because of him. When he was active, he never required people to come to his house for a meeting. Rather, he would go and meet them at a place of their choosing. Although he could have easily remained fully occupied writing his own books, he was always willing to help edit and organize the works of others. In fact, he used to insist that it was a part of his duty to promote the work of other deserving scholars. His first concern was to help the Hindu cause. He was a selfless man.

Can you tell us a little about your mother?

My mother was always at home looking after us and performing her *puja* (worship). She was a pious lady. Her primary duty was to take care of the family. She was not really concerned with what my father was doing. She had a high regard for Ram Swarup and took him to be an enlightened person. She always assumed that, because my father was always working with him, nothing could go wrong. She died in 1981.

How did your father's work impact you and the rest of his family?

By 1980 my father had fulfilled his familial obligations and had lived a full life. All of his children were married and further business dealings were of no interest to him. He told us that he wanted to go full-time into writing and explained why. "There are four types of debts", he said: "*bhuta rin, deva rin, pitra rin* and *rishi rin*. (*Rin* means 'debt'.) *Bhuta rin* is one's debt toward the ancestors. *Deva rin* is one's debt toward the Gods. *Pitra rin* is one's debt to the father, which includes taking care of the family. *Rishi rin* is one's debt to the saints and rishis." My father felt that he was at the stage in life when he should be working to settle his debt with the rishis and saints by spreading their message. He felt that the *vidya* (knowledge) of the rishis should be passed on to mankind. He used to emphasize that he was doing this work without hope of getting a reward or becoming famous.

(...)

Other well-known scholars have extracted extravagantly from my father's writings but have neglected to give him credit. This is plagiarism, no doubt. But my father used to insist that he was not bothered by it, so long as the right idea got promoted. Initially, I had our publication rights drawn up with a copyright clause, but my father directed me to remove it and let the people use the material any way they wanted.

Why did your father write only in English?

Many people asked my father why he did not write in Hindi. His response was that because the Christians and Muslims were using English to put forward their message, and the media supporting them was English-based, he felt it was appropriate that his work should be published in English. He also made the point that the people who spoke Hindi as a first language were already with him ideologically and did not need to be educated or persuaded.

(...)

How would you assess the current response to VOI publications?

Today, the response is quite satisfactory, but our publications are fairly low priced and therefore yield low profit margins for book sellers, which means the books are not usually kept in stock in the stores but rather are kept on display so that orders can be made directly to us by interested parties. Today, we have 95 titles in print. Twenty-nine are authored by Sita Ram Goel himself. To be honest, the literary value of a book has little significance in the book selling business. The physical value of the book is what counts. If you want books by Aurobindo, you have to buy them from the Aurobindo Ashram. They are not available anywhere else. Books on Gandhi are only published by the government. It is the same with most good Hindu literature. If Gita Press does not publish it, no one will. There is just not much money in it.

What guidelines did your father set up for you to do this work, yet make a good living and support your family?

My father's guidelines stipulated first that I fulfil my responsibilities to my family. Then as time and resources allowed, I was to perpetuate the services of the VOI. To earn my livelihood, I manage Biblia Impex, a book export business that my father formed in 1964 to provide financial security for our family. My father started Biblia Impex from a small table in a friend's office. He would sit on one side of the table, and his typist would sit on the other side. He was one of the first Indian publishers to send books abroad without asking for advance payment. Other export businesses would never do this. They would always require money in advance. My father understood European integrity. He knew they were trustworthy.

Father used to tell me that I should not work for more than I required. Years ago, I had an opportunity to purchase some properties that could have made us very wealthy, but I did not do so.

(...)

Can you summarize your father's legacy?

My father created an awareness of certain surreptitious forces threatening Hinduism and the fundamental culture of India. He made it his life's mission to expose the real intentions of people who were disguised as benefactors but were secretly intent upon serving selfish ends. In his book entitled *Hindu Society Under Siege*, he clearly laid out how we Hindus are under attack from many fronts. He emphasized that the biggest problem was a lack of awareness of the problem. He and Ram Swarup were always challenging Christian and Islamic tactics, and in their analyses of these strategies did much to clarify Hinduism. Initially people did not know how to compare Hinduism with Christianity and Islam. People assumed that because the Christians set up hospitals and schools, they were good people with well-meaning intentions. They did not understand that they might have ulterior motives.

My father realized that, to expose these Christian missionaries, it was necessary to analyze their literature and critique them in a logical manner. This in itself was a big revelation that brought about many positive results. The people also did not understand Islam. None of us knew about Mohammed Sahib, Akbar, Babar and Aurangzeb. We just thought that they were rulers of India. We had no idea about the many injustices they had ruthlessly inflicted upon

Hindus. Ram Swarup and my father presented the activities of these people clearly and within a historical perspective. They won our hearts with their minds.

(On 13 January 2005, Shri Pradeep Goel himself left this world, unexpectedly and too soon. The care for his father's publishing house passed on to his son and his brother.)

2. India's only communalist: A brief biography of Sita Ram Goel

Koenraad Elst

2.1. Is there a communalist in the hall?

A lot of people in India and abroad talk about "communalism", often in grave tones, describing it as a threat to secularism, to regional and world peace. But can anyone show us a communalist? If we look more closely into the case of any so-called communalist, we find that he turns out to be something else.

Could Syed Shahabuddin be a communalist? After all, he played a key role in the three main "Muslim communalist" issues of recent years: the Babri Masjid campaign, the Shah Bano case and the Salman Rushdie affair (it was he who got *The Satanic Verses* banned in September 1988). Surely, he must be India's communalist par excellence? Wrong: if you read any page of any issue of Shahabuddin's monthly *Muslim India*, you will find that he brandishes the notion of "secularism" as the alpha and omega of his politics, and that he directs all his attacks against Hindu "communalism". The same propensity is evident in the whole Muslim "communalist" press, e.g. the Jamaat-i Islami weekly *Radiance*. Moreover, on *Muslim India*'s editorial board, you could find articulate secularists like Inder Kumar Gujral, Khushwant Singh and the late P.N. Haksar.

For the same reason, any attempt to label the All-India Muslim League as communalist would be wrong. True, it is the continuation of the party which achieved the Partition of India along communal lines. Yet, emphatically secularist parties like the Congress Party and the Communist Party of

India (Marxist) have rarely hesitated to include the Muslim League in coalitions governing the state of Kerala. No true communalist would get such a chance.

On the Hindu side then, at least the *Rashtriya Swayamsevak Sangh* (RSS, "National Volunteer Corps") could qualify as "communalist"? Certainly, it is called just that by all its numerous enemies. But then, when you look through any issue of its weeklies *Organiser* and *Panchjanya*, you will find it brandishing the notion of "positive" or "genuine secularism", and denouncing "pseudo-secularism", i.e. minority communalism. Moreover, in order to prove its non-communal character, it even calls itself and its affiliated organizations (trade-union, student organization, political party etc.) "National" or "Indian" rather than "Hindu". The allied political party, the *Bharatiya Janata Party* (BJP, "Indian People's Party"), shows off the large number of Muslims among its cadres to prove how secular and non-communal it is. Even the Shiv Sena shows off its token Muslims. No, for full-blooded communalists, we have to look elsewhere.

There is only one man in India whom I have ever known to say: "I am a (Hindu) communalist." To an extent, this is in jest, as a rhetorical device to avoid the tangle in which RSS people always get trapped: being called "communalist!" and then spending the rest of your time trying to prove to your hecklers what a good secularist you are. But to an extent, it is because he accepts at least one definition of "communalism" as applying to himself, esp. to his view of India's history since the 7th century. Many historians try to prove their "secularism" by minimizing religious adherence as a factor of conflict in Indian history, and explaining so-called religious conflicts as merely a camouflage for socio-economic conflicts. By contrast, the historian under consideration accepts, and claims to have thoroughly documented, the allegedly "communalist" view that the major developments in medieval and modern Indian history can only be understood as resulting from an intrinsic hostility between religions.

Unlike the Hindutva politicians, he does not seek the cover of "genuine secularism". While accepting the notion that Hindu India has always been "secular" in the adapted Indian sense of "religiously pluralistic", he does not care for slogans like the Vishva Hindu Parishad's advertisement: "Hindu India, secular India". After all, in Nehruvian India the term "secular" has by now acquired a specific meaning far removed from the original European usage, and even from the above-mentioned Indian adaptation. If Voltaire, the secularist par excellence, were to live in India today and repeat his attacks on the Church, echoing the Hindutva activists in denouncing the Churches' grip on public life in christianized pockets like Mizoram and Nagaland, he would most certainly be denounced as "anti-minority" and hence "anti-secular".

In India, the term has shed its anti-Christian bias and acquired an anti-Hindu bias instead, a phenomenon described by the author under consideration as an example of the current "perversion of India's political parlance". Therefore, he attacks the whole Nehruvian notion of "secularism" head-on, e.g. in the self-explanatory title of his Hindi booklet *Saikyularizm: Râshtradroha kâ Dûsra Nâm* ("Secularism: the Alternative Name for Treason"). The name of India's only self-avowed communalist is Sita Ram Goel. Our position is that he is one of the bravest and most important intellectuals in modern India.

2.2. Formative years

Sita Ram Goel was born on 16 October 1921 in a poor household, though belonging to the merchant Agrawal caste, in Chhara, a village in Haryana. As a schoolboy, he got acquainted with the traditional Vaishnavism practised by his family, with the Mahabharata and the lore of Garibdas and other Bhakti saints, and with the major trends in contemporary Hinduism, especially the Arya Samaj and Gandhism. He took an MA in History at Delhi University, winning prizes and scholarships along the way. In his school and early university days he was a Gandhian activist, helping a Harijan Ashram in his village and organizing a study circle in Delhi.

In the 1930s and 40s, the Gandhians themselves came in the shadow of the new ideological vogue: socialism. When they started drifting to the Left and adopting socialist rhetoric, S.R. Goel decided to opt for the original rather than the imitation. In 1941 he accepted Marxism as his framework for political analysis. At first, he did not join the Communist Party of India, and had differences with it over such issues as the creation of the religion-based state of Pakistan, which was actively supported by the CPI but could hardly earn the enthusiasm of a progressive and atheist intellectual. He and his wife and first son narrowly escaped with their lives in the Great Calcutta Killing of 16 August 1946, organized by the Muslim League to give more force to the Pakistan demand.

In 1948, just when he had made up his mind to formally join the Communist Party of India, in fact on the very day when he had an appointment at the party office in Calcutta to be registered as a candidate-member, the Government of West Bengal banned the CPI because of its hand in an ongoing armed rebellion. A few months later, his friend Ram Swarup came to stay with him in Calcutta and converted him as well as his employer, Hari Prasad Lohia, out of Communism. Goel's career as a combative and prolific writer on controversial matters of historical fact can only be understood in conjunction with Ram Swarup's sparser, more reflective writings on fundamental doctrinal issues.

2.3. With Ram Swarup against Communism

Born on 12 October 1920 as the son of a private banker in Sonipat, Haryana, Ram Swarup (formally Ram Swarup Garg, his gotra name, and equally belonging to the Agrawal caste) earned a degree in Economics from Delhi University in 1941. He joined the Gandhian movement and acted as the overground contact or "postbox" for some underground activists including Aruna Asaf Ali during the Quit India agitation of 1942. He spent a week in custody when a letter bearing his name was found in the house of another activist. After his release and until 1944, he worked as a clerk in an American office set up in Delhi to coordinate the Allied war effort against Japan.

Meanwhile, his wit made him quite popular in progressive circles. He was a declared socialist, a great fan of Aldous Huxley and a literary imitator of George Bernard Shaw. In 1944, he started the "Changers' Club", alluding to Karl Marx's dictum that philosophers have interpreted the world instead of changing it. Of course, it was never more than a discussion forum for a dozen young intellectuals, including the future diplomat L.C. Jain, the future Planning Commission member Raj Krishna, future *Times of India* editor Girilal Jain, and Sita Ram Goel. At that time, Ram Swarup was a committed atheist, and in the Changers' Club manifesto he put it in so many words: "Butter is more important than God." In 1947, the club disbanded because its members plunged into real life.

In 1948-49, Ram Swarup worked for Mahatma Gandhi's English disciple Mira Behn, née Madeleine Slade, when she retired to Rishikesh to edit her correspondence with Gandhiji, a project that was not completed. He would continue to explore the relevance of Gandhism to real-life problems (even as late as 1977, in his booklet *Gandhian Economics*), as an alternative to the ideology which was rapidly gaining ground among the intelligentsia around him: Communism. Just about the time of Independence, Ram Swarup developed strong opinions about Communism. When the CPI defended the Partition scheme with contrived socio-economic arguments, he objected that the Partition would only benefit the haves among the Muslims, not the have-nots. He moved in a direction opposite to the ideological fashion of the day, and became one of India's leading anti-Communists.

It is at this point that he came to "save" his friend Goel from the temptation of totalitarianism. Ram Swarup's first books,

Let Us Fight the Communist Menace (1949) and *Russian Imperialism: How to Stop It* (1950), were published by Prachi Prakashan, an anti-Communist publishing house which he and Goel set up in Calcutta as part of their *Society for the Defence of Freedom in Asia* (SDFA).

The books drew attention in high places. In 1949, Home Minister Sardar Vallabhbhai Patel decided to found a think-tank specifically devoted to monitoring Communism, the *Democratic Research Service*, formally started in November 1950. It was sponsored by the industrialist Birla family, and initially led by the later Prime Minister (1977-79) Morarji Desai, who passed the job on to Minoo Masani. It was as secretary of the DRS that Ram Swarup prepared a *History of the Communist Party of India*, which Masani published in his own name. A lot of bad blood developed between them, so that later, in his memoirs of the anti-Communist struggle, *Against the Tide* (Vikas, Delhi 1981), Masani managed to leave Ram Swarup and Sita Ram Goel unmentioned. Ram Swarup quit the DRS to rejoin Goel in Calcutta.

Though routinely accused of being lavishly financed by the CIA, the SDFA started with just Rs.30,000, half of which was brought in by Goel personally, and continued its work with the help of donations by Hari Prasad Lohia and other friends, its budget seldom exceeding Rs.10,000. It published some important studies, which were acclaimed by leading anti-Communists in the West and Taiwan, and on one occasion vehemently denounced in the *Pravda* and the *Izvestia*. Until its closing in December 1955, the centre was the main independent focus of ideological opposition to Communism in the Third World. Ram Swarup's book *Gandhism and Communism* (1954), which emphasized the need to raise the struggle against Communism from a military to a moral and ideological level, was brought to the attention of Western anti-Communists including several US Congressmen, and some of its ideas were adopted by the Eisenhower administration in its agenda for the Geneva Conference in 1955.

In some ways, Ram Swarup was Sita Ram Goel's polar opposite. He was a quiet and reflective type of person. He never married, never went into business, hardly ever had a job, never stood for an election. He had been living with the Lohia family in their Calcutta or Delhi property since 1949; only in his last years did he move to his deceased brother's house. At any rate, his biography was not very eventful apart from his daily yoga practice and his pioneering intellectual work.

Much later, in a speech before the Yogakshema society, Calcutta 1983, Sita Ram Goel explained his relation with Ram Swarup as follows (*The Emerging National Vision*, p.1.): "In fact, it would have been in the fitness of things if the speaker today had been Ram Swarup, because whatever I have written and whatever I have to say today really comes from him. He gives me the seed-ideas which sprout into my articles. (...) He gives me the framework of my thought. Only the language is mine. The language also would have been much better if it was his own. My language becomes sharp at times; it annoys people. He has a way of saying things in a firm but polite manner, which discipline I have never been able to acquire."

2.4. Anti-Communist publications

S.R. Goel's first important publications were part of the work of the SDFA:

* *World Conquest in Instalments* (1952, an annotated reprint of chapters 3 and 7 of Josef Stalin's *Foundations of Leninism*, 1924);
* *The China Debate: Whom Shall We Believe?* (1953);
* *Mind Murder in Mao-land* (1953);
* *China is Red with Peasants' Blood* (1953);
* *Red Brother or Yellow Slave?* (1953);
* *Communist Party of China: a Study in Treason* (1953);
* *Conquest of China by Mao Tse-tung* (1954, an annotated reprint of some of Mao's writings on strategy);

* *CPI Conspire for Civil War* (1954);
* *Netaji and the CPI* (1955);
* *Nehru's Fatal Friendship* (1955).

Goel also published books on Communism by other authors, including *Blowing Up India: Reminiscences of a Comintern Agent* by Philip Spratt (1955), who, as an English Comintern agent, had founded the Communist Party of India in 1926. After spending some time in prison as a convict in the Meerut Conspiracy case (1929), Spratt had come under the influence of Mahatma Gandhi, and ended as one of the best-informed critics of Communism.

Then, and all through his career as a polemical writer, the most remarkable feature of Sita Ram Goel's position in the Indian intellectual arena was that nobody even tried to offer a serious rebuttal to his theses. The only counter-strategy has always been, and still is, "strangling by silence", simply refusing to ever mention his name, publications and arguments.

An aspect of history yet to be studied is how such anti-Communist movements in the Third World were not at all helped, and in fact often opposed, by Western interest groups whose understanding of Communist ideology and strategy was just too superficial. Most US representatives starkly ignored the SDFA's work, and preferred to enjoy the company of more prestigious (implying: fashionably anti-anti-Communist) opinion makers in India. Goel himself noted in 1961 (*Genesis and Growth of Nehruism*, p.212) about his Western anti-Communist contacts like Freda Utley, Suzanne Labin and Raymond Aron, who were routinely dismissed as bores or CIA agents: Communism was "opposed only by individuals and groups who have done so mostly at the cost of their reputation. (...) A history of these heroes and their endless endeavour has still to be written."

In the 1950s, Goel was not active on the "communal"

battlefield: not Islam or Christianity but Communism was his priority target. Yet, under Ram Swarup's influence, his struggle against Communism became increasingly rooted in Hindu spirituality, the way Aleksandr Solzhenitsyn's anti-Communism became rooted in Orthodox Christianity. Gradually, they moved from the Gandhian version of Hinduism to a more comprehensive understanding of the ancient Hindu tradition.

Goel also co-operated with (but was never a member of) the Bharatiya Jana Sangh, the RSS-affiliated political party, and he occasionally contributed articles on Communism to the RSS weekly *Organiser.* In 1957 he contested the Lok Sabha election for the Khajuraho constituency as an independent candidate on a BJS ticket, but lost. He was one of the thirty independents fielded as candidates by Minoo Masani in preparation for the creation of his own pro-Western and anti-socialist *Swatantra Party*, which was to become the leading opposition party in the late 1960s, only to fade away during the Emergency in 1975. Masani had selected Goel for being one of the rare men deemed able to stand up to Nehru in parliamentary debate.

2.5. Sita Ram Goel and the RSS

In 1952-60, apart from the topical SDFA books in English, Goel wrote and published 18 titles in Hindi: 8 titles of fiction and 1 of poetry written by himself; 3 compilations from the Mahabharata and the Tripitaka; and Hindi translations of these 6 books, mostly of obvious ideological relevance:

* *The God that Failed*, a testimony on Communism by Arthur Koestler, André Gide and other prominent ex-Communists;
* Ram Swarup: *Communism and Peasantry*;
* Viktor Kravchenko: *I Chose Freedom*, another testimony by an ex-Communist;

* George Orwell's *Nineteen Eighty-Four*;
* *Satyakam Sokratez* ("Truth-lover Socrates"), the three Dialogues of Plato centred round Socrates' last days, i.e. the *Apology*, *Crito* and *Phaedo*;
* *Shaktiputra Shivaji*, a history of the seventeenth-century Hindu freedom fighter, originally *The Grand Rebel*, by Denis Kincaid.

There is an RSS aspect to this publishing activity. RSS secretary-general Eknath Ranade had asked Goel to educate RSS workers about literature, and to produce some literature in Hindi to this end. The understanding was that the RSS would propagate this literature and organize discussions about it. Once Goel had set up a small publishing outfit and published a few books, he had another meeting with Ranade, who gave him an unpleasant surprise: "Was the RSS created to sell your books?" Fortunately for Goel, his friend Guru Dutt Vaidya and son Yogendra Dutt included Goel's books in the fund of their own publishing-house, Bharati Sahitya Sadan. This is Goel's own version, and Ranade is not there to defend himself; but Goel's long experience in dealing with the RSS leadership translates into a list of anecdotes of RSS petty-mindedness, unreliability and lack of proper manners in dealing with fellow-men, especially fellow Hindu activists.

In May 1957, Goel moved to Delhi and got a job with a state-affiliated company, the Indian Co-operative Union, for which he did research and prospection concerning cottage industries. The company also loaned him for a while to the leading Gandhian activist Jayaprakash Narayan, who shared Goel's anti-Communism at least at the superficial level. His was the position that used to be called "anti-Stalinism": rejecting the means but not the ends of Communism.

During the Chinese invasion in 1962, some leftist politicians including P.N. Haksar, Nurul Hasan and I.K. Gujral (the later Prime Minister, 1997-98), demanded Goel's arrest. But at the same time, the Home Ministry invited him to take a leadership role in the plans for a guerrilla war against the then widely-expected Chinese occupation of eastern India. He made his co-operation conditional on Nehru's abdication as Prime Minister, and nothing ever came of it.

In 1961-62, Goel wrote a series in *Organiser* under the pen name *Ekaki* ("solitary"), criticizing Nehru's consistent pro-Communist policies. In 1963, he had it published as a book under his own name: *In Defence of Comrade Krishna Menon.* An update of this book was published in 1993: *Genesis and Growth of Nehruism.* In it, he questioned the current fashion of attributing India's Communist-leaning foreign policy to Defence Minister Krishna Menon, and demonstrated that Nehru himself had been a consistent Communist sympathizer ever since his visit to the Soviet Union in 1927.

Nehru had stuck to his Communist sympathies even when the Communists insulted him as Prime Minister with their unbridled scatology. He was too British and too bourgeois to opt for a fully authoritarian socialism, but like many European Leftists he supported just such regimes when it came to foreign policy. Thus, Nehru's absolute refusal to support the Tibetans even at the diplomatic level when they were overrun by the Chinese army ("a Far-Eastern Munich", according to Minoo Masani: *Against the Tide*, p.45), cannot just be attributed to circumstances or the influence of his collaborators: his hand-over of Tibet to Communist China was quite consistent with his own political convictions. While refuting the common explanation that the pro-Communist bias in Nehru's foreign policy was merely the handiwork of Minister Krishna Menon, Goel also drew attention to the harmfulness of this policy to India's national interests.

For all its pertinence and depth, the article serial in *Organiser* was discontinued after sixteen instalments because RSS overseers Eknath Ranade and Atal Behari Vajpayee feared that if any harm came to Nehru, the RSS would be accused of having "created the climate", as in the Mahatma Gandhi murder case. Next, though Goel's critique of Nehru's pro-

China policies was eloquently vindicated by the Chinese invasion in October 1962, it also cost him his job. He withdrew from the political debate, went into business himself and set up Impex India, a company of book export with a modest publishing capacity.

In 1964, RSS general secretary Ranade invited Goel to lead the prospective Vishva Hindu Parishad, founded later that year. Goel set as his condition that he would be free to speak his own mind rather than act as a mouthpiece of the RSS leadership. The RSS could not accept this, and the matter ended there.

Goel's only subsequent involvement in politics was in 1973 when he was asked by the Jana Sangh leadership to mediate with the dissenting party leader Balraj Madhok in a last attempt at conciliation (which failed); and in the opposition to Indira Gandhi's Emergency regime in 1975-77. Though he was under watch and his correspondence was censored, he managed to stay out of the Emergency jails and worked as a member of the think-tank of the Janata alliance until it defeated Mrs. Gandhi in the 1977 elections.

2.6. Sita Ram Goel as a Hindu Revivalist

As a commercial publisher, Goel did not seek out the typical "communal" topics, but nonetheless kept an eye on Hindu interests. That is why he published books like Dharampal's *The Beautiful Tree* (1983, on indigenous education as admiring British surveyors found it in the 19th century, before it was destroyed and replaced with the British or missionary system); Ram Swarup's apology of polytheism, *The Word as Revelation* (1980, republished by Voice of India, 2001); K.R. Malkani's *The RSS Story* (1980); and K.D. Sethna's *Karpasa in Prehistoric India* (1981; on the chronology of Vedic civilization, implying decisive objections against the Aryan Invasion Theory). It may also be said that he thrived as a businessman and earned considerable wealth, an asset which was to make possible the next step.

In 1981 Sita Ram Goel retired from his business, which he handed over to one of his sons and one of his nephews. With donations from sympathizing businessmen, he started the non-profit publishing house Voice of India. In a later stadium, when its reputation had been established, it would attract contributions from a variety of historians and thinkers. But initially its main purpose was to provide a platform to Ram Swarup:

* *Hinduism vis-à-vis Christianity and Islam* (1982, revised 1992, also in Hindi: *Hindû Dharma, Isâiat aur Islâm*, 1985);
* *Understanding Islam through Hadis: Religious Faith or Fanaticism?* (1983, revised by court order 2001);
* *Buddhism vis-à-vis Hinduism* (revised 1984, originally 1958, a reflection occasioned by the mass conversion of Dalits led by Dr. Bhimrao Ambedkar to Buddhism in 1956);
* Introduction to a republication of D.S. Margoliouth: *Mohammed and the Rise of Islam* (1985, original in 1905);
* *Hindu-Sikh Relationship* (1985);
* *Ramakrishna Mission in Search of a New Identity* (1986, occasioned by the RK Mission's symptomatic attempt to redefine itself as a non-Hindu religion);
* *Cultural Alienation and Some Problems Hinduism Faces* (1987);
* Introduction to Anirvan: *Inner Yoga* (1988, reprint 1995);
* Introduction to the republication of Sardar Gurbachan Singh Talib, ed.: *Muslim League Attack on Sikhs and Hindus in the Punjab* 1947 (1991), also separately published as *Whither Sikhism?* (1991);
* Foreword to a republication of William Muir: *The Life of Mahomet* (1992, original in 1894);
* *Hindu View of Christianity and Islam* (1992, a republication of the above-mentioned introductions to

books on Mohammed by Muir and Margoliouth plus an enlarged version of *Hinduism vis-à-vis Christianity and Islam*);

* *Woman in Islam* (1994);
* *Pope John-Paul II on Eastern Religions and Yoga: A Hindu-Buddhist Rejoinder* (1995);
* *On Hinduism: Reviews and Reflections* (a collection of essays posthumously published, 2000);
* *Meditations: Yogas, Gods, Religions* (a collection of essays posthumously published, 2000).

Goel also accepted *Organiser* editor K.R. Malkani's offer to contribute some articles once more, and these articles were later collected into Voice of India booklets. Apart from numerous articles, letters, contributions to other books (e.g. Devendra Swarup, ed.: *Politics of Conversion*, Deendayal Research Institute, Delhi 1986) and translations (e.g. the Hindi version of Taslima Nasrin's Bengali book *Lajja*, published in instalments in *Panchjanya*, summer 1994), Goel has contributed the following books to Indian historiography and the inter-religious debate through Voice of India:

* *Hindu Society under Siege* (1981, revised 1992);
* *Story of Islamic Imperialism in India* (1982, revised 1994);
* *How I Became a Hindu* (1982, enlarged 1993);
* *Defence of Hindu Society* (1983, revised 1987 and 1994);
* *The Emerging National Vision* (1983);
* *Heroic Hindu Resistance to Muslim Invaders* (1984, revised 1994);
* *Perversion of India's Political Parlance* (1984, revised 1995);
* *Saikyularizm, Râshtradroha kâ Dûsrâ Nâm* (Hindi: "Secularism, another name for treason", 1985), also available in English translation by Yashpal Sharma as *India's Secularism, New Name for National Subversion* (1999);

* *Papacy, Its Doctrine and History* (1986);
* Preface to *The Calcutta Quran Petition by Chandmal Chopra* (a collection of texts alleging a causal connection between communal violence and the contents of the Quran; 1986, enlarged 1987 and again 1999);
* *Muslim Separatism, Causes and Consequences* (1985, revised and enlarged 1995);
* Foreword to *Catholic Ashrams, Adapting and Adopting Hindu Dharma* (a collection of polemical writings on Christian inculturation, 1988, enlarged 1994 with a new subtitle: *Sannyasins or Swindlers?*);
* *History of Hindu-Christian Encounters* (1986, enlarged 1996);
* *Hindu Temples, What Happened to Them* (1990 vol.1, enlarged 1998; 1991 vol.2, enlarged 1993);
* *Genesis and Growth of Nehruism* (1993, a revised reprint with new preface of the book *In Defence of Comrade Krishna Menon*, 1963);
* *Jesus Christ: An Artifice for Aggression* (1994);
* *Time for Stock-Taking* (1997), a collection of articles critical of the RSS and BJP;
* Introduction to the reprint of Matilda Joslyn Gage: *Woman, Church and State* (1997, ca.1880), an early feminist critique of Christianity;
* Introduction to *Vindicated by Time. The Niyogi Committee Report on Christian Missionary Activities* (1998, reprint of the full report from 1956);
* *Pseudo-Secularism, Christian Missions and Hindu Resistance* (1998), the separately available editorial introduction to *Vindicated by Time.*

Goel's declared aim was to defend Hinduism by placing before the public correct information about the situation of Hindu culture and society, and about the nature, motives and strategies of its enemies. For, as the title of his book *Hindu Society under Siege* indicates, Goel claimed that Hindu society has been suffering a sustained attack from Islam since the 7th century, from Christianity since the 15th century, in the 20th century also from Marxism, and that all three have carved out a place for themselves in Indian society from which they besiege Hinduism. The avowed objective of each of these three world-conquering movements, with their massive resources, was diagnosed as being the replacement of Hinduism with their own ideology, or in effect: the destruction of Hinduism.

Goel's writings have always been as good as boycotted in the media, both by reviewers and by journalists and scholars collecting background information on the communal problem. An exception of sorts is Mitsuhiro Kondô's paper "Hindu Nationalists and their Critique of Monotheism: The Relationship between Nation, Religion and Violence", included in Mushirul Hasan & Nariaki Nakazato: *The Unfinished Agenda* (Manohar, Delhi 2001, pp.79-100), partly based on an interview by the young woman scholar from Japan with Goel at his house in March 1998. For objectivity and a correct rendering of the Hindu positions discussed, it is better than most academic papers on any aspect of "Hindu communalism", but still seriously wanting (as I have argued in a review included in my book *Ayodhya: The Case Against the Temple*, Voice of India, Delhi 2002, pp.189-196).

Physical methods to silence Sita Ram Goel and his school of thought have been tried only sporadically, probably because rioters and terrorists rarely read a book and thus spare themselves any indignation over its contents. On one occasion, the police had to be called when a Muslim mob gathered at the binders' workshop where the freshly printed Hindi translation of Ram Swarup's book *Understanding Islam through Hadis: Religious Faith or Fanaticism?* was being bound. In October 1990, the Hindi version of the book was banned by court order, followed by the English version in March 1991, all for the sake of preventing communal tension. In 2001, the book was unbanned and republished after a few passages had been removed, as directed by the court.

In 1993, Syed Shahabuddin, who had managed to get Salman Rushdie's provocative novel *The Satanic Verses* banned in India, tried to get Ram Swarup's book *Hindu View of Christianity and Islam* banned as well. A prompt reaction by Arun Shourie in his weekly newspaper column and a petition of intellectuals led by Prof. K.S. Lal contributed to the defeat of this attempt. People had not forgotten the result of Shahabuddin's earlier book-banning endeavour, which spinned out of control to entail violent demonstrations in many countries, an Islamic death sentence against the author and several murders and murder attempts on people connected with the book's distribution. So, even the secularists who had supported Shahabuddin on that occasion were in no mood for a repeat performance. They simply looked the other way. Why should they bother to intervene in such a conspicuous manner, one which would only draw attention to the offending book? After all, their dominance in the academic institutions and the media could ensure that very few people would ever get to hear of the book's existence.

2.7. Differences with the RSS outlook on hostile religions

Though most Hindutva stalwarts have some Voice of India publications on their not-so-full bookshelves, the RSS Parivar is reluctant to offer its organizational omnipresence as a channel of publicity and distribution. Since most India watchers have been brought up on the belief that Hindu activism can be identified with the RSS family of organizations, they are bound to label Sita Ram Goel (the day they condescend to mentioning him at all, that is) as "an RSS man". It may, therefore, surprise them that the established Hindu organizations have so far shown only limited interest in his work.

It is not that they would spurn his services, though. In its Ayodhya campaign, the Vishva Hindu Parishad has routinely referred to a "list of 3000 temples converted into or replaced by mosques", meaning the list of nearly 2000 such cases collected and presented in Goel, ed.: *Hindu Temples*, vol.1. Goel also published the VHP argumentation in the government-sponsored scholars' debate of 1990-91 (titled *History vs. Casuistry*), and he straightened and corrected the BJP's clumsily drafted *White Paper on Ayodhya*. But organizationally, the Parivar is not using its networks to spread Ram Swarup's and Sita Ram Goel's books and ideas. Twice, in 1962 and 1982, the RSS leadership intervened with the editor of *Organiser* to have ongoing serials of articles by Goel, on Nehru and on Islam, halted (the second time, the editor himself, the long-serving arch-moderate K.R. Malkani, was sacked as well). And ideologically, it has always turned a deaf ear to their analysis of the problems facing Hindu society.

Most Hindu leaders expressly refuse to search Islamic doctrine for a reason for the observed fact of Muslim hostility. RSS leader Guru Golwalkar once said: "Islam is a great religion. Mohammed was a great prophet. But the Muslims are big fools." (speech in Delhi attended by Ram Swarup and Sita Ram Goel, ca.1958) This is not logical, for the one thing that unites the otherwise diverse community of Muslims, is their common belief in Mohammed and the Quran: if any wrong is attributed to "the Muslims" as such, it must be situated in their common belief system. Therefore, Goel's position was just the opposite: not the Muslims are the problem, but Islam and Mohammed.

In the Ayodhya dispute, time and again the BJP leaders have appealed to the Muslims to relinquish all claims on the supposed birthplace of the Hindu god Rama, arguing that destroying temples is against the tenets of Islam, and that the Quran prohibits the use of a mosque built on disputed land.

In fact, whatever Islam decrees against building mosques on disputed property, can only concern disputes within the Muslim community or at most with its temporary allies under a treaty. Goel has demonstrated in detail that it is perfectly in conformity with Islamic law, and established as legitimate by the Prophet through his own example, to destroy Pagan establishments and replace them with (or turn them into) mosques. For an excellent example, the Kaaba itself was turned into a mosque by Mohammed when he smashed the 360 Pagan idols that used to be worshipped in it.

Therefore, S.R. Goel was rather critical of the Ayodhya movement, witness his preface to *Hindu Temples*, vol.1: "The movement for the restoration of Hindu temples has got bogged down around the Rama Janmabhoomi at Ayodhya. The more important question, viz. *why* Hindu temples met the fate they did at the hands of Islamic invaders, has not been even whispered. Hindu leaders have endorsed the Muslim propagandists in proclaiming that Islam does not permit the construction of mosques at sites occupied earlier by other people's places of worship (...) The Islam of which Hindu leaders are talking exists neither in the Quran nor in the Sunnah of the Prophet. It is hoped that this volume will help in clearing the confusion. No movement which shuns or shies away from truth is likely to succeed. Strategies based on self-deception stand defeated at the very start."

Goel's alternative to the RSS variety of "Muslim appeasement" was to wage an ideological struggle against Islam and Christianity, on the lines of the rational criticism and secularist politics which have pushed back Christian self-righteousness in Europe. The Muslim community, of course, is not to be a scapegoat (as it is for those who refuse to criticize Islam and end up attacking Muslims instead), but has to be seen in the proper historical perspective: as a part of Hindu society estranged from its ancestral culture by Islamic indoctrination over generations. Their hearts and minds have to be won back by an effort of consciousness-raising, which includes education about the aims, methods and historical record of religions.

2.8. Conclusion

One of the grossest misconceptions about the Hindu revivalist movement is that it is a creation of political parties like the BJP and the Shiv Sena. In reality, there is a substratum of Hindu activist tendencies in many corners of Hindu society, often in unorganized form and almost invariably lacking in intellectual articulation. To this widespread Hindu unrest about the uncertain future of Hindu civilization, Voice of India has provided an intellectual focus.

The importance of Ram Swarup's and Sita Ram Goel's work can hardly be over-estimated. I for one have no doubt that future textbooks on comparative religion as well as those on Indian political and intellectual history will devote crucial chapters to their analysis. They were the first to give a first-hand "Pagan" reply to the versions of history and "comparative religion" imposed by the world-conquering monotheisms, both at the level of historical fact and of fundamental doctrine, both in terms of the specific Hindu experience and of a more generalized theory of religion free from any prophetic-monotheistic bias. Their long-term intellectual importance is that they have contributed immensely to breaking the spell of all kinds of ingrained Christian, Muslim and Marxist prejudices and mis-representations of Hinduism and the Hindu revivalist movement.

If you plant a tree, you'll be gone by the time it reaches its full height. The men whose work is only now beginning to make its influence felt, are no longer around to witness its fruition. Ram Swarup died unexpectedly on 26 December 1998 during his afternoon nap. Sita Ram Goel left this world equally quietly, though after suffering a deteriorating health condition for several years. His mind was sharp till the last and he continued to take daily morning or evening walks, yet for most of the time, he was confined to bed. On the morning of 3 December 2003, he passed away in his sleep.

(Dr. Koenraad Elst is a Belgian Indologist. The introduction, here reproduced verbatim as ch.2.1, and an earlier version of the biographical note, here updated as ch.2.2-8, were included, along with a survey of Sita Ram Goel's scholarly contributions and ideological positions, in Koenraad Elst: "India's Only Communalist: an Introduction to the Work of Sita Ram Goel", in Arvind Sharma: *Hinduism and Secularism: After Ayodhya*, Palgrave, New York 2001, pp.135-158. Another version of the biographical note was given in Koenraad Elst: *Decolonizing the Hindu Mind*, Rupa, Delhi 2001, pp.208-215.)

3. A case study in "eminent" historiography

Vishal Agarwal

3.1. Opening Remarks

This review[1] deals with the textbook on history authored by the eminent historian Romila Thapar: *Ancient India, A Textbook of History for Middle Schools*, published by the National Council for Educational Research and Training (NCERT), New Delhi 1987. Until 2001, the textbook was mandatory reading for students of Standard VI in schools affiliated to the Central Board for Secondary Education (CBSE).

When the text of the first edition of the book, published in 1966, is compared with its current edition, published in July 1987 and reprinted 13 times till January 2000, we do not find any significant differences between the two. The changes are primarily cosmetic — sentences added here and there, a word or two changed, and so on. A few errors are corrected, a subtle shift in emphasis made here and there (in some cases clearly motivated by the changing political climate of India), and so on. This means that in the 34 years from1966 to 2000, Thapar did not see the need to revise completely her understanding as well as her presentation of history of ancient India to middle-level school children of India. In contrast, NCERT textbooks for other disciplines such as Chemistry, Mathematics, Physics etc., were replaced regularly and periodically without raising any national controversies.

[1]Acknowledgement: I have benefited considerably from constructive criticisms that were offered by Shibaji Kar, Professor Yashwant Malaiya and Professor Shishir Thadani on the first draft of this paper.

As indicated in the foreword of the 1966 edition of the book, we find that the Chief Editor was S. Gopal, whereas the other editors of the series were Romila Thapar, S. Nurul Hasan[2] and Satish Chandra. Nurul Hasan is dead, S. Gopal passed away a few years ago, but Thapar and Chandra continued to be authors or editors for NCERT even 35 years later. It appears that India did not produce better or equally good historians who could write history texts for school children, in all these 3´decades! The hegemony of this small group of Marxist historians (or their fellow-travellers) in producing school history texts for impressionable schoolchildren in India all these years is quite alarming. After being withdrawn by the inimical NDA government in 2001, it appears that at least some of these textbooks will be reinstated by the present UPA government ruling from New Delhi.

The foreword to the 1987 edition, written by P.L. Malhotra, claims that the major objectives of these textbooks are "inculcation of the scientific temper, and egalitarianism, democracy and secularism, equality of the sexes and removal of social barriers. It is also of crucial significance in combating obscurantism, religious fanaticism, superstition and fanaticism." The second sentence contains all the buzzwords used frequently by Marxist historians to characterize

---

[2]Dr. Nurul Hasan was the Education Minister appointed by Prime Minister Indira Gandhi, and later the Governor of West Bengal. Concerning him and his protégés, archaeologist Dilip Chakrabarti remarks (*Colonial Indology*, Munshiram Manoharlal, Delhi 1997, p.13): "To thwart the strength of the old Congress party stalwarts, the then Prime Minister of the country, Mrs. Indira Gandhi, came to depend significantly on the support of the 'left' political parties, and recruited in the process to her cabinet a History professor, putting him in charge of education. This professor, an Oxford D.Phil. with a firm belief in the 'progressive', i.e., 'left' ideas, was also the son of an important government functionary of British India and related by marriage to one of the powerful 'native' princely houses of the north. Till his date in harness as the governor of a left-controlled Indian state, he acted as the patron saint of a wide variety of historians claiming 'progressive' political beliefs and hoping for a slice of the establishment cake."

Hinduism as such. The present review makes it amply clear how the past of our people is demonized and misrepresented by this influential textbook.

Unless stated otherwise, this review pertains to the 1987 edition of the textbook that continued to be in use till 2001. A few references will however be made to the 1966 edition for various reasons.

3.2. "The Study of Indian History"

The introductory chapter alone in the current edition is quite different from the 1966 edition. It stresses the current trends in historiography of ancient India — such as a greater emphasis on the lives of common men rather than on aristocrats and kings only in older texts of history. It discusses how history of ancient periods is reconstructed, the various sources of information for the same, and how civilization in ancient India could have begun. The chapter as such, makes very dry reading for a 6th Std. student, because there are so few illustrations.[3] For instance, from a pedagogical perspective, it is quite questionable whether the following remarks will make much sense to a ten or eleven year old student, especially because Thapar has not furnished any illustrations to clarify her point (p.3):

> "The correct understanding of history depends on two things. One is a careful and critical use of source material. Historians of ancient periods have to use a variety of sources, some of which are more reliable than others. Therefore it is necessary to give priority to the reliable sources. The second is that the arguments given by historians defending certain statements should be based on rational analysis. (...) Above all, even the past must be subjected to a critical analysis. It is only in this way that historical knowledge will advance."

---

[3]On page 2, there is a chart showing some Indian scripts. Curiously, the 1966 edition of the book omitted the Devanagari script! This omission of the most widely prevalent script of India has been rectified in the current edition.

Study aids such as well-demarcated sections with section headings are missing in this chapter. The chapter is one continuous text divided into several paragraphs running over 5 pages. A significant omission from the chapter is a map of India, which could have greatly facilitated the understanding of the essay-type text where it discusses the topography of the subcontinent. The book makes no attempt to relate the present to the past, even though the author remarks on page 1 that one of the reasons for studying history is to understand our present. A misleading statement is made that Sanskrit documents were written in Devanagari script (p.4) when in fact they were written in numerous scripts such as Brahmi, Grantha, Sharada and so on.

3.3. "Early Man"

The first chapter opens with a remark of questionable accuracy (p.9):

> "It took almost 300,000 years for man to change from a food-gatherer to a food-producer."

As even the Marxist historian Irfan Habib's recent book points out, the *Homo Erectus* had probably started gathering food 700,000 to 500,000 years ago, or even earlier.[4] Since the Neolithic revolution involving large-scale production of food occurred about 10,000 years before the present, it is reasonable to suggest that man took 500,000 years or perhaps a longer time to switch from food-gathering to food-producing, and not a mere 300,000 years as the textbook teaches.

The chapter again makes very boring reading, due to the paucity of illustrations. Instead of just giving illustrations of tools used by Palaeolithic and Neolithic man, the author could have also given schematic depictions of primitive nomads,

---

[4]Irfan Habib: *People's History of India,* vol.1 *(Prehistory)*, Tulika , Delhi 2001, pp.25-27.

early villages and so on to facilitate comprehension and memorization and to promote interest in the minds of children. The text of this chapter in the 1987 edition differs from the 1966 edition only in a few sentences here and there. The only significant addition, in my opinion, is a section on the standard anthropological explanation for the rise of religious beliefs in primitive human societies. This description is quite similar to her description of the Vedic religion in chapter III.

3.4. "Man Takes to City Life"

Chapter II of the book deals with the Harappan culture. In her 1966 edition, Thapar had made an erroneous remark (p.30):

> "The earliest city to be discovered in India was Mohenjo-daro on the river Indus in Sind. Further up the Indus valley another ancient city was excavated and this was Harappa near the modern Montgomery."

This has fortunately been corrected in the latest edition to read (p.24):

> "The earliest city to be discovered in India was Harappa in Punjab (presently in Pakistan). Further down in the Indus valley another ancient city was excavated and this was Mohenjo-Daro in Sind."

The present edition however still gives the wrong reason for calling the Indus Valley Civilization as 'Harappa culture' (p.24):

> "The archaeologists called the civilization of these ancient cities the Indus Valley Civilization, because both of these cites and other sites sharing the same culture were found in the Indus valley. But for the last forty years archaeologists have been digging in other parts of northern and western India and have found more cities that resemble those of the Indus valley. Therefore the Indus Valley Civilization is now also called the Harappa culture since the pattern of living in these resembles that of Harappa..."

The correct reason for calling the Indus Valley Civilization alternately as the Harappan Culture or Harappan Civilization is the accepted model of naming archaeological cultures after the names of the sites where they are discovered or first identified.[5] In other words, the Indus Valley Civilization is alternately referred to as Harappan Civilization because Harappa was the first site belonging to the culture that was discovered.

The paragraph ends with a meaningless statement (p.24):

> "It is also called the Indus Civilization because it spread over areas beyond the Indus valley."

Perhaps, Thapar intended to provide a rationale for distinguishing the term 'Indus Civilization' from the 'Indus Valley Civilization'. The name 'Indus Civilization' was actually the title of the book on Mature Harappan Civilization (with its fully developed urban character), written by Sir Mortimer Wheeler, and first published in 1953 when the dense concentration of Harappan sites along the Hakra-Ghaggar plains and in Gujarat was not appreciated yet. In fact, there is a contemporary view that the name of this civilization should be changed to 'Indus-Sarasvati Civilization' or something similar. This view is dismissed by Marxist historians in India as a Hindutva fantasy, but its logic is nevertheless accepted by apolitical, sober American scholars such as Jane McIntosh:[6]

> "Suddenly it became apparent that the 'Indus' Civilization was a misnomer — although the Indus had played a major role in the development of the civilization, the 'lost Saraswati' River, judging by the density of settlement along its banks, had contributed an equal or greater part to its prosperity. Many people today refer to this early state as the 'Indus-Saraswati Civilization' and continuing

---

[5]Dilip K. Chakrabarti: *India — An Archaeological History, Paleolithic Beginnings to Early Historic Foundations*, Oxford University Press, Delhi 1999, p.152.

[6]Jane R. McIntosh: *A Peaceful Realm — The Rise and Fall of the Indus Civilization*, Westview Press, Boulder (Colorado) 2002, p.24.

references to the 'Indus Civilization' should be seen as an abbreviation in which the 'Saraswati' is implied."

Thapar rightly notes that the IVC also extended over northern Maharashtra (p.24) but her maps given on the next page show the culture extending only till Gujarat, leaving out even the site of Daimabad in Maharashtra.

Listing the civilizations contemporaneous with the Indus Civilization, Thapar remarks (p.26):

"In the region now called Iraq, there was the Sumerian Civilization."

The nomenclature is wrong and misleading, and needs to be corrected as follows. Mesopotamia comprises two parts: the northern part called Assyria, and the southern called Babylonia. The latter itself is subdivided into a northern region called Akkad and the southern remainder known as Sumer. Babylonia is normally taken to mean the flood plain of Tigris and Euphrates.[7] In other words, 'in the region now called Iraq', only one of the civilizations was Sumer.[8]

Thapar claims that Sind and Rajasthan were not deserts then but were moist and humid (p.26) — a claim that is contested by many scholars.

On the storage of surplus food in the Harappan Civilization, she writes (p.26):

---

[7]For the use of this standardized nomenclature, see e.g. Juris Zarins: *The Domestication of Equidae in Third Millennium B.C. Mesopotamia*, a Ph.D. thesis submitted to the Department of Near Eastern Languages and Civilizations, University of Chicago, 1976.

[8]One might argue that Sumer is mentioned specifically by Thapar because of its trade relations with Harappan Civilization. Such an argument would be incorrect, because she mentions Egyptian Civilization in the same paragraph, even though this civilization did not trade with the Harappans. Therefore, the sentence mentioning Sumer as a civilization 'in the region now called Iraq' is misleading and inaccurate, because it overlooks the presence of Babylonian, Akkadian and other civilizations in that region.

"More grain was grown that was actually eaten by the people in the villages. This extra or surplus grain was taken to the cities to feed the people of the towns and was stored in large granaries or buildings specially made for storing grain."

Later, Thapar speculates on the existence of granaries at Harappa. She remarks (p.27):

"In the citadel at Harappa, the most impressive buildings were the granaries."

While Thapar devotes several sentences to a hypothetical description of how grain was transported in boats along the river, the identification of certain structures at Harappa, Lothal etc., as granaries is in fact purely speculative and tentative.[9]

The chapter contains a few pointless statements, which would bore the reader by their flatness. For instance, in discussing the construction of Harappan homes, Thapar says (p.29):

"The roofs were flat. There were few windows but plenty of doors, which were probably made of wood. The kitchen had a fire-place (...)."

The monotonous discussion could have been made a lot more lively and memorable by relating it to modern housing patterns in India. As an example of this approach, let me cite an analogous passage from another textbook describing Harappan homes:[10]

---

[9]In fact, Thapar herself has implied in a recent article ('The Rgveda: Encapsulating Social Change', in K.N. Panikkar, Terence J. Byres, and Usha Patnaik, eds.: *The Making of History — Essays Presented to Irfan Habib*, Tulika, Delhi 2000, pp.11-40) that the identification of the structures as granaries is tentative. She says: "Huge storage structures have been identified, *possibly* as granaries or as warehouses." (p.13, emphasis mine). And now of course, a recent authoritative work also states that the identification of these structures as granaries (especially in Harappa) is not proven, see Gregory Possehl: *The Indus Civilization*, Alta Mira Press, Walnut Creek (California) 2002, pp.247-248.

[10]Jane R. McIntosh: *A Peaceful Realm — The Rise and Fall of the Indus Civilization*, Westview Press, Boulder (Colorado) 2002, pp.100-101.

"Despite the differences in size, the housing in the major Indus settlements was generally of a high standard, suggesting that even the least important individuals led a comfortable existence. There were many features that were common to all or most of the houses. Often, especially in the larger houses, a small janitor's room faced directly on to the house doorway so that the visitor was first confronted and checked out by a doorkeeper. Once within the house, the visitor would turn immediately left or right into a passage that led into the courtyard, the center of the household, as it is in modern India."

"A stair led from the courtyard to the upper part of the house — generally one and in some cases two upper stories. The stair probably continued upward to give access to the roof. Constructed of wooden beams covered by matting and plaster, the roof provided an additional space for the family to sit, talk, and sleep, as they do today. (...) In some settlements, namely Kalibangan, Banawali and Lothal, the houses also included a room set apart as a domestic shrine, a feature also common in modern Indian homes, although such shrines have not been found at Mohenjo Daro."

"Houses of any size at Mohenjo Daro would also have a private well, sturdily constructed of wedge-shaped baked bricks — those without a well of their own, however, were well served by the public water supply. (...) Other cities were less generously provided with wells but also had an excellent drinking water supply in the form of reservoirs and cisterns. The area immediately inside the walls of the great settlement at Dholavira was taken up by enormous reservoirs that covered around a fifth of the enclosed area of the settlement. Water played an important — indeed a vital part in the life of the Indus people, and their management and use of the domestic and urban water supply were way ahead of those of any other civilization of their time. Not for another 2,000-odd years were hydraulic engineers of this caliber to reemerge, with the Romans in the Old World and Chavin in the New."

"One of the most impressive rooms of the Indus house was the bathroom. (...) Bathing would have followed the custom that still holds today, of pouring water over oneself with a small pot — but in some households there was the refinement of a "shower": a small stair along one side of the bathroom allowed another person to ascend and pour a steady stream of water over the bather. The bathroom floor, constructed of stone or sawn baked bricks, allowed the water to flow off into the efficient drainage system that served the city; via pottery drainpipes or drainage chutes. Wastewater was collected into small open drains in the lanes and from there flowed into the main drainage system. This ran along the main streets hygienically covered by bricks or stone slabs. At intervals there were inspection covers so that the free flow of the drains could be checked and maintained."

In this version above, the repeated references to the similarity of the Harappan dwellings to modern Indian homes, and how the drainage system in the Harappan cities was well ahead of its times, makes the reading more interesting for students. In contrast, Thapar's book is replete with dry passages that make for a tedious reading, and are difficult for the student to retain in his mind, or relate to his own immediate society and environment. No attempt is made to relate the continuity of Harappan elements to our own times. Thus, the accuracy of weights and measures found at Harappan sites is mentioned (p.33), but the continuity of these measures to present times is not stated. Amongst the modes of disposal of the dead listed by Thapar, cremation is not mentioned even though it seems to have been practiced widely in Harappan culture.

And on the fall of Harappan culture, she says (p.34):

"The Harappa culture lasted for about a thousand years. By 1500 BC, when the Aryans began to arrive in India, the Harappa culture had collapsed. Why did this happen? The cities may have been destroyed by floods, which came regularly; or there may have been an epidemic or some terrible disease which killed the people. The climate also began to change and the region became more and more dry and like a desert. Or else the cities may have been attacked and were unable to defend themselves."

The Aryan Migration Theory that Thapar alludes to is also contested. In fact, prominent archaeologists, anthropologists as well as Indologists, now dismiss any large-scale migration of the 'Aryans' into India. Not only is the concept derived from nineteenth-century theories of 'races', it is based on the assumption that languages spread only by migration of peoples speaking them, as Thapar seems to hold.[11]

There is no description of various Chalcolithic cultures in the interior of India before she jumps straight to the Aryans in the next chapter.

It is a real pity that Thapar did not revise her book between 1987 and 2000, because the chapter could have greatly benefited from the reports on excavations at several new Harappan sites within India (such as Kunal, Malvan, Surkotada, Dholavira etc.). A prominent omission in the textbook is the fact that the greatest concentration of these sites is found along the Ghaggar-Hakra river basin, identified by most archaeologists and non-Marxist historians today with the Vedic Sarasvati. Moreover, there is hardly any attempt in this chapter to correlate features of the Harappan culture with the present Indian culture with concrete examples.

3.5. "Life in the Vedic Age"

It should be interesting to read Romila Thapar's presentation of the Vedic Aryans, in Chapter III, titled "Life in the Vedic Age", since historiography of this era has become highly politicized in India. The very first paragraph of the chapter in the 1966 edition gave misleading information (p.43):

> "Aryans came from outside India, from north-eastern Iran and the region around the Caspian Sea. Those that came to India are called Indo-Aryans to distinguish them from the other Aryans who went to various parts of western Asia and Europe."

This has been modified slightly in the present edition (p.37) as:

> "It was during this period that a people speaking an Indo-Aryan language (which is the basis of Vedic Sanskrit) emerged in north-western India. We do not know where they came from; perhaps

---

[11]Thus, elsewhere in the textbook (p.6), she remarks: "One way of discovering who came from where is by studying the languages of an area. People who move or migrate carry their language with them..."

they came from north-eastern Iran or the region near the Caspian Sea or Central Asia."

The central idea, that there were migrations of Indo-Aryan speakers into India from the Northwest remains, despite the absence of evidence for any such migration around 1500 BCE. Thapar then discusses the fact that the concept of race as applied to Aryans has been called into question, and so on. However, the entire description of Vedic peoples in her chapter is nothing but a euphemistic version of the colonial-racist Aryan Invasion Theory, showing how the 'Aryans' subjugated the 'indigenous Dasas and Dasyus'.[12]

Thapar continues (p.37):

> "They are called 'Indo-Aryans' to distinguish them from others who spoke various Aryan languages and went to western Asia and Europe."

The statement is pointless, because the use of the word 'Aryan' to denote speakers of Indo-European tongues other than Indo-Aryan and Iranian has been given up several decades ago. Scholars of historical linguistics rather say that the 'Indo-Iranians' (who were themselves a branch of Indo-Europeans) split into 'Iranians' and 'Indo-Aryans'. Thapar is also completely wrong in asserting that there were no Indo-Aryans in Europe or in western Asia. Oleg Trubachev has recently written a book on the Indo-Aryans in Ukraine.[13]

---

[12]This back-door revival of the Aryan Invasion Theory by Thapar et al. even in her earlier publications has not fooled many people. Speaking of an old publication of hers, for instance, Edmund Leach ("Aryan Invasions over Four Millennia", in E. Ohnuki-Tierney, ed.: *Culture Through Time, Anthropological Approaches*, Stanford University Press, Stanford 1990) remarks: "Why is this sort of thing so attractive? Who finds it attractive? Why has the development of early Sanskrit come to be so dogmatically associated with an Aryan invasion? In some cases, the association seems to be matter of intellectual inertia. Thus, Thapar (1969), who provides a valuable survey of the evidence then available, clearly finds the whole 'movement of peoples' argument a nuisance, but at the end of the day she falls into line."

[13]Oleg N. Trubachev: *Indoarica*, Nauka, Moscow 1990 (in Russian).

As for Indo-Aryan in western Asia, certain words that clearly belong to some Indo-Aryan dialect, are attested in archaeology even before the well-known Mitannic chariot-driving manual. Even with regard to the Hittite texts, it should be noted that although they were written between the 16th and the 14th centuries BCE by and large, it appears that some of them are copies of the originals that were written between 17th and 16th centuries BCE.[14] Indo-Aryan names are also found in a tablet dating from the Agade dynastic period (2300-2100 BCE). J. Harmatta reconstructs two of the names in the table as 'Arisen' and as 'Somasen'.[15]

Even R.S. Sharma, a Marxist historian like herself, has accepted the presence of Indo-Aryans in western Asia in the third millennium BCE.[16] Therefore, Thapar's explanation of the term 'Indo-Aryans' is wrong, or misleading at best.

Romila Thapar continues (p.38):

> "The Aryans at first settled in the Punjab. Gradually they moved south-eastwards into the region just north of Delhi. There used to be a river flowing nearby called Sarasvati but the water of this river has now dried up. Here they remained for many years, and here they prepared the collection of hymns known as the Veda. In the same region is the plain of Kurukshetra where, it is believed, the great battle between the Pandavas and the Kauravas was fought. Sometime later, the Aryans moved still further eastwards into the Ganga valley, clearing the thick forests as they went along."

The mention of Sarasvati as a river along whose banks the Aryans dwelt is very noteworthy. Currently, Thapar's colleagues like Irfan Habib and R.S. Sharma brand anyone who mentions this river in north India as 'communal', 'Hindu fascist' and 'anti-Dravidian'.

---

[14] I.E.S. Edwards et al., eds.: *The Cambridge Ancient History*, Vol.I, Pt.II, 3rd edn., Cambridge University Press, Cambridge 1971, p.831.

[15] J. Harmatta: "The Emergence of the Indo-Iranians: the Indo-Iranian languages", in Dani and Masson eds.: *History of Civilizations*, vol.I, 1992, p.374.

[16] Ram Sharan Sharma: *Looking for the Aryans*, Orient Longman, Hyderabad 1995, pp.36-40

Thapar equates the Painted Grey Ware Culture with the Vedic Age (p.38), and adds (p.39; also in the 1966 edition, p.43-44):

> "Our knowledge of the Aryans is not based, as it is in the case of the Harappa people, mostly on digging up their habitation sites. We know about the Aryans from the hymns and the poems and stories which they composed and which were recited and passed on from generation to generation until they were finally written down. We call this "literary evidence", and it provides the clues to their history. But recently digging in certain places such as Hastinapur and Atranji-Khera (in western Uttar Pradesh) has also supplied further information about their culture."

It is thus clear that the association of Hastinapur and Atranji-Khera with the Aryans was apparently accepted by Thapar herself up to 1987 at least on the basis of excavation reports by archaeologists like B.B. Lal. However, subsequent to the demolition of the Babri Masjid in 1992, Thapar has taken a somersault and she spares no efforts to lampoon B.B. Lal for searching for Aryans in archaeological records. Ever since Lal has taken the stand that the Babri mosque did stand atop a pre-existing temple, the entire gang of 'secular' historians has been maligning him, to no avail. Thapar's criticism of Lal should be seen in this context as a subtle, politically motivated attempt to link Lal with the so-called Upper Caste Hindu fantasies of being superior 'Aryans'.[17]

[17]For instance, she says: "The theory of the Aryan race has not only served cultural nationalism in India but continues to serve Hindu revivalism and, inversely, anti-Brahmin movements. At the academic level, the insistence on ascribing Indo-European roots to all aspects of Vedic culture has acted as a restraint on the analysis of mythology, religion and cultural symbols from the historical point of view. The intellectual history of a period as rich as that of Upanishads and early Buddhism, approximately the mid-first millennium BC, has been hemmed in by the constraints of seeing it in terms of an internal movement among dissident Aryans, rather than from the more meaningful perspective of a period of seminal change. The perennial search for 'the Aryans' continues apace, with archaeologists still attempting to identify a variety of archaeological cultures as Aryan." ('Ideology and Interpretation of Early Indian History', pp.1-22 in Section I of Romila Thapar: *History and Beyond*, Oxford University Press, Delhi 2000, p.18.)

In other words, considering that Thapar has herself linked the PGW culture at Hastinapur and Atranji-Khera with the Aryans in the past even in school textbooks, it is hypocritical and dishonest on her part now to criticize B.B. Lal now for the same fault.[18]

The sole reason for equating the PGW with late Aryans is the assumption that the late Vedic literature is contemporary with this ware, dated archaeologically in the first half of the first millennium BC. Archaeologists however find nothing particularly 'Aryan' about PGW. If PGW represents the Indo-Aryans then, according to accepted theories, similar or antecedent/precursor types of pottery should be located west of the Ganga-Yamuna region on the Iranian Plateau. Yet, B.K. Thapar has noted the absence of any PGW antecedent types of pottery anywhere along the route supposedly taken by the Aryans, and he has outlined the chronological problems associated with the accounts.[19] Similarly, Dilip Chakrabarti points out that the traits of PGW indicate an eastern rather than a western origin:[20]

> "The Painted Grey Ware culture, thus, with its traits of rice cultivation and the use of domestic pig and buffalo, seems to suggest a culture distinctly eastern in bias and not a western one as its suggested Aryan authorship would indicate."

---

[18]B.B. Lal has now himself given up his earlier linkage of the PGW with the Aryans. In fact, he is currently a staunch opponent of the Aryan Invasion Theory or its euphemistic versions these days, which makes him an even greater enemy of Thapar and her fellow Marxist historians.

[19]B.K. Thapar: 'The Aryans: A Re-appraisal of the Problem', in L. Chandra, S.P. Gupta, D. Swarup, and S. Goel, eds.: *India's Contribution in World Thought and Culture*, Vivekananda Rock Memorial Committee, Madras 1970, pp.147-164

[20]D.K. Chakrabarti: 'The Aryan Hypothesis in Indian Archaeology', p.333-358 in *Indian Studies, Past and Present*, 4 (1968), p.353.

American archaeologist Jim Shaffer states some additional objections against relating PGW with the late Aryans.[21] According to archaeologist Shereen Ratnagar, an ex-student of Thapar herself, it is even debatable if the PGW constitutes a 'culture'.[22] We see here how the failure of Thapar to revise textbooks in a timely and regular manner has resulted in the teaching of outdated theories to students for several years.

Thapar obviously could not fail to mention that Vedic Aryans ate beef, even in her brief discussion on their foot habits (pp.40-41):

> "The cow held pride of place among the animals because the Aryans were dependent on the produce of the cow. In fact, for special guests beef was served as a mark of honour (although in later centuries, brahmanas were forbidden to eat beef)."

The assertion that only Brahmins were forbidden to eat beef, and not other sections of Indian society, seems to be politically motivated, because it promotes anti-Brahminism and would tend to discredit any modern day anti-cow-slaughter movements in India as 'Brahminical'. Thapar has obviously not offered any proof that other sections of the Indian society, the Kshatriyas and Vaishyas for instance, were allowed to eat beef in 'later centuries'.

And then, Thapar perpetuates this Aryan fantasy of their love for horses (p.41):

---

[21]Jim G. Shaffer: 'The Indo-Aryan Invasions — Cultural Myth and Archaeological Reality', pp.77-90 in John R. Lukacs, ed.: *The People of South Asia — The Biological Anthropology of India, Pakistan, and Nepal*, Plenum Press, New York and London 1984, p.85.

[22]Shereen Ratnagar: 'Archaeology and State', pp.157-166 in *The Indian Historical Review*, vol.27.2 (2000), p.165.

"The horse is an animal which was not native to India and was brought in by the Aryans from Iran and Central Asia. The horse was used largely for drawing chariots. Chariot racing was a favourite amusement. The chariot-maker was a respected member of the society."

The notion that the horse was brought to India only by the Aryans has been controverted by archaeology. Remains of horses have been found in several Harappan sites and have been identified as such by competent zoologists at Kuntasi,[23] Shikarpur,[24] Malvan[25] etc.

The statement that the chariot maker was a respectable member of the Vedic society is inaccurate, because by the later Vedic age, his 'twice-born' status was certainly brought into question.[26] Clearly, Thapar has confounded the early Vedic age (i.e., the time of the Rigveda) with the later Vedic age.[27] The assertion that chariot racing was a favourite amusement of the Aryans is also questionable, despite the fact that many antiquated books mention it. In fact, the impression one gets on reading the mention of chariots in the Vedas is

---

[23] M.K. Dhavalikar: *Cultural Imperialism (Indus Civilization in Western India)*, Books & Books, Delhi 1995, pp.116-117.

[24] P.K. Thomas, P.P. Joglekar, Arati Deshpande-Mukherjee, and S.J. Pawankar: 'Harappan Subsistence Patterns with Special Reference to Shikarpur, a Harappan Site in Gujarat', *Man and Environment*, vol.XX.2 (1995), pp.33-41.

[25] F.R. Allchin and Jagat Pal Joshi, eds., with contributions from A.K. Sharma, K.R. Alur, J.P. Srivastava, K.T.M. Hegde, Vishnu Mittre and D. Shah: *Excavations at Malvan (Memoir of the Archaeological Survey if India no. 92)*, published by the Director-General of the Archaeological Survey of India, Delhi 1995, p.95.

[26] The status of the '*rathakara*' became so dubious in the later Vedic period that it was debated whether he even has the right to perform the *agnyadhana* rite for establishing the ritual fires.

[27] Similarly, it might be pointed out that PGW is not equated generally with the Vedic Age *per se*, as Thapar has done in the textbook. Rather, it has been equated with the 'Later Vedic Period'.

that it was reserved for gods, for the elites and for ritual and military purposes. Its use for recreational chariot races was rare.[28]

The author then proceeds to describe the Aryan invasion in a fully-blown manner for impressionable young students (p.41):

> "*The Aryans and the Dasyus* — The Aryans, when they settled in various parts of north India, were hostile to the indigenous people whom they referred to as 'Dasas' and 'Dasyus'. The Dasas and Dasyus did not worship the same gods as the Aryans and spoke a language which was different from Vedic Sanskrit. Some Dasa chiefs were treated with great respect, but many of the Dasa people were enslaved so that eventually the word 'dasa' came to mean slave. The Dasas who were enslaved had to do the most difficult and lowly work and were not treated kindly. But the Aryans also mixed with local people and married into local families. The word 'Aryan' came to refer to any person who was respected."

In reality, the Vedic texts do not offer any evidence that

[28]Mercifully, Thapar leaves out the following misleading statement present in the earlier version of her book (1966, p.48): "The chariot has been described often in the hymns. It was a light two-wheeled chariot which was exciting to race, and was useful in battle." The reality is that the Vedic chariot is typically described in hyberbolic terms as a vehicle of the gods with all types of fantastic features. Thus, it is made of gold (Rigveda 1.30.16), the chariot of Ashwins is pulled by three horses (Rigveda 1.34.9 etc.), it is pulled by 10 horses (Rigveda 2.18.4), it carries 67 people (Rigveda 3.6.9). Chariots are even said to be pulled by bullocks (Rigveda 10.131.3) and so on. On the rarity of chariots in the Rigvedic milieu, Edmund Leach remarks *(ibid.)*: "It is true that the two-wheeled chariot, in a crude form, is likely to have been invented in Central Asia. But the appearance of chariots as grave goods and the pictorial representation of chariots in other contexts suggest that it was a rare object, a ceremonial carriage rather than a piece of normal military equipment. The characters in the Rgveda ride in chariots because they are divine beings."

the Aryans[29] were migrants or invaders in India, nor do they suggest or state that the Dasas were indigenous Indians. Such an inference can be drawn only from the prior assumption of the Aryan Invasion Theory.

There is also no evidence that the Dasa were the native Indians who were enslaved, and forced to do all the menial work. The use of the word 'slave' to describe them in the Rigvedic context is most unfortunate, as it creates the impression that the economy in the Vedic Age was based on production by enslaved people. Rather, at best, the impression one gets from the Vedic texts is one of dasas being domestic servants. Many Indologists, such as Asko Parpola, also equate the Dasas with earlier Indo-Aryan migrants in India and Iran, or with the old Iranians. The statement that the Dasas spoke a language that was different from the Vedic Aryans, is also based on tendentious and erroneous interpretations of the Rigveda.[30] Thapar's description is

---

[29]Interestingly, in her other publications, Thapar even suggests dropping the use of the word 'Arya' to denote a race or a group of people: "The notion of an Aryan race identified on the basis of an Aryan language has now been discarded. Language and race are distinctly different categories. Perhaps it would be more appropriate to discard the term 'Aryan' as well, using only Indo-Aryan to identify the language, or else staying strictly within the definition of *arya* from Sanskrit texts where it is a linguistic and social qualifier, without the overlay of nineteenth century theories." Thus Romila Thapar: 'The Theory of Aryan Race in India — History and Politics', pp.1108-1140 in Romila Thapar: *Cultural Pasts*, Oxford University Press, Delhi 2000, p.1134. According to the footnote on p.1108, this paper is an expanded version of the text of a lecture delivered at the 40th International Conference of Eastern Studies in Tokyo, 26 May 1995.

[30]On p.410 of her earlier article 'The Image of the Barbarian in Ancient India' (*Comparative Studies in Society and History*, Volume 13.4, October 1971, pp.408-436), Romila Thapar says: "In the Rg Veda, the earliest of the Vedic texts, there is no mention of the *mleccha* as such but there are references to the Dasa or the Dasyu, the local peoples who were subordinated and regarded as alien and barbaric. They are compared with demons, with one reference to being black-skinned (*krsna-tvaca*) and snub-nosed, speaking a strange language or speaking incorrectly (*mrdhra-vac*)..." If this is not the full blown racist-colonial Aryan Invasion Theory, what else is it?

therefore crude and draws too much on antiquated colonial-racist theories.

It would be interesting to reproduce here the parallel passage of the earlier edition of her book (1966, p.48):

> "*The Aryans and the Dasyus* — When the Aryans first arrived in India, they had to fight for land with the people already living in India. These people were called the Dasyus or Dasas. The Aryans were fair-skinned and the Dasyus are described as being dark-skinned with flat noses. The Dasyus did not worship the same gods as the Aryans. They spoke a language which the Aryans did not understand, because the latter spoke Sanskrit. The Aryans who fought and defeated the Dasyus did not treat them kindly and enslaved many of them. The Dasyus had to work for the Aryans and were made to do the most difficult and lowly work. The Aryans made it a rule that no Aryan could marry a Dasyu."

The differences between the two versions are too obvious to be repeated here. According to this older edition of the textbook, the Aryans even practiced apartheid (1966, p.48):

> "*Society* — The Aryans and the Dasyus lived in separate parts of the same village and in the beginning they were not allowed to mix with one another. The Aryans were also divided amongst themselves into three classes. The most powerful people were the king and his warriors who were also called *kshatriyas.* Equally important were the priests or *brahmans*; and then came the craftsmen and cultivators or *vaishyas.* There was in addition a fourth group called the *shudras.* This consisted of Dasyus and those Aryans who had mixed with the Dasyus and married Dasyus; so they were looked down upon..."

In the current edition, the last sentence is presented in the following edited version (p.42):

> "This consisted of Dasyus and those Aryans who were looked down upon."

Although this version is more correct, it still relies on

the twin equations of 'Aryans = foreigners' and 'Dasyus = indigenous Indians'.[31]

Every possible opportunity is availed of by Thapar to ridicule or mock Vedic learning. For instance, she picks up 1 out of more than 1000 hymns in Rigveda, and then misinterprets it (p.42):

> "Young boys stayed with the priests who taught them how to recite the hymns of the Vedas. There is an amusing description of the pupils in one of the hymns. It is said that the pupils repeating the lesson after the teacher sound like frogs croaking before the coming of the rains."

The view that Rigveda VII.103, alluded to by Thapar above, is somehow 'amusing' is refuted by current scholarship, which sees a fairly serious rain-charm here.[32] In fact, this hymn does not intend to ridicule Veda-reciting Brahmins at all.[33] It is unfortunate that as a specialist in ancient Indian history, Thapar is ignorant of the language of the original texts (such as the Vedas) or even of significant secondary literature on them.

The description of the Vedic religion is quite reductionist (p.43-44) and might well have been taken from a Christian Missionary propaganda booklet. There is no attempt to relate Vedic religion with modern Hindu religious practices, an omission that contributes to dullness of the chapter. The

---

[31]The reader must not think that it is impossible to write a history for the Vedic period without invoking the Aryan Invasion Theory or its euphemistic versions. Such works have indeed been written by competent scholars, and as an example, one may refer to Dilip K. Chakrabarti: *India — An Archaeological History, Paleolithic Beginnings to Early Historic Foundations*, Oxford University Press, Delhi 1999.

[32]See Walter H. Maurer: *Pinnacles of India's Past — Selections from the Rgveda. University of Pennsylvania Studies on South Asia*, vol.2, John Benjamin's Publishing Company, Amsterdam/Philadelphia 1986, p.208.

[33]See the extensive discussion on the purport of this hymn in H.D. Velankar: *Rgveda Mandala VII*, Bharatiya Vidya Bhavan, Bombay 1963.

description of the Vedic religion also bears a striking resemblance to her description of the religious beliefs of the stone-age man earlier in the textbook. Intelligent students would obviously link the two and conclude that the Vedic religion was very primitive and barbaric.

There are many academically sound ways of studying religion[34] and religious rituals. Thapar however indulges in a wholesale negative stereotyping of rituals, and spares no opportunity to refer to them in a contemptuous or in a politically loaded manner. Amongst the various faults of Vedic rituals mentioned by Thapar, bluntly or subtly, is that they made religion difficult to practice, promoted Brahminical hegemony, promoted the theory of the divine right of kings to rule, promoted superstition, were costly and an unnecessary drain on cattle and other wealth, were too lengthy, were a fiction created by crafty Brahmins, and so on. Not one positive role of rituals in human life is mentioned. The entire treatment of Vedic ritualism is therefore slanted and makes the student averse towards Vedic religion per se.

Having discussed the preceding two chapters of the textbook in detail, let me now pass over the remaining chapters briefly.

3.6. "India from 600 BC to 400 BC"

The fourth chapter deals with the rise of the Kingdom of Magadha. Unfortunately, here also we see no description of culture and civilization in Peninsular India and the focus is still the Ganga valley.

Contrasting Vedic religion with Buddhism and Jainism, Thapar says (p.57):

> "Buddhism and Jainism had followers among the craftsmen, traders, peasants and untouchables, because they felt that these religions were not difficult to practice. The brahmans on the other

---

[34]See e.g. Russel McClutcheon and Willi Braun: *Guide to the Study of Religion*, Cassell, New York and London 2000.

hand had made their religion difficult to practice because of the many ceremonies and rituals..."

The statement has a subtle bias against the Brahmin community. It could have been ignored as a statement of a historical fact, but alarmingly, the subtle bias appears so often in the text that the student can scarcely miss her emphasis on the Brahminical hegemony. Thus, the Brahmins are mentioned as recorders of laws that promoted casteism and discrimination against lower castes (p.53), they bestowed a divine right to rule upon kings only if they submitted to Brahminical ceremonies (p.50), their influence was great because they were king's advisors and without them the king could not rule (p.50), the king collected taxes for various reasons among which the support of Brahmins was one (p.50), as priests they became messengers between gods and men, and 'so were naturally powerful' (p.43), the Brahmins became more important than other castes, and the Kshatriyas in particular, by 'making religion very important' (p.42), only the Brahmins were forbidden to eat beef in later ages (p.40-41) and so on.[35] One can hardly assume that Thapar has made all these remarks in a matter-of-fact manner or in a dispassionate manner considering that her own publications say that she is very 'sensitive in the way the past is used by the present'.[36] Apparently, Thapar does not have anything positive to say about this community, and appears to have a penchant for back-projecting current politically and socially fashionable ideas about inter-caste relationships into ancient India. It is entirely questionable whether ancient Indians who

---

[35]Moreover, the Vedic religion is consistently equated with Brahmins, and therefore gets condemned in the minds of impressionable students through 'guilt of association' with the crafty Brahmins.

[36]Romila Thapar, ed.: *India, Another Millennium*, Viking, Delhi 2000.

were not Brahmins perceived their Brahmin neighbors in the manner that Thapar is trying to depict them.

The entire discussion conveys the false impression that the bulk of the membership of the Buddhist Sangha and the Jaina community came from the Shudra and Vaishya classes. Historians such as her own Guru, A.L. Basham (1989, p.66) clearly dispute this:

> "There is a general view, largely inspired by Marxist theories on the relations of religious philosophy with the prevailing class system, that the rise of the heterodoxies such as Buddhism and Jainism was concomitant with the rise of an influential mercantile class that gave its support to these new movements, which were less expensive than orthodoxy and gave a greater place to the laity in religious activities. There may be some truth in this, but there were many other factors in the rise of these sects, and the idea that the main supporters of early Buddhism were well-to-do merchants is not wholly borne out by the evidence of the early Buddhist texts. Though many members of the middle classes gave support to Buddhism, it appears that *brahmans* formed the largest group of both the monks and the lay supporters of Buddhism. Buddhism in its early form appealed chiefly to the intellectuals and rulers, and few members of the lower orders supported it."[37]

It is surprising that there is hardly any worthwhile discussion of Upanishadic doctrines in the book although much space is devoted to Jainism and Buddhism. One would expect that after frequent criticisms of Vedic ritual in subtle and not so subtle ways, Thapar would have dwelt upon the advantages or the positive aspects of Upanishadic thought. However, only a reductionist anthropological statement is made on the Upanishads. Even elementary foreign texts on

---

[37]A.L. Basham: *The Origins and Development of Classical Hinduism (edited and annotated by Kenneth G. Zysk)*, Beacon Press: Boston 1989, p.66.

ancient Indian history do better in this regard. Any positive presentation of any aspect of Hinduism and Hindu spirituality as such has no place in Indian 'secularism', and therefore the omission is not surprising.[38]

The mention of untouchability as arising from Brahmanical laws (p.53) in the pre-Buddhist period seems somewhat anachronistic.

3.7. "The Mauryan Empire"

In Chapter V, discussing the Buddhist-leaning Maurya emperor Ashoka's Prakrit edicts, Prof. Thapar creates a subtle bias in the minds of students by stating, where there is otherwise no need to do so, that Prakrit was spoken by the common people and Sanskrit by the educated upper classes (p.62). So: Brahmins bad, Buddhists and their emperor good, for the latter spoke to the people in their own language. However, Ashokan inscriptions in Prakrit are found as far south as Mysore. Is it Thapar's case that people in that Dravidian part of India spoke Indo-Aryan Prakrit in Ashoka's times? Thapar's own ideological slant becomes obvious when one notices how in the relevant Chapter VI, she will fail to mention that the Buddhists and Jains themselves composed their texts in Sanskrit in later times.

Rather, in Chapter VIII of the textbook (p.114), Thapar does not fail to mention that:

> "The Vedic religious texts were in Sanskrit which only the priests and the few who were educated could understand... Writers such as Dandin wrote in Sanskrit, since they were writing for the court circles and the upper castes."

---

[38] I want to emphasize very strongly that I do not advocate a blind adoration of everything that is Vedic or Hindu, nor am I supporting the caste system or its inherent inequities. Rather, I am questioning Thapar's tendency to bash Hinduism selectively, rightly or wrongly, while treating other faiths with kid gloves. Such a slanted treatment of various religions in a school textbook is unfair to Hindus.

She never asks how many Buddhists and Jains continued to understand Pali and Prakrit in later centuries, or how many Muslims in India understood Arabic, the language of the Koran. This constant linkage of Sanskrit with 'upper castes' and 'Brahmins' serves to create hatred against this language in the impressionable minds of students. There is no mention at all in the text that Sanskrit is a beautiful language with a very systematic grammar compiled by Panini, or that scholars of various faiths all over India wrote in Sanskrit because it served as a link language. In fact, it is surprising that Thapar should promote prejudice against Sanskrit when she herself writes her books (and addresses her audiences in various public talks) in English — another elitist language! In fact, the period under which Thapar makes the above remark also saw Buddhists and Jains often switching to Sanskrit for composing their own texts.

The lengthy description of the rule and policies of Ashoka is inspiring. After all, he and Moghul emperor Akbar are the two greatest royal heroes of the 'secular' historians. No Hindu ruler even comes close to them in greatness according to our Marxist historians.

3.8. "India from 200 BC to AD 300"

Chapter VI has a misleading statement near its beginning (p.71):

> "India south of the Vindhya mountain and the Narmada river was known in ancient times as Dakshinapatha; now it is called the Deccan. South of the Deccan is the land of the Dravidian speaking people."

The statement is false because there are crores of speakers of Dravidian languages (Kannanda and Telugu) even on the Deccan plateau. Anyway, it is still an improvement over what she wrote in the first edition, where she seemed to subscribe to the Aryan-Dravidian binary with regard to Indian culture and population. For instance, she said (1966, p.83):

"India south of the Vindhya mountains and the Narmada river was known in ancient times as Dakshinapatha; now it is called the Deccan. South of the Deccan is the land of the Dravids or Tamils. Form ancient times these lands were the homes of Indian peoples of non-Aryan origins..."

On page 78, she makes an anachronistic statement –

"The southeast region came to be the land of the Tamils, because Tamil was the language spoken there."

In reality, Tamil and Malayalam did not become two separate languages till the end of the first millennium AD, so that even the southwest region was very well a part of the 'land of Tamils' in the period of time under discussion.

On page 83, Thapar unnecessarily lends credence to the legend that Christianity arrived in India in the first century AD. As a historian, she should have been a little more skeptical because competent scholars reject this legend and generally place the arrival of Christianity into India three centuries later. Apparently, secular historians must display excessive skepticism when discussing Hinduism, but the standards can be relaxed a little for other faiths.

The contrast in Thapar's treatment of Hinduism with her treatment of other faiths becomes very evident when she describes Christianity (p.83), and later Islam (p.122-123) in her textbook. These two faiths are described just as their own followers would like to describe them ('*emic*'). In contrast, Hinduism is primarily described as how an outsider anthropologist ('*etic*') would. To illustrate this point better, let me discuss what a similar *etic* treatment of Christianity would yield:[39]

"...believed that one great male god ruled the world. Sometimes they divided him into three parts, which they called father, son, and holy ghost. They ate crackers and wine or grape juice,

[39]James W. Loewen: *Lies My Teacher Told Me. Everything Your American History Textbook Got Wrong*, Touchstone, New York 1996, p.115.

believing that they are eating the son's body and drinking his blood. If they believed strongly enough, they would live forever after they died."

Needless to say, Christians would be offended at such a description. Likewise, Thapar's description of the Vedic religion and at times even of classical Hinduism are offensive to devout Hindus. Thapar names the two major schools of Buddhism as Hinayana and Mahayana (p.88). Hinayana Buddhists however consider this name derogatory and prefer to call themselves Theravada Buddhists.

3.9. "The Age of the Guptas"

The 1966 edition of the textbook mentioned in Chapter VII (p.101) that the Gupta period has sometimes been referred to as the "Golden Age" because this period saw great achievements of Indian culture. The present edition however omits the phrase, consistent with the historiography of D.D. Kosambi, D.N. Jha and other Marxist historians, who find all kinds of pedantic reasons for downgrading the evaluation of this period and who reject the term "Golden Age". Note however that the Std. VII NCERT textbook on medieval India did not fail to give the title '*The Age of Magnificence*' to the chapter dealing with the Mughal period.

Unlike Jha, Thapar does not discuss in detail why the period should not be termed as the "Golden Age", since this very phrase is missing in the text. Rather, she summarizes some of the reasons against this nomenclature (p.103, last para) that are found in Jha's books on ancient India.[40] Although in her recent book *Early India*, Thapar says that the term "Golden Age" has been replaced with "Classical Age" by a scholarly consensus, the obvious but unstated reason

[40]For a refutation of the thesis of Indian Marxist historians that the Gupta Period was not a Golden Age, refer Shankar Goyal: *Marxist Interpretation of Ancient Indian History*, Bhandarkar Oriental Research Institute, Pune 2000, pp.74-95.

that prevents Thapar c.s. from labeling the Gupta Age as the Golden Age is their phobia of Hindu pride and Hindu Nationalism. These historians think that they could promote Hindu fundamentalism in India even by remotely alluding to the greatness and glory of any period of Indian history that could be linked with Hinduism.

Not surprisingly, Thapar now includes the following disclaimer-type statement in her textbook, a statement that was absent in the first edition of the book:[41]

> "In the Gupta period, Hinduism became a powerful religion. The word 'Hindu' was however not used until a later time by the Arabs when they referred to the people of Hind, i.e. India. The Hindus were worshippers of Shiva, Shakti and Vishnu. Since the worship of Shiva and Vishnu became very popular at this time, we refer to it as Hinduism even during the Gupta period."

Thapar is wrong in stating that the word *Hindu* was used first by Arabs. It was first used by the Persians to refer to people of India in the inscriptions of the Persian Emperor Darius I as early as 6th century BCE[42] Cognates of 'Hindu' and 'India' also occur in Chinese and Greek writings several centuries before Arabs used the words.

One wonders why Thapar is so extra-cautious here to point out the anachronistic usage of the word 'Hindu' and 'Hinduism' by her, when her entire textbook is so full of such anachronistic terms? Was the 'Kashmir valley' termed as such

---

[41]The statement is clearly motivated by Thapar's political considerations, her antipathy towards Hindus and Hinduism. It is a subtle form of the kind of hate-mongering against Hinduism that permeates the textbook as such. It should be seen in the light of her other political writings in recent years, such as '*Syndicated Hinduism*', '*Syndicated Moksha*', '*Imagined Communities*', '*The Tyranny of Labels*' and so on. It is really disturbing to see how school children have been subjected to such a subtle propaganda all these years through their history textbooks published by the NCERT.

[42]For additional information, see David N. Lorenzen: 'Who Invented Hinduism', *Comparative Studies in Society and History*, Vol.41, No.4, Oct. 1999, pp.630-659.

in prehistoric times (p.12)? Did 'India' exist as an entity (religious, cultural or political) in pre-Harappan times (p.13)? Is there any evidence for the existence of 'Jainism' and 'Buddhism' before 400 BC (ch.IV) more than there is evidence for the existence of 'Hinduism' in the Gupta Age? Did the Kushanas arrive from 'Chinese Turkestan' (p.85) in the first century AD? Did Zoroaster really preach 'Zoroastrianism' (p.111) in 'Iran' and 'sometime before 600BC', as the textbook claims? (Most specialists now settle for at least 900 BCE and consider Afghanistan as his main area of activity.)

My point is that the ancient past is necessarily described with the help of modern terms and names, and this is obviously the case with Thapar's textbook also. However, the selective manner in which Thapar makes a special case of the late nature of the word 'Hinduism' clearly indicates her intention. She wishes to indoctrinate the Hindu students that their faith is not as old as they believe it to be, and that their religion did not exist as such before the Gupta Age.[43]

It is really amusing to see how Thapar and other Marxist historians first accept the hegemony of Protestant Christian terminology in defining religious 'isms' and then proceed to declare that the *religion* 'Hinduism' did not exist till recent centuries. From an orthodox Hindu perspective, one could assert even today that the Semitic religions are nothing more than '*panthas*' or sects in relation to Sanatana Dharma. So why impose Western and Eurocentric concepts on Indian students? One could argue that the very category 'religion' is inappropriate to describe the sacred traditions of India and China, just as the category '*dharma*' may not apply to Christianity, Judaism and Islam.

---

[43]Nor surprisingly, the cited statement on the lateness of Hinduism is absent in the older editions of Thapar's textbook. Clearly, the political ascendancy of Hindu Nationalism in the late 1980s motivated her to introduce this disclaimer-type statement on the term 'Hinduism' in her 1987 edition.

3.10. "India and the World"

After the eighth chapter, which deals with the less controversial post-Gupta fragmentation into smaller kingdoms, the ninth and final chapter introduces the touchy subject of the entry of Islam into India. It has a 3-page-long section summarizing the historical evolution of Islam as well as its religious tenets. The description conforms to the Muslims' self-definition of their faith and its genesis, and like Thapar's description of Christianity, it is marked by a lot of sensitivity. This relatively lengthy treatment of Islam was totally unnecessary as it does not have much of a bearing on ancient Indian history. It will be noted that while long sections in the book have been devoted to Buddhism, Jainism and Islam, the references to Hinduism are perfunctory or incidental. In the entire book, there is no meaningful discussion of fundamental Hindu doctrines of Brahman, karma, rebirth, yoga, ashrama etc. The Upanishads, Ramayana, Mahabharata, Gita and Puranas are mentioned only in a peripheral manner, and there is not even a brief summary of their contents and teachings. Considering the profound impact of the epics and Puranas on Indian culture, it is a shame that Thapar restricts herself to stating that they are records of battles between Aryan chieftains and that they were redacted in the Gupta period. There is not even a mention of Adi-Shankaracharya, who lived in the period covered by the text.

Thapar presents the advent of Islam to India singularly as an enriching experiencing. The destruction brought by Islamic armies is totally blacked out. In fact, the advent of Islam to India is balanced with the advent of Buddhism/ Hinduism in Southeast Asia in the following words (p.125):

> "The Arabs not only introduced Islam but also a number of new cultural influences to India, which were to grow and develop in later centuries. Thus, on one side, India was exporting its culture and, on the other side, it was importing a new culture."

Need I even comment on this false equation? Indians exported their culture to Southeast Asia through trade and via peaceful acculturation. The advent of Islam into the Indian subcontinent was to a great extent marked by violent invasions.

3.11. Closing Remarks

I would like to end this review with the confession that as a sixth grade student in 1981-82, I too read an earlier version of the textbook at school, because it was mandatory reading. I was a good student, and have a clear recollection that I had found the text boring, verbose, tedious and also difficult to relate to my surroundings. There was practically nothing in the text that enthused me to study more on the subject. The story in the text was quite detached, dispassionate to the extent that it was dejecting, and demotivating. The prose was stilted and dense. There was just too much material that a student of Std. VI could grasp and retain. When I read the textbook as a more mature person today, I can articulate my impressions much better and add a critique of the text as well.

When the two editions (1966 and 1987/2000) of the textbook are compared, as I have done here to some extent, one is simply amazed to see how similar they are, as if NCERT history as understood by Thapar c.s. is more *sanatana* or eternal than Hinduism. The instances of erroneous or slanted statements (not all of which are listed in this review) are more in the first edition, but a considerable number continued to exist in the 1987 edition that was used at least till the year 2000. Romila Thapar 'revised' the textbook assigned to her in 1987 with only a few minor changes to the 1966 edition, primarily cosmetic and sometimes politically motivated.[44] This

[44]Since I have not examined any intermediate versions or editions of the textbook, I cannot comment on possible revisions contained in them. Nevertheless, they could not have been numerous or even significant considering that the 1987 edition is so similar to the very first edition printed in 1966.

'revised' textbook, already outdated in 1987, was then allowed to continue in thousands of schools without any further revision for at least 14 more years, till the year 2001.

The textbooks have a subtle slant against Brahmins, Hinduism, Sanskrit, Vedas and Hindu philosophy and religion as such. The bias, which is certainly related to the author's Marxist affiliations, appears in the form of:

1. A selective overemphasis of certain aspects of ancient India (such as Brahminical hegemony, or the elitist status of Sanskrit);
2. Misrepresentation of certain facts or blatant errors (notably in the treatment of Vedic Aryans), suppression of inconvenient facts (such as the devastation brought by Islamic armies);
3. A one-sided presentation (such as excessive dwelling on the negative aspects alone of Vedic ritual);
4. A lack of discussion on aspects of Hinduism (such as Upanishadic philosophy, or the themes of Ramayana and Mahabharata), other than the sectarian worship of Vishnu and Shiva.[45]

There is no significant attempt in the textbook to relate India's past with our present. The illustrations in the book are too few, to begin with. They are not chosen judiciously (some

[45]S.K. Gupta (*The Prejudiced Past: Rewriting Indian History*, Indus Publishing Company, Delhi 1998, p.20) closes his assessment of Marxist historiography with these words: "The Marxist historians do lay a lot emphasis on pluralism, nationalities, wide variety of identities, including the autochthonous groups, yet they deny the significance of culture, tradition, religion — regarded by others as a social force — and indulge in shibboleths and rhetoric rooted in their universal framework of historical materialism. Thus, the kind of empathy one requires in mapping the social reality and understanding a people's past remains largely missing." This characterization of Marxist historiography in India is definitely applicable to Thapar's perfunctory treatment of Hinduism in the textbook. She gives only a very brief description of the Vaishnava and Shaiva sects and refers to them as 'cults' (p.78).

instances are pointed out by me in notes on earlier chapters) and are often not referred to directly in the text as such.

The task of imparting quality education to intermediate school children is a very important building block in the creation of any forward-looking nation. It is a very serious responsibility vested with the authors of these study materials. Textbooks should be revised and updated periodically and regularly, at least once every five years. The revisions should be guided by advances in the field of study concerned, not by one's political affiliations. The fact that Romila Thapar has failed to revise textbooks authored by her in a timely fashion,[46] and has continued to brainwash generations of impressionable school students with slanted versions of history, is a serious dereliction of duty. Writing textbooks for school children in one's country is a privilege, a privilege that Thapar has abused severely to promote her own political agenda and to indulge in a subtle hate-mongering against Hindus and their faith.

One hopes therefore that the present political dispensation will take the task of educating Indian schoolchildren more seriously, and that the new authors will revise their own textbooks more frequently and keep them free of ideological slants and political propaganda.

(Mr. Vishal Agarwal is a US-based biomedical device engineer and an independent scholar of Sanskrit and Hindu Dharma.)

---

[46] One can hardly invoke a lack of time on her part for her inability to revise the textbooks in a timely fashion. After all, she has never been found wanting when it came to political propaganda in the form of addressing press conferences hosted by Communist organizations like SAHMAT, or contributing articles to Leftist publications such as *Frontline*.

4. Sri Sita Ram Goel

Lokesh Chandra

Sri Sita Ram Goel was a child of the centuries and millennia of his holy land Bharat, that in his own words was the playground of our Perennial Dharma (*Sanatan Dharm ki Lilabhumi*). His prime being was India's eternity, in which the political, historical, cultural and religious mirrors were a continuing inspiration and guidance, where ancient sagas and future utopias mingled in creative evolution. The counter-worlds that threatened a millennium were distortions and destructions of historical continuity.

Goelji instinctively inherited the territorial imperative in its multiple expressions of space and time. One of the strangest discoveries of the biological scientists is that the bond between a man and the soil he walks on is more powerful than his bond with the woman he sleeps with. Goelji saw that this territorial imperative, so basic to life itself, had been violated in more ways than one. The sanctity of the motherland had vanished from the political vocabulary of India.

Goelji had taken upon himself to restore two words: honour was one, glory another. While some romantics believed that amity grew on trees, Goelji was a pioneer in opening up the amity-enmity complex as it found expression in the venom of our history. His was the first documented presentation of the destruction of India's heritage, spread over several volumes. His works challenge the history of parochial in-group mentality. His documented works authentically lay before us: disobey the code of enmity and the society will be crushed. He wanted to take India out of its enslavement to modern intellectual prejudices that had emerged from imperialist as well as communist thought. He was a soldier of India's perennial conscience. The duty of a soldier is to save his own people and it is equally his duty to destroy their enemies. Human existence has a dual constitution: to hate as well as to love. To quote Sigmund Freud: "men are not gentle, friendly creatures wishing for love, Ö a powerful measure of desire for aggression has to be reckoned as part of their instinctual endowment".

Goelji overlooked nothing, forgot nothing of the tears of centuries or the tortures of a millennium. His researches establish the integrity of India in a cultural whole. Violent reactions ensued among his contemporaries who upheld political absolutes and socio-economic certainties under the garb of moral convictions. Goelji devoted his life to reveal the intrusions that have threatened the integrated territorial society and culture of India. Goelji was the big bang of politics, who saw the ancient cataclysms of invasions, their devastating effects on life and land, economy and polity. He was appalled at the political establishment that failed to discern the forces that threaten existence, or identity, or stimulation.

Just as Prometheus stole fire from heaven to give to man, the struggle of Goelji was to give fire to India, to awaken the mystic fire, the Agni from the depths of Rigvedic time, in the conscience of contemporary India. He detailed the untold tortures of invasional medievalisms, in order to transform and rejuvenate the vitality of spirit, glory and heroism of future generations. He wanted the catastrophic events of the millennium to become a blessing, a transition to life's better side. Winter lays a blanket of ice over the autumnal harvest, and spring spreads a carpet of fruits and flowers on the barren flow of winter. The writings of Goelji are the spring, a symbol that the torn spirit of India be reborn in glory.

Realist to the core, he saw our Classical Sanskrit tradition overflowing with life, with a considered 'no' and an unconditional 'yes'. The modern Indian with a penchant for the 'synthetic' harmonizing of opposites into an 'imagined' greater whole forgets the real earthly world, his duty to the present, the interests of his nation, and falls into the trap of tragic and demonic forces. Goelji chronicled the historic setbacks, the deluge of catastrophes, and the role of history in the present and future. He showed the dynamics of our centuries to forge ahead a cultural autonomy that alone could become the amazing power of a scintillating vision. Culture is a flood-tide of energy, a powerful stimulation, a glorious vision of eternal values. Culture is a Covenant between Man and his Progress.

The historic studies of Goelji regarding the mediaeval period provide clarity by the formulation of a counter-image of genocidal annihilation of human beings and of our cultural system. No self-image of India can be complete without understanding the aggressive cultural paradigms that emphasized physical destruction on a gigantic scale and tried to erode the inner being of India. This diminution of Classical autonomies inherited over the millennia created conflicts and tensions under the pretext of theological dogmas, that continue to plague our country to this day. Goelji has chronicled in his extensive and well-documented works this arrogance of Religion responsible only to God and that negates the deep reality of Life.

Goelji is the Voice of those mute and unsung millions who perished for the Eternity of their Land, under the heels of the imperialism of the mind. His message is: when we advance with courage we make new history. His writings are the future of a new thinking of perestroika or re-structuring, heralding a spring of India's eternal values. A persona of great courage, he discarded the shallow shibboleths of the day and wrote to disseminate the profound being of our land. Goelji provides the facts and figures of the web of events to bring an awareness of the darkness, death and sorrow of history that still shrouds our lives. He illuminates the complexity and nuance of time to bring sanity to the politics of realism. His unmatched data bring out the creative validity of cultural content in civilization, and sublime sensitivity to the demands of power. Power and values, well-being and security cannot be distanced from the flux and passions of history.

Luke 1.52 says: "God has put down the mighty from their thrones and exalted those of low degree." Likewise, Goelji put down the anti-national misconceptions and exalted the meta-historical vision of our society and polity, culture and economy. Future India will have to read him, understand him, without being seized by prevalent prejudices and threatening dogmas lest they sunder our culture, our values and our very existence. His is the *Brahmajala*, the cosmic lineaments that form the fabric of our life, light and well-being.

Sri Goelji's magisterial volumes point out at length how our centuries are strewn with ruins, with agonies and wailings of genocides and above all the entombment of the mind in the reflex images of the saintly orders of *Bhakti*, who in unknowing crushed the martial spirit of India. The negations of the Bhakti movement are the darkness of the spiritual order. The Sumerian word for the departed soul is *gidim*, 'creation of darkness'. This darkness of self-righteousness has become euthanasia. The saintly tradition (*Santa-vada*) tried to convert this darkness into spiritual hygiene of non-hatred, and opined that God in the ultimate is one and there is no conflict or contradiction between the victor and victim. The analysis of these distortions of willful misunderstanding, with disastrous consequences, can be read in Goelji.

Alexis de Tocqueville writes: "Religion... is mingled with all the habits of the nation and all the feelings of patriotism, whence it derives a peculiar force." Samuel Huntington confirms: "Civil religion enables Americans... to marry God and country, so as to give religious sanctity to their patriotism and national legitimacy to their religious beliefs." The writings of Goelji shape and define the future of India that will be established on the principles of culture and humanity for which Indians have sacrificed their lives for several centuries.

Sri Goelji was a friend of my father Prof. RaghuVira. They had a circle of cultural dialogue in which multifarious questions of the day were discussed. One day in May 1963, the discussion veered around language and content. Sri Goelji asked my father: "Would you prefer Rahulji [Sanskrityayana] who writes on Communism in Hindi to Sri Aurobindo who employs English to communicate India's unalloyed culture?" My father said: "We shall discuss it when I get back." Father told me: "Sri Sita Ram has raised a question about outer form and inner content, about significance and signifier, about the relationship of the inner core to the outer crust. It is a philosophical question with wide-ranging implications. Sri Sita Ram always brings up fundamental points that bear upon vast areas. His mind is imbued with the depths of Indic thought and is dazzling in his understanding of modern Western concepts." My father succumbed to a car-crash and never returned to answer Sri Goelji.

To raise provocative questions was the forte of Sri Goelji. He spent a half-century of his life to pen bold and provocative books that dealt with denationalization of the elite, blurring and fading of identity, the deconstruction of cultural values, confusion of national and 'universal' categories, cultural core or deculturization, the surgeonry of hegemonic monocentrism, and so on. Goelji is, in the words of the *Kena Upanishad*, the splendour of Ourselves, other than the known and above the unknown.

(Prof. Dr. Lokesh Chandra is a scholar of Buddhism and a former member of the Rajya Sabha.)

5. Hindus owe a great debt to Sita Ram Goel

Ashok Chowgule

Destroying a civilization, not just its physical existence but also its spirit, is easy. It has been achieved a number of times in centuries past, e.g. today one knows very little about the Mayas, the Incas etc., except their massive monuments lying in ruins. These monuments attest to the greatness of their civilization, but we know vert little about their history or their philosophy. In their case, this destruction has happened only in the last five hundred years, which demonstrates how the application of massive force can make people forget their past. If the Hindu civilization has survived in spite of similar attempts to annihilate it, this is because it has given birth to great souls who worked for the larger cause of Hinduism. The late lamented Sita Ram Goel ranks among this category.

5.1. Hindu civilization under siege

For hundreds of years, Hinduism was banished to *vanvas* (exile from society). First it was attacked physically. More recently, attempts were made to make Hindus feel bad about Hinduism. This forced Hinduism to go into an internal exile and to become introvert.

Of course, there were many great souls who rose to the defence of Hinduism. Heroes like Chhatrapati Shivaji Maharaj took to arms to defeat the enemies, and heroes like Swami Vivekanand went to different parts of the earth to explain the true meaning of Hinduism, not just to the non-Hindus but to the Hindus themselves as well. Each such person came into being to meet the challenges of the time, and each was successful in his own way.

When it became obvious that India was going to win her independence, some people thought of what the state of affairs for the Hindus would be in the new situation. Would they have the wherewithal to govern, given the history of being ruled by others for such a long time? Are they united to face up to the challenge provided by this new opportunity? Dr. Keshav Hedgewar and his friends thought that the state of affairs prevailing in the early 1920s did not give them the confidence that was needed. So the Rashtriya Swayamsevak Sangh came into being, which got Hindus together *as Hindus* without making distinctions on the basis of caste, language or region.

Yet, India's political decolonization did not immediately lead to a proud assertion of her native civilization. Until the early 1980s, the Hindus silently kept their Hinduness under wraps. This is because immediately after independence they gave an opportunity to Jawaharlal Nehru to put in place what he said was his vision for the society. Just so as not to give Nehru any excuses, they tolerated his appeasement of religious minorities, an economic programme based on centralized planning, a social programme in which Hinduism was denigrated, etc. And Nehru told them that these other issues and not Hindu civilization were the immediate priority. He said that India being poor, these other issues had to be kept aside, at least for the time being.

The Nehruvian experiment was an attempt to emphasize the materialist aspects of life and downplay the philosophical dimension. But, as the Christians say, man does not live by bread alone. It tried to foist on the people an artificial identity, disconnected from the past. This could have succeeded only if Hindu philosophy was destroyed. Since this did not happen, the experiment failed. Being the oldest surviving civilization, Hinduism with its philosophy was part of the lives of the Hindus and they were not willing to give it up. This unwillingness was not due to any cussed outlook on their part, but because they genuinely believed that the philosophy had immense merit even in today's world.

In their shallowness, the Nehruvian policies ignored the essential greatness of the Hindu philosophy and tried to wean the Hindus away from their civilizational norms. The Hindus were told that there is nothing in the past that they should feel good about so the past should not become a beacon for the future. But they were not able to relate to the new plan because it went against everything that they believed in at heart. When the failures of the policies that were tried became apparent, and changes would not come forward willingly, the Hindus started to revolt, in a metaphoric sense. There was no economic progress, nor was the social climate any better than before. The Ram Janmabhoomi movement became a rallying-point for expressing the revolt. A festering wound in the Hindu society became a movement not just to recover a site, but to recover Hindu pride.

The Hindu resurgence is not a secret — that is not the way Hindus operate. One person who recognized this was Sir Vidyadhar Surajprasad Naipaul, the 2001 Nobel laureate for Literature. He has expressed the essential ethos of the Sri Ram Janmabhoomi movement like few others have. We must give credit to Sir Vidia for doing so despite the tremendous campaign of calumny that the English language media and academics have been waging against the Ayodhya liberation movement. But Sir Vidia has been able to sift the wheat from the chaff and appreciate the Hindu passion that is the driving force.

These developments clearly indicate that the foresight of the founders of the RSS has been vindicated, and it is not only in India but all over the world that the Hindus are united and willing to fight for what is rightfully due to them. Over the last twenty years, Hinduism is slowly coming out of its self-denial, and is claiming its kingdom back. Just as the Pandavas were willing to make a compromise when they sought just five villages instead of the area rightfully due to them, Hindus are willing to bend over backward to accommodate even those who hate them. True to type, their enemies treat even this magnanimity with the same contempt that they have for Hinduism itself. But an awakened Hindu is no longer willing to tolerate this state of affairs. And so he is fighting back.

5.2. The frontline of the mind

In some cases, as in the opposition to conversion activities, Hindus have on occasion resorted to force. But to many, it has come as an even greater shock that the fight to restore Hinduism to its rightful place has also been taken to the intellectual level. This is something new, and the opponents are just not able to understand how it has come about. For a long period of time, they thought that they were succeeding in making Hindus feel mentally ashamed of being Hindus. The truth of the matter was that the Hindus were neither accepting nor ignoring what these opponents were saying, but they did not express their resistance openly.

Meanwhile, a new class of what Vamadev Shastri calls the "intellectual Kshatriya" was slowly being created. And here the work done by Sita Ramji has made the whole difference. Through his own writing, and by publishing in a professional manner the works of others like Ram Swarup, Sita Ramji has compiled a set of literature which lays the theoretical foundation for Hindutva. It is a monumental compilation — not so much in the number of publications, but in the variety of subjects as well as the depth of the coverage. And thousands of aspiring intellectual Kshatriyas have benefited from it.

Those who were uncomfortable about the veracity of the information that was provided by the academic establishment started to disseminate the newly available insights, and even those who had blindly accepted the conventional wisdom slowly started to change their opinions. For example, the people's way of looking at the Ram Janmabhoomi movement

— not as a structure but as a means towards Ram Rajya — began to be put forward in a modern idiom. The struggle between the head (which wanted to keep the apparently divisive issues aside) and the soul (which wanted to keep the civilization alive at all costs) got resolved. The people no longer saw the Ram Janmabhoomi movement as an obstacle for progress, but as a means towards progress.

What Sita Ramji has successfully done is to bring the Hindu consciousness from the heart to the mind. However, this has been possible only because there is merit in what the Hindu is seeking to achieve today. Sita Ramji has given shape to this consciousness that has resonance with the Hindu philosophy. And the mind has started to accept it because Sita Ramji also expressed it in a language and idiom that the Hindu of today is comfortable with. The heart will accept the location of the birthplace of Sri Ram on the basis of a feeling, but the mind would like to see historical and archaeological proof.

In the life of Sita Ramji, as he has expressed in his autobiography *How I Became a Hindu*, we come across episodes of personal inquest and exploration so characteristic of Hindu tradition. They led him into some dark alleys too, esp. his juvenile involvement with Communism. It is a reflection of his greatness that he was not apologetic about his time as a Communist and that he changed when he found that this ideology was in fact a criminal experiment in manipulating people and society. People do make mistakes, but it requires great character to admit the mistakes, which is the primary prerequisite for undertaking the corrective moves. And he did even more: he used his personal experience with a poisonous belief system to understand it better and inform his reading fellow-countrymen about it, inoculating them against it.

Another extremely important contribution of his, under inspiration from Ram Swarup, has been the reformulation of the antagonism between the conquering monotheistic religions and "Pagan, polytheistic" Hindu Dharma. In the past,

Hindus have tried to acquire respectability and to preserve their self-respect with attempts to explain many of the concepts of Hinduism in terms defined and imposed by its declared enemies. So the Brahmo Samaj set out to say that Hinduism is not polytheistic but monotheistic like Islam and Christianity. The Arya Samaj said that Hindus do not believe in idol worship. When recasting Hinduism in the idiom of Islam and Christianity, we lose the essence of its philosophy. Instead of upholding the very essence of why its philosophy is great, we seek to dilute it, making it unable to withstand the pressures both physical and intellectual.

Sita Ramji changed the terms of this debate. He wrote and published literature that gave the proper Hindu perspective of Christianity and Islam. In this way the essential message of Hinduism was kept at the top of the debate, and the others were forced to take cognizance of it. The expression of Hindu thought in the language and idiom of today gave confidence to thousands of Hindus who were slowly making their presence felt in various corners of society including academe. For the first time they could refer to literature that presented Hindu concerns in a cogent formulation and met the standards set by the intellectual authorities. This confidence enabled even the Hindus in academe to put forward their views without being afraid of owning up their Hindu identity.

5.3. Still a long road back from exile

In normal circumstances, the research done by Sita Ramji and the authors he encouraged should be part of the mainstream academic study programme. But the facts that were collected and the interpretation of these facts were contrary to the then conventional wisdom. In a process amounting to negationism, they were dismissed as being factually untrue. Then, when the facts could not be disputed any longer, it was alleged that the interpretation was wrong. And when even this did not hold water, the works were labelled as polemical.

A serious effort was made to ensure that the Voice of India publications are not read.

However, *satyameva jayate* (truth will prevail). Over the last few years, with a rising Hindu awareness, people started to realize that the information provided to them did not match with what their collective memory told them, nor with the teachings of the Sants, the sages and the respected philosophers steeped in ancient knowledge. So they went to look for proper information in other places. Students of history or political science started asking their Nehruvian teachers difficult questions. The academic establishment could no longer afford to ignore the works of Ram Swarup, Sita Ram Goel and their school of thought.

They also found to their great discomfort that they could not refute either the facts or the interpretation, witness their impotence regarding the wealth of data which Goelji (in his two-volume work *Hindu Temples, What Happened to Them*) marshalled in evidence of the sordid story of Islamic iconoclasm. How badly they would have liked to refute it, but instead they are reduced to the default tactic of strangling it by silence. The only vocal weapon available to them is one that no respectable scholar would use: argument by labels. So they are saying that those who disagree with their party line are members of the Sangh Parivar — as if such membership would automatically disqualify the opponent. Before captive audiences of uninformed outsiders, a category that includes most Western "experts" on India or Hinduism, they just use spurious claims of "proof" and "scholarly consensus" to bluff their way through the argument against a pro-Hindu position that remains strictly unrepresented on their farcical "debating" forums.

This explains the anomalous disproportion between the objective historical importance of Sita Ram Goel's life and work, and the total silence following his demise in the dominant intellectual circles. The more penetrating his insights and the more compelling his logic, the more pressing became their need to pretend that he didn't exist. Silence is golden, and this deafening silence among Hindu Dharma's numerous enemies is now paradoxically a measure of his greatness. But for us, who learned from him, it is also a measure of the work cut out for us. The enemy is still in control of the institutional and mediatic environment, so there is still a long campaign of Truth ahead of us before we will have liberated our rightful Kingdom.

(Mr. Ashok Chowgule is an entrepreneur and president of the VHP-Maharashtra.)

6. Some recollections from my acquaintance with Sita Ram Goel

Koenraad Elst

Now that the trail-blazing Hindu publisher and historian Sita Ram Goel has left this world, it would be meritorious for all who knew him to commit to writing their memories of him. On his earlier years there is extremely little documentation save perhaps for some school records, since all the relatives of his own generation have already passed away. As for his student and early working days, if anyone were to write his biography, his surviving friends would urgently need to be traced and interviewed, before they too leave this world.

Mr. Goel abhorred myth-making. And there is no dearth of myth-making in biographical notes about well-known people, such as the spurious claims about Ramakrishna Paramahansa's so-called Christian and Muslim mystical experiences concocted posthumously by some of his disciples converted to the agenda of the "equality of all religions". He also used to laugh at attempts by modern disciples to know better what great authors intended than can be gleaned from their own explicit utterances, as in "What Marx *really* said". Therefore, concerning his years as an acknowledged guide of vigilance against Communism and of Hindu awakening, we had better record those of his words not yet available in print lest they get either forgotten or misrepresented, though of course without giving them the same status as the published works which carried his own imprimatur. As a matter of practical history-writing, we ought to compare our memories before time gets a chance to corrode and distort them.

6.1. First meetings

My own acquaintance with the leading light of Hindu awakening goes back to the end of the *annus mirabilis* 1989, when the dominoes of the Soviet bloc had been falling one after another. I was living with my wife in a little groundfloor apartment in Goyanka Gali near Assi Ghat in Varanasi, but I had come to Delhi for a few days to settle some administrative matters. Wandering around in the booksellers' area of Daryaganj, I walked into Uppal Publishers' bookstore and bought Mr. Goel's book *History of Hindu-Christian Encounters*, an obvious title of interest for a lapsed Catholic studying Hindu philosophy. A day or two later, I had finished reading it and found myself back in the same bookshop. Off-hand, I mentioned to Mr. Uppal what a great read I had found the book he had recommended to me. To my surprise, he said that the book's author could be found in an office just around the corner. He telephoned at once and Mr. Goel's nephew informed me that the author was expected in the office by 1 p.m. and that I was welcome to come over and meet him.

All afternoon, I was sitting at the feet of the master, taking notes. Mr. Goel was very generous with his knowledge and with his time, though not in the sense of sacrificing his working hours. Ever one of the most active people I have known, he often kept up a lively and witty conversation all while writing letters and signing documents which secretaries presented to him.

A few months later, my wife and I were back in Delhi, and before revisiting Mr. Goel, we dropped by the BJP office and the RSS bookshop Suruchi Prakashan. That way, we got to meet some of the leading Hindu nationalists, such as the helpful Mr. J.P. Mathur and the thoroughly friendly Mr. K.R. Malkani. The bookshop was a shabby affair, but the fortunate implication was that I could buy the gist of RSS thought for little paper weight to carry and little money to pay. We also tried to meet Mr. Syed Shahabuddin, leader of the anti-temple campaign, but he pretended not to be in his office.

Though the media always identified Hindu activism with the RSS, it took an ordinary listener less than five minutes to notice that Mr. Goel was an entirely different kind of Hindu activist with an entirely different approach from what I had come across in the RSS pamphlets. Thus, he was rather carefree about one of Hindutva's biggest scarecrows: the Muslim demographic offensive. Alright, Hindu society was in trouble, but not so deeply as to have no option left except outbreeding the Muslims. When asked about his relations with the RSS, he smiled wearily and said that RSS men were very good at physical locomotion, but that their achievements for Hindu society were limited.

Mr. Goel also took us to the rooftop apartment of his friend Ram Swarup. By then, we started realizing how lucky we were to be introduced to such exceptional company. Listening to their explanations of both the timeless profundities and contemporary weaknesses of Sanatana Dharma, we experienced what Mr. Goel's son Pradeep would later describe in his *Hinduism Today* interview: "They won our hearts with their minds."

Having gathered sufficient material for a preliminary write-up on the Ayodhya affair before flying home in April 1990, I promised Mr. Goel he would hear back from me. I sent him my manuscript two months later, and it was rushed into print: *Ram Janmabhoomi vs. Babri Masjid, a Case Study in Hindu-Muslim Conflict*. Looking back, I don't find it very well-written, it was a mere journalistic introduction to the subject and it did not contain much new information for any Indian attentively following the news on the communalism front. Yet it filled a gaping hole in the market, viz. a brief account of the controversy untainted by the Marxist-cum-Islamist agenda which dictated the dominant discourse at the time.

Former *Times of India* editor Girilal Jain chaired the press meeting presenting my book. It was on this occasion that BJP leader L.K. Advani gave a speech on his Ayodhya policy, waving my book in his hand, and that he made his offer to persuade the VHP to confine their campaign for the liberation of Hindu temple sites to the Ayodhya site, i.e. to drop their claim on the mosque-occupied Krishna Janmabhoomi site in Mathura and Kashi Vishvanath site in Varanasi. That way, my puny first book made the front page of most Indian newspapers.

Fortunately, the opportunity more or less forced Mr. Advani to equally draw attention to a more important new book on the same subject, viz. a collection of scholarly papers and analytical columns on the Ayodhya evidence edited by Mr. Goel: *Hindu Temples, What Happened to Them*, vol.1. So, indirectly I could do something in return for Mr. Goel's favour of publishing my book. The *Hindu Temples* book contained his preliminary list of nearly two thousand mosques built on the sites of destroyed temples. Mr. Advani had initially not been too keen on highlighting this research, for it raised the issue of Islamic iconoclasm as an intrinsic feature of Islam, whereas the Sangh Parivar preferred a superficial anecdotal approach confining the debate to just three disputed sites and formulating it in terms of "the national hero Rama" versus "the foreign invader Babar" rather than Hindu versus Islamic. The list of destroyed temples became a classic illustration of the treatment which the media and academe always gave to Mr. Goel's work: it was only mentioned in whispers and never openly discussed.

In November 1990, I was back in Delhi and Mr. Goel proposed that I write a sequel to my Ayodhya book. I could stay in the guest room and was provided with a computer. I dropped all the other plans I had made for my sojourn in India and stayed behind that computer screen for nearly three months, except for trips downtown to meet various Hindu leaders and attend press conferences related to the ongoing Ayodhya crisis. Most Europeans return from India with a sun tan, but I had never been as pale as I was after the writing of *Ayodhya and After.*

Ever since, I have returned to Delhi at least once a year, but never for very long, as my family responsibilities and other social ties in my home society were increasing. But I could always stay in the same guest room and spend lots of time with Mr. Goel. In the office, I was also a witness to his interaction with all manner of visitors, a very instructive insight into the inner kitchen of the broader Hindu movement, Sangh and non-Sangh. Though my writings on Islamo-"secularist" policies, largely inspired by Sita Ram Goel, were to cause me some trouble in my professional and social life, I shall ever remain grateful for the privilege of a close association with one of modern India's greatest men.

6.2. His justice

The overriding recollection I have of Sita Ram Goel is his outstanding generosity. You could always divulge your doubts to him, he was sure to come up with a reassuring though often unexpected answer, one that would really help you on your way forward. His sense of humour could wash away any blues. He was also generous as well as attentive in the material sense, e.g. unlike the proverbial cold-hearted Bania, he never forgot to take care of the material needs of servants, having food brought to a driver waiting in the car or paying sizable tips to door-keepers.

Yet, Mr. Goel could also be very stern in his judgment. In my case, for example, he could reprimand me when I wasn't careful with the financial side of things, as when I was allowing myself to get fleeced by a certain type of Indian often found around the supposedly rich Westerner. Normally an ocean of calm, he also wouldn't hide his annoyance when I failed to keep up with agreed-upon deadlines, though he never let such irritations come in the way of the realization, even if belated, of Voice of India projects.

On the other hand, if there is any point on which I would criticize him with the benefit of hindsight, it would be for being too lenient with me in one important respect. He was insufficiently strict as an editor, at least in my own case. When I look at my first Voice of India books now, I find they are insufficiently structured, insufficiently meticulous in identifying sources, sometimes also bringing into the discussion topics that disturbed the book's proper focus. I suppose he was overly respectful of Western sensibilities, especially those of my own anti-authoritarian generation that had never learned to accept corrections from older people who know better.

He could be stern with people in the sense of making them face their responsibilities instead of accomodating their self-serving excuses. When the Mohajirs were getting butchered by fellow Muslims in Karachi, he pointed out that they were the creators of Pakistan, a state based on communal hate. So, if they became the targets of communal violence in the country of their own making, they could hardly deny they had it coming.

Now, to say this of a Muslim group and of Pakistan is not all that original in Hindu circles. But Goelji took the logical next step. When the Kashmiri Pandits were expelled from Kashmir by the local Muslims and a handful of Pandits visited his office seeking financial help, he did give some money to a refugee organization of theirs, but not without showering them with a very stern sermon. He recounted to their faces the less than glorious record of the Kashmiri Pandit community in the establishment of an anti-Hindu secularism as India's state religion. Leaders of the Kashmiri refugee self-organizations turned out to have been staunch Communists who only remembered their Hindu identity as soon as they needed to solicit the solidarity of the wider Hindu society.

A few times, Goel's stern judgment even became a factor in some bad blood developing between him and his mentor: "Ram Swarup sees through ideas like no one else, but he doesn't see through people. He always manages to join hands with the wrong people." During his anti-Communist activism, Ram Swarup's analysis stood out by its profundity and its spiritual dimension, yet he was cordially in touch with Westerners whose anti-Communism was either of the superficial or of the conspiratorial kind, lacking in serious analysis as well as in spiritual depth. Goel, by contrast, tended to keep aloof or to maintain a palpably sceptical attitude even when cooperating with people if he considered them as not meeting his standards. He wasn't a diplomat, and his rule of thumb was: talk straight to scoundrels, avoid contact with fools.

6.3. His kindness

Secularists like to bandy about the hateful stereotype of Hindu revivalists as anti-Muslim and anti-Christian hate-mongers. The type does exist in reality, here and there, though in most cases it is more alive in the eye of the beholder. At any rate, it does not describe Mr. Goel at all.

Alright, I'll concede a single instance where Mr. Goel explicitly expressed his "hate" for a non-Hindu. However, this didn't concern a real human being but an icon: Mother Teresa. He had met her in person in Kolkata long before she became that icon, and had formed a distinctly negative opinion of her. In 1992, on the India-bound airplane, I had met a former fellow-student of mine in the company of her fiancé, out for a tropical holiday before getting married. I checked with Mr. Goel if they were welcome and then took them along to his house for dinner. Rather naïvely, the young lady enumerated the handful of things she knew about India, inevitably mentioning the venerated Mother Teresa. She wasn't ready for the oration which Mr. Goel gave in reply, listing in a crescendo everything that was wrong with Teresa's saintly aura, and culminating in a total condemnation: "I *hate* her!" Oddly, this was the opening to a very fruitful conversation, of which my friend related afterwards: "God, this man seems to know everything! In his presence, I feel so *small*."

As a critic of destructive ideologies and their mendacious cant, Sita Ram Goel was sharp and unforgiving. Yet, when it came to the people who were the captives of these ideologies, he could be very mild. At the office, he frequently entertained a Shiite Muslim friend, one Mr. Naqvi, who conspiratorially revealed to me a belief apparently extant among some Shiites, viz. that the Quran hadn't really been revealed to Mohammed, but to Ali, who in his generosity left the honour to Mohammed. He was also friends with some Christian clerics and served for years as the treasurer of the Christian-dominated Abhishiktananda Society for Hindu-Christian dialogue. When he heard of riots, he cynically observed how they were logical extensions of Islamic politics in India, but at the same time his heart shrunk at the thought of all those people dying, Muslims as well as Hindus.

In fact, these two seemingly contradictory traits were logically connected. Being hard on ideology allows for being mild on people. Conversely, those who are harsh on Muslims are typically softbrains in their judgment of Islam. In the post-Godhra riots of 2002, Gujaratis brought up on a diet of Gandhian sentimentalism burst out in violence against their Muslim neighbours. On some Hindu nationalist forums, you can see outpourings of resentment against Muslims, vows to "teach them a lesson", interspersed with laudatory claims about Islam and the Prophet, purportedly the pitiable objects of "distortion" by fanatical mullahs.

I gathered the impression of a direct causal connection between Mr. Goel's fellow-feeling for his countrymen, Hindu as well as non-Hindu, and his deep knowledge of his society. He truly had the finger on the pulse of his people. Real knowledge predicts, and Mr. Goel was rarely wrong in his predictions about the performance of public figures nor even about election results. Thus, the BJP's actual conduct in government in 1998-2004, while making a total mockery of all the dramatic predictions by the secularist and Western "experts", fully bore out his own assessment of the clueless Hindutva politicians. After talking with him, most of us always came away with the feeling that *this man really has the answers.*

6.4. Fascism vs. freedom

About Mr. Goel's formative years, the only information I dispose of is what he himself told me, except for a few stray utterances by Ram Swarup and by Girilal Jain. He himself used to say that all consequential details of his young days can be found in his writings, esp. in the booklet *How I Became a Hindu.* There is absolutely no reason to disbelieve or doubt his testimony, but for the sake of historiographical propriety, I call on the few surviving people who knew him then to come forward with their story.

Since in the present heated climate it is nearly impossible to discuss Hindu revivalism without some Communist dinosaur shrieking and hissing "fascism" somewhere, it may be useful to mention some anecdotes from the 1940s. Starting with one from the 1950s.

Once during his years as an anti-Communist writer in Kolkata, Mr. Goel was approached by a couple who praised him for his anti-Communist work, a compliment gracefully accepted. But when they, a *bhadralok* gentleman and his European wife, started saying how Hitler had been right all along in fighting Communism, Mr. Goel ended the conversation. He wanted no business with Hitler nor with his nostalgics. Later on, when editing chapter 5 of my book *The Saffron Swastika,* he mentioned this meeting to me and remarked (possibly only realizing right then) that they had been none other than the subjects of that chapter, Dr. Asit Krishna Mukherji and his French wife Dr. Savitri Devi, née Maximiani Portas, India's foremost Nazi enthusiasts.

While few other Indians ever understood and supported Nazism as a full-blown ideology, there were millions who had applauded the military successes of the Axis powers. At some point in World War 2, one of Goel's professors in Delhi University announced to the students that the Japanese army was marching through the Gangetic plain and was expected to liberate Delhi in the next few days. There was jubilation in class, for many Indians were hoping for a defeat of Britain at the hands of the Axis powers. Only Goel remained sceptical. It was but one of the many silly wartime rumours that were doing the rounds then and exciting the minds. When the German and Japanese Armies were in retreat, people in the tea stalls were speculating that the gains made by the Allies were only temporary: "Now Hitler will use his secret weaponÖ" But young Goel laughed it off, pointing out that the Axis powers were locked in and cut off from basic supplies like petrol and, increasingly, even food: no matter how bravely they might fight, the basic material data of their situation made their defeat inevitable.

That was the quintessential Sita Ram Goel: deeply realistic, always with an eye for the basic material facts which constrain the options available to the human players on the world stage. Later on, he was to develop an analogous attention for basic doctrinal data whenever evaluating confrontations between competing political or religious movements. Thus, it is silly to judge or predict the moves by Islamic leaders purely from circumstantial or generally-human considerations, for there is bound to be at least a component of specifically Islamic doctrine in their motives and actual behaviour. Jihad was not the personal idiosyncrasy of some odd mullah, but a central component of Mohammed's own normative teachings, bound to have some role in *any* Islamic strategy.

Goel's realism was not a one-way attitude invariably resulting in conclusions we might consider alarmistic. Sometimes, on the contrary, it was reassuring. When people warned him that his anti-Communist writing might invite an assassination attempt from the notoriously pro-violence Communists, he calmly replied: "No, I've read my Lenin." In

Communist doctrine, violence is not to be used at random and on a whim, but should be confined to the actual revolutionary phase of the struggle. (As I recall Herbert Marcuse commenting on the terror campaign by his German followers Ulrike Meinhof and Andreas Baader in the 1970s: "Terror can be useful to rouse the masses and trigger events in a revolutionary situation, but not in the counterrevolutionary situation we now have.") Mr. Goel rarely speculated, he dealt in facts. His closeness to basic facts was to provide a refreshing contrast with the free-for-all of history-writing and wishful political analysis by the Nehruvian secularists, who always ignored the borderline data in favour of their own dogmas.

At the end of World War 2, Ram Swarup, who was to become Goel's mentor in anti-Communism but was then a rising star among leftist intellectuals, quit his job as a clerk for the British-Indian government. He felt that with the Axis powers' defeat on the horizon, working for the Allied war effort was changing its character from a fight against Fascism to mere collaboration with the British colonialists. A colleague asked him how he could abandon the struggle against a monster like Hitler. One sufficient answer would have been that by then, Hitler had practically been defeated already, apart from the fact that a few little Indian clerks weren't very material to the outcome of the war anyway. But Ram Swarup preferred to keep the debate at the level of principle and made a point about the Allied perception of Hitler instead: "The devil is never as black as he is made out to be."

At a time when the socialist leader Subhas Bose was fighting alongside the Axis powers, this was actually a very moderate thing to say for an Indian socialist. Much to the despair of Western leftists, the Indian left has never accepted the Nazi-centric moral universe of the post-1945 West, with Hitler or collaboration with Hitler as the ultimate evil. On the contrary, the Indian Communists have incorporated Bose's heritage, included his Forward Bloc party in their Bengal coalition, named an airport after him and proposed one of his aged lieutenants (of the INA women's brigade) as their candidate for the Indian presidency in 2002. Official Nehruvian India has also made its peace with Bose and included him in its pantheon of anti-colonial leaders. It counts as only a minor circumstance that he collaborated with the Axis, for in essence he was an Indian freedom fighter, just as Japanese collaborator Ahmed Soekarno is revered as a freedom fighter and father of the nation in Indonesia. With his incurable scepticism, Ram Swarup likewise refused to buy the Allied line that World War 2 was a holy war between good and evil. And to be sure: as bogeymen, Adolf Hitler and Josef Stalin were in the same league, except that Stalin was the bigger killer, while Winston Churchill and Franklin Roosevelt weren't exactly choir boys either. Denouncing Hitler as evil was easy, but evaluating his enemies as *good* was very difficult, at least for a man of Ram Swarup's perceptiveness.

By contrast, Sita Ram Goel never shared this slightly relativistic position and kept Nazism firmly in his demon cabinet, even if sharing it with Communism from 1949 onwards. Unlike most Indians, he had judged Nazism negatively not only from the viewpoint of democracy and humanism, but also from the angle of India's freedom. "The enemy of my enemy is my friend": this was a seductive but simplistic principle, and it didn't apply to Nazi Germany as the supposed enemy of colonial Britain. Hitler strongly favoured the continuation of the British empire as a model of Germanic domination over the darker races. "If Britain wins, she will soon quit India, but if Hitler wins, we will never get our freedom", the young historian Goel told his fellow-countrymen.

6.5. Clash of civilizations

The now-fashionable expression "clash of civilizations" was already in use in India well before Samuel Huntington gave it currency in the West. Girilal Jain, for one, already used it in his analysis of the Ayodhya crisis in 1988-92. Sita Ram Goel wasn't inclined to using trendy expressions, but the clash between Hinduism and Islam had always been a central theme in his reading of medieval and modern Indian history. Contrary to the fog-blowing of the secularists and their loudspeakers in Western academe, who always try to blur the lines between Hinduism and Islam, a line laid out ever so clearly by Islamic doctrine, Goel firmly stuck to the facts: Islam had waged a declared war against infidelism in India since its first naval invasion in AD 636 and continuing to the present.

However, about the future of Hinduism, at least in its confrontation with Islam, Mr. Goel was not overly pessimistic. In spite of its demographic growth and its successful extraction of concessions from secular governments in India and the West, Islam may really be a paper tiger. Not only is its impending demise a mathematical certainty, but it may even happen sooner than we would normally think possible. The Muslims themselves will question Islamic beliefs, and some of them are already doing so (Mr. Goel kept contact with Ibn Warraq, apostate and author of *Why I Am Not a Muslim*). For most, the occasion will probably be the conspicuous failure of Islamic culture to keep up with the requirements of the modern world.

Recently, some mainstream politicians in Europe have broken a taboo by calling Islam "a backward religion". For the present purpose, not the character but the impact of Islam is important, so let us rephrase that: *Islam is a factor of backwardness.* Successive UN reports on the state of the Arab countries have documented how in spite of their God-given oil wealth, they are hopelessly behind in practically every respect: enterprises set up, original research conducted, inventions patented, internet access per head, books published, sales per book, foreign books translated etc. Likewise in the past, in its first and most creative centuries, the Arab world had a non-Muslim majority and the grip of Islam on the minds of even the Muslims was not yet very firm; but when Islam solidified and penetrated the culture more thoroughly, a thousand years of stagnation set in. Today in Malaysia, the Muslim population enjoys increasing prosperity by redistributing the wealth generated by the non-Muslim minorities. And not to look too far, just compare India's creativity and progress in the last decade with the persistent obscurantism in the failed state of Pakistan.

The worldwide Islamic propaganda and mosque-building boom is financed by the buyers of petrol, not by Muslim economic achievement. As Mr. Goel remarked: "When their oil runs out, they will go back to tending goats." Or more seriously: they will reject that retrograde option, drop Islam in disappointment, and seek access to the real world.

On the conversion front, Christianity has better trump cards than Islam. Its missionary effort is very systematic and puts to use the latest knowledge from psychology and marketing. But both belief systems are ultimately doomed by their delusional core doctrines. In the long run, mankind won't keep on believing that Jesus was God's only-begotten Son and that His death and resurrection delivered us from sin; nor that God gave private and exclusive messages to Mohammed now preserved in the Quran. Unfortunately, even while their time runs out, they can still do serious harm to Hinduism. That is why the prospect of ultimate success is no reason for complacency.

6.6. Last meetings

In Sita Ram Goel's last years, I purposely telephoned or mailed him less often than I used to in the preceding decade. His diminishing health as well as my own sudden heart disease were conditions that made us less prone to communication. But more importantly, I was embarrassed for not meeting his standards. I had gotten divorced, a very ordinary occurrence in the contemporary West but still an object of scorn for a serious Hindu. I remembered the disapproving smirk in his comments on the family life of his

American acquaintances ("I met Mr. Y at the wedding of Mr. X's son, who is of course divorced by nowÖ"), and I felt reduced to being yet another specimen of the decadent Westerner species. Not that he ever expressed himself to that effect, but I wouldn't have found it unjust if he had. His own family life had always struck me as a model of harmony or at least of successful conflict resolution, to the great benefit of all members young and old, a standing challenge to the individualistic mores of the modern West.

When I was in Delhi, he didn't come to the office anymore and the only place where we talked was at his bedside. His mind was lively as ever and often even full of plans for new books, including a sequel to his book on Nehru, but pain had become his permanent companion. He still proofread the writings of others but didn't manage to realize his own writing projects anymore. More than in the past, he talked about his spiritual life.

Mr. Goel had never been much involved in conventional religion, never went to temples or performed devotional rituals, and could possibly be described as an atheist. However, he practised a few simple meditation techniques. Though troubled by physical discomfort, at least he finally had plenty of time for his sadhana. I understand that he also rediscovered the devotional verses of his family's guru Garibdas.

These last years, every time when I took leave of him on my way to the airport to fly back home, I realized that this could be the last I would see of him. Yet, he held out for several years longer than I expected (kicking the habit of smoking had clearly helped). For an old man, there is nothing abnormal in dying, as he himself had said on the occasion of Ram Swarup's peaceful and unexpected passing on 26 December 1998. In principle, then, it was nothing surprising when the phone rang and news of Mr. Goel's own death came. But then it always takes us by surprise.

At Ram Swarup's cremation, I recall seeing many Delhi

intellectuals, including some otherwise fierce polemicists, unable to contain their tears. But Mr. Goel remained perfectly collected. Any preacher could perfunctorily have spoken the following words, but Mr. Goel fully meant it when he told me: "The Ram Swarup who was born in Sonipat wasn't the real Ram Swarup. The important part of Ram Swarup hasn't left us." I don't think I can say a similar thing now. Perhaps the real Mr. Goel is still with us somehow, but like many of us, I do miss him. Even as the moment of his passing recedes in time, it remains quite a task to find in ourselves the counsel for which we used to turn to Sita Ram Goel.

7. Sitaram Goel, modern India's greatest intellectual kshatriya

David Frawley

Sitaram Goel, who passed away in early December 2003, was one of India's most important thinkers in the post-independence era. His writings are central to the recent Hindu awakening in the country that is now growing rapidly to world prominence. While his guru and colleague, Ram Swarup, laid the spiritual and philosophical basis for the movement, the detailed analysis and in-depth articulation was supplied by Sitaram. The current generation of Hindu writers owes much to Goel for charting a clear course for them to follow. As this movement develops, his work is bound to become yet more significant.

While I was traveling in England several years ago, giving talks on Hindu dharma, the idea of the importance of a new intellectual *kshatriya* or intellectual warrior class for Hindu society dawned upon me. Yet returning back to the USA, where I live, I almost forgot about it. Somehow Sitaram Goel, with whom I had already been working for some time, heard of it and asked me to develop the idea further, which I did in various books and articles.

The idea of an intellectual kshatriya is that of a person who defends Hindu dharma with intellectual power and unwavering discrimination, which is the real need of this information age and in the clash of cultures occurring today. It requires critical thinking and original insight, not a mere repetition or imitation of past systems or past thinkers. It requires that one is incisive, even harsh if necessary in order to counter wrong views, like a surgeon working to remove a cancerous tumor, particularly relative to groups whose vested interests prevent them from looking at Hindu culture with an open mind.

In this regard an intellectual kshatriya reflects the diplomatic approach of Hindu thought known as *shama, dama, danda, bheda*. One offers peace to friends who may be temporarily alienated by misunderstandings (*shama*). One controls by strength (*dama*) those who are wavering in support but not necessarily inimical in their views. One uses strict rules and punishments (*danda*) for those who are hostile but can still be brought in line. And one creates division and destruction (*bheda*) for those who are unwilling to be reconciled. This is the traditional Hindu kshatriya approach going all the way back to the Vedas.

If we stop short at *shama* in all circumstances, afraid that we might offend someone by speaking the truth, we may not be able to deal with the powerful and insidious forces that strive to dominate this planet and will seek to undermine Hindu dharma in any way that they can. A Hindu voice is important today, as is a Hindu critique of civilization, now that the world is trapped between a regressive religious fundamentalism on one side and a destructive consumerism on the other. The Hindu mind can show how to change the world in a direction that is in harmony with dharma and transcends the limitations of both politics and organized religion with their misleading ideologies.

I can think of no other modern writer who fulfills this role of intellectual kshatriya better than Sitaram Goel, who perhaps pioneered this approach. He realized the necessity of challenging and countering the forces seeking to destroy Hindu culture, exposing their wrong ideologies and biased theologies as well as the misguided actions these beliefs must result in. The book company that he founded and guided, Voice of India, remains probably the most cogent Hindu voice on current and historical affairs and is a good model for other Hindu publishers and publications to emulate.

Some people may recoil at Sitaram's frank language and bold critiques. Such people are usually those who do not understand the harshness of the intellectual battle that has been going on in India for some decades. While Hindu dharma is regularly denigrated and distorted by missionary and Marxist forces (which often have foreign funding), Hindus are expected to be kind and tolerant in return and not criticize anyone in their self-defense, should they speak out at all. Such a defeatist attitude is what Sitaram reacted against and provided a clear alternative to.

Sitaram was writing from the frontlines of the battle, not from a convenient view on the sidelines. He had to speak loudly to awaken Hindus, who were passively accepting the undermining of their culture even in their own homeland. Sitaram himself was the subject of many campaigns of vilification, including by groups asking Hindus to be more tolerant of them! And he did not seek to placate anyone. In this regard, he could be quite strong if not strident in his criticism of Hindu groups that he felt were on the wrong track or intellectually deficient. He was never an apologist and never made excuses, but always held to the truth regardless of who might not be comfortable with it.

Sitaram was a prolific writer with several dozen books to his name, covering a broad range of social, historical and religious issues. A communist in his youth, his own intellectual journey back to Hindu dharma is an important story in its own right. He was one of the main Hindu writers who challenged communism in India, when it was fashionable for everyone to be a leftist, starting with Nehru himself. Sitaram also inspired and helped many new writers, myself included. He took up difficult issues like the massive Islamic destruction of Hindu temples, which others preferred to ignore or gloss over. He warned of the danger of Islamic terrorism long before it erupted on the world scene after 9/11, which type of events he predicted years ago. He similarly challenged the Christian missionary assault on India, exposing its agenda of conversion in the guise of social service, and its exclusivist dogma using Hindu tolerance to hide its aggression. Whatever he examined, he dealt with directly, thoroughly and rationally, letting the facts speak for themselves.

Sitaram Goel deserves more appreciation for the great service that he has rendered not only to Hindu society but to the cause of truth. In any deeper study of the social and historical aspects of Hindu dharma, one should first examine his works. While the truth is not always pleasant to face, one must do so in order to go forward. May many others follow Goel's example and create the type of Hindu intellectual class he showed was necessary, not only for India but for the entire world.

(Dr. David Frawley, initiated into Hinduism as Vamadeva Shastri, is an American practitioner of and writer on Vedic lore and history, Ayurveda and the Hindu spiritual disciplines.)

8. Sita Ram Goel: some reminiscences

Shreerang Godbole

8.1. Personal encounters

My first encounter with Sitaji probably took place some time in 1982. I was closely following his articles in *Organiser*. In one of these, he had defended Mahatma Gandhi. The gist was as follows: "Partition would have occurred in spite of Mahatma Gandhi. Appeasement of Muslims was not something the Mahatma had started. Even Lokmanya Tilak, Swami Shraddhananda had done the same before him." I had rebutted some of his points in a rejoinder in *Organiser*. Sitaji never replied to my rebuttal. Little did I know that one day, I would become a life long admirer of Sitaji. Several years later, he was to change his opinion on Gandhiji. The first edition of his *History of Hindu-Christian Encounters*, published in 1986, was fairly effusive about Gandhiji. A larger and revised edition of this book which appeared in 1996 contained a postscript to the chapter on Gandhiji wherein he had severely criticized the Mahatma. Gandhi formed one of the points of disagreements between Ram Swarup and Sitaji (see below).

My first meeting with Sitaji took place in his office sometime in 1992. I was studying in Delhi and had accompanied my father Dr. Arvind Godbole, Mumbai, to meet him. We had gone to present him with an award named after noted Marathi author (and staunch Savarkarite) P.B. Bhave. I remember Sitaji asking us how he came to be chosen for the award. He said that his writings were being eagerly received south of the Vindhyas and there was a thirst in Hindus to know the truth (about Islam and Christianity). However, very few people in the North seemed to read his writings. There was total darkness in the North, he said. I remember being quite shocked at his suggestion that Hindus would be better off if certain states like Bihar were given to China. I was (and still am) a Sangh swayamsevak who had grown up with a firm belief in the ideal of *Akhanda Bharat.* But that was Sitaji. For him, Bharat was merely a cradle of Hindu civilization. For him, Hindu civilization came first, the territory was incidental!

I vividly remember how Sitaji came to see us off that day right outside the gate and walked some distance with us. I whispered to my father that we should ask Sitaji for his autograph. Sitaji asked us what we wanted. When we voiced our desire, he politely refused saying he never signed autographs. This was of course in tune with his impersonal nature, something he seemed to share with Ram Swarup. To those who considered him opinionated and egoistical, my statement may come as a surprise. A few years later, I was to have regular correspondence with Sitaji. I have preserved all that correspondence, not only because of the numerous insightful remarks contained therein but also because it was written in his handwriting and contained his signature. I have not been able to destroy even the envelopes that have his handwriting. I don't think Sitaji would have approved my hero-worship.

My second meeting with Sitaji was telephonic. I was in Delhi between 1990-92 and the Ayodhya controversy was at its peak. There were several articles in the secularist press that were spreading misinformation on the Hindu position. I liked Koenraad Elst's book on the subject and had used it as a basis to rebut Harbans Mukhia's article in *The Pioneer.* I telephoned Sitaji sometime in 1992 to clarify certain doubts. He complimented me on my effort and said that I seemed to be familiar with the Hindu argument.

My lasting association with Sitaji however was sparked off by my criticism of the position of Hindu organizations (especially the RSS) vis-à-vis the problem of Islam. A seminar was held in Pune under the aegis of Prajna Bharati on 27-28 July 1996. Participants included K.S. Sudarshan, Dattopant

Thengdi, Murli Manohar Joshi, K.R. Malkani, S. Gurumurthy, Devendra Swarup, P. Parameshwaran, M.G. Vaidya and Muzaffar Hussain, among others. I was attending the seminar as an ordinary RSS swayamsevak. Of course, by then, I had hungrily read most of the VOI publications and was deeply influenced by them. At the conclusion of one of the sessions, the organizers asked if anyone else wanted to speak. I got up and put forth eight pet formulations of the Sangh Parivar vis-ë-vis the Muslim problem and proceeded to rebut them. Subsequently, I wrote a letter to Sudarshanji questioning the wisdom of the Bharatiya Mazdoor Sangh in starting a *Sarva Panth Samadar Manch* (platform for equal validity of different religions).

I sent a summary of my short speech and the letter to Sitaji. He in turn showed them to Ram Swarup who also liked them immensely. Sitaji asked me if he could circulate the material widely and elicit responses, which could then be published. Sitaji himself had been collecting material on the Sangh Parivar vis-à-vis the Islamic problem. Koenraad Elst was also writing a book on the BJP at that time. Sitaji hoped to publish both these books at the same time. A brief exchange of letters between Sudarshanji and me followed. A similar exchange also took place between RSS activist S.D. Laghate from New Delhi and me. I sent all these letters to Sitaji. In a letter dd. December 7, 1996, he wrote: "Responses are piling up. All of them are in tune with you. (Ö) Let no one say that the Sangh leadership surrendered to Islam without warning, as in the case of Gandhiji. He threw up his hands after having assured Hindus that Pakistan will take place over his dead body, — the greatest betrayal in human history. Sangh leaders may live to beat his record."

In a letter to me dd. Jan.1, 1997, Sitaji wrote: "I wonder if the RSS leaders have ever known such straight talk from one of their own fold. Yours is a revolutionary step. The RSS is doomed unless the rank and file stands up. My own experience of the RSS leadership has been: the higher you go, the greater the duffer you meet. My own experience of Thengadi has been particularly revealing... I have also received some poetry (meaning using words without saying anything) from a few others of the same sort. It is revealing — the poverty of mind. When Arun Shourie showed me the typescript of his *Missionaries in India*, I had observed, 'Now I can die in peace, others are coming up to take the battle'. Your letter to Laghate makes me doubly sure. The responses I have received show that Hindus are waking up."

In his letter dd. February 2, 1997, he wrote: "I shared your letter to Sudarshanji with several friends. They all liked it immensely, and said that it was time for some people to stand up." In his letter dd. April 15, 1997, Sitaji wrote: "The two books (*Time for Stock-Taking: Whither Sangh Parivar?* and Elst's *BJP vis-à-vis Hindu Resurgence*) have been completed in the first draft. I had a heap of press cuttings regarding BJP wooing Muslims. All these have gone in our appendix to *Time for Stock-Taking*, which starts with the working paper *Ideological Defence of Hindu Society*, which I had prepared in 1983 at the behest of Sudarshanji."

Thus were born the above-mentioned books. Though I had sparked off the responses that led to *Time for Stock-Taking*, it was Sitaji who truly deserved credit for bringing out the book. However, he began the introduction to the book by giving me the entire credit for it. He used to invariably send me complimentary copies of all VOI publications. When I once asked him for names of suitable reference books on the Sufis, he generously gifted me Sayid Athar Abbas Rizvi's two-volume *A History of Sufism in India*. Such was his magnanimity. This again may come as a surprise to those who judge him on the basis of his combative and at times harsh language. I also spent a memorable day with Sitaji on February 21, 1997. From his office, we drove to Ram Swarup's residence. Ram Swarup's in-house library had far fewer books than I had expected. He must have sensed the surprise on my face. Putting his hand on my shoulder, Ram Swarup said:

"Form an idea and develop your own thoughts around it. My book *The Word as Revelation* has no bibliography." I was delighted to receive a copy of his *Communism and Peasantry*, which remains one of my prized possessions.

The three of us then drove to Sitaji's residence and had dinner. Sitaji generously made all arrangements for my transport back to my residence. That day is etched on my mind. I shall cherish the time spent in the company of these two rishis to the end of my life! Sitaji made many important observations and remarks in his correspondence and conversations. I am now putting them, or my memory of them, on record. That is to say, I have tried to faithfully put down Sitaji's remarks in conversation, while those made in his letters have been quoted verbatim. I do not necessarily endorse all of them. They also represent only his side of the story; many of the people concerned are dead and cannot offer their version of events. At any rate, what follows are some observations of his which I think are worth preserving.

8.2. On Christianity and Islam

On closed creeds (letter dd. December 7, 1996): "Islam and Christianity are not ways of worship; they are ways of waging war on humanity — both in the qualitative and quantitative sense. That has to be our mantra. Those who divide the human family — Moses, Jesus, Muhammad, Marx, Ambedkar, Nehruvian secularists — are criminals and should be nailed as such, no matter how high the pedestal on which they have been perched."

On peripheral criticism of Christianity's behaviour as distinct from the critique of its core doctrine (in conversation): "I think Dr. N.S. Rajaram is reading too much into the Dead Sea Scrolls scandal." After all, once you penetrate the core of these belief systems, they aren't hard to debunk: "I have no time to read more on Christianity. I am busy demolishing it." (letter dd. September 9, 1996, in reply to my plan to send him a copy of *The Life and Witness of the Churches in Mizoram*)

On the Quran and the biography of Muhammad (letter dd. August 22, 1996): "Pickthall's translation of the Quran is as good (or as misleading) as any other. I have used it in my *Hindu Temples II.* A chronological account is not available except in a book by Noldke, *A History of the Quran*, which I have not yet been able to find. It was published long ago but has been reprinted a few decades back. If there is a good Christian library in Pune, it may be there. In any case, I am putting some of the verses straight in my new edition of *The Calcutta Quran Petition*, which is under way. I have read 18 volumes of orthodox Hadis collections in Urdu, and found a number of Hadis which provide the context. It is revealing."

Further (letter dd. May 22, 1995): "I would request you not to take interest in Muhammad's personal life such as his wives and children. What matters to the Kafirs like us is his doctrine of terrorism. He might have married a hundred wives and produced a thousand children, for all we care. But he would not have become the scourge he has been had he not borrowed his god and his theology from the Bible and imposed it on the Arabs so that they became brutalized. But I will answer your questions: 1) All orthodox biographies of Muhammad link revelations with his life at every stage. Allah confirms in the Quran whatever Muhammad has done or is planning to do. One of them, Ibn Ishaq alone, is available in English. Muir whose *Life of Mahomet* we have published, has done the same. 2) Ayesha's observation about Allah making things convenient for Muhammad occurs in all orthodox compilations of the Hadis. Bukhari, Muslim and Daud are now available in English translation. I have studied in detail the Urdu translations of all the six authentics."

On Sufism (letter dd. August 22, 1996): "I wish I could recommend to you some book on Sufism. There is none written so far about their true character and role. Hindus have written the greatest nonsense about them. But as you can read between the lines, I recommend *History of Sufism in India* by S.A.A. Rizvi published in two volumes by Munshiram

Manoharlal, New Delhi. I can get them for you. They are expensive. *Sufis of Bijapur* [by Richard Eaton] has only a few lines which say something true about this gang. Rest of it is descriptive. In any case, the same author has written another book meanwhile and withdrawn whatever he had said a little earlier. Must have been paid handsomely. Scholars by and large have axes to grind. Some of them have been for sale also. I wish I could write my book on Sufis. A whole shelf is lined with source material in Urdu and Persian."

On Urdu poetry (in conversation): "What Muslim poets dared not write in prose, they wrote in verse. Urdu poetry is more often than not a revolt against Islam." Few people are aware that Sitaji was a great lover of Urdu poetry.

On renaming towns (in conversation): "It is my desire that Daulatabad be renamed Deogiri. That was the first Hindu city to be given an Islamic name." I could sense that Sitaji felt very strongly about this. He asked me who in Maharashtra could be depended upon to do this renaming. In the same vein: "I have always felt repelled by the names *Balasaheb* and *Babasaheb* occuring too often in Marathi names and honorifics. No one seems to know what these words stand for in Islamic parlance." (letter dd. April 15, 1997)

On historian P.N. Oak, known for claiming the Taj Mahal and other Muslim buildings as Hindu creations, Sitaji recalled his reply when Oak had asked him whether he had described him as a taint on Hindu scholarship (in conversation): "No, that's not true. You are in fact a big black blot on Hindu scholarship." Sitaji used to bemoan the fact that the marvellous sculpture in Hindu temples is never appreciated while the Taj Mahal, which is just a vulgar piece of marble, is described as a wonder.

On Islamic history, after K.R. Malkani had cited a story to prove that *namaz* offered on a disputed site is unacceptable to Allah (letter dd. September 24, 1996): "The story about Umar refusing to do namaz inside a Church (not a Jewish place of worship, Jerusalem was already a Christian city by this time) in Jerusalem after its conquest in 636 is found in all Muslim histories of the medieval Caliphate. It is supposed to prove the tolerant character of Islam. But critics of Islam have always asked a very valid question: 'What could be tolerant about a creed whose adherents claim a place simply because one of their heroes used it briefly for namaz?' The story proves the opposite of what it is supposed to prove. Muhammad had laid down: 'Once a mosque, always a mosque.' The argument was used by many Muslims during the Ayodhya controversy. In any case, Malkani should have asked, 'What happened to the Church even if Umar did not do his namaz there? Did it remain a Church?' History records that it was converted into a mosque before long, as soon as the Muslims felt strong after the Christian population was driven out. Moreover, Umar's character and reign are no secret. They have been thoroughly documented, and tell us that he was the Stalin of the Lenin that was Muhammad — a bloodthirsty hoodlum of the most despicable sort."

On Wahiduddin Khan (letter dd. November 1, 1996): "W. Khan has been the blue-eyed boy of the Sangh Parivar for quite some time. Malkani and Nanaji Deshmukh consider him an authority on Islam they like to believe in. W. Khan is the leading light of Tablighi Jamaat, a wide-ranging organization working since 1920 for wiping out all traces of Hindu culture in the consciousness and behaviour of Hindu converts to Islam. Muslims are made to 1) eat beef in a public meeting; 2) marry within degrees prohibited in Hindu tradition; 3) take authentic Muslim names. They have to stop wearing *dhoti* etc. See my chapter on Wahabis and Faraizis in *Muslim Separatism*."

8.3. On "secularism"

On secularist censorship (in conversation): "In India, there is freedom to praise Islam. There is no freedom to criticize it. There is an undeclared curfew on any critical discussion of Islam."

On Nehru and the secularists (letter dd. November 1, 1996): "Ganesh Shankar Vidyarthi was a typical Congressman of the Gandhi-Nehru brand — hard on 'Hindu communalists'. He was killed in the Kanpur riots in 1931. The Congress appointed a Committee for inquiry with Dr. Bhagvan Das as Chairman. But the report was written by Sunderlal of *Bharat mein Angrezi Raj* fame. He had plagiarized the anti-British part of this book from Maj. Basu's *Rise of Christian Power in India.* His own contribution was the portion praising Muslim rule to the skies. The Committee recommended revision of India's history to show Muslim rule as a great benefit. Pandit Nehru took the cue and wrote his *Glimpses of World History*, eulogizing Ghaznavi, Babar and Aurangzeb and denouncing Hindu freedom fighters like Shivaji. Akbar became the father of Indian Nationalism and so on. I have collected a lot of material for the 2nd volume on Nehru — *The Confluence of All Imperialist Ideologies.*" Note that Sitaji's proposed second volume never saw the light of day. A great loss for the Hindus!

On Arvind Ghosh, Houston-based publisher of the *Sword of Truth* booklets and a fierce critic of the Nehru-Gandhi family (in conversation): "I told him that we should fight Nehru's philosophy and not bother about his private life. He did not listen. The result was that his book on Nehru was banned."

8.4. On Hindu nationalists

On Shivaji (in conversation): "Shivaji cannot be over-glorified, he was *aapaadmastak shaktiputra*". Shivaji was Sitaji's foremost hero.

On Veer Savarkar, when I had asked Mr. Goel to give reference to a disputed Savarkar statement (pleading, contra Shivaji's gentlemanly magnanimity, to give tit for tat to Muslim captors of Hindu women) that he had mentioned elsewhere: "Savarkar's statement about Shivaji's failure to distribute captured Muslim women among Hindu soldiers has been read by me with my own eyes in one of the chapters in [Savarkar's early book] *Six Periods*, published by an RSS set-up in Lucknow with a footnote, 'We do not agree with this.' That was years ago. I may have the book in my library but it may take a whole day to find it out. But a single statement does not undo his vision on India's history." (letter dd. March 12, 1997)

On Shyama Prasad Mookerjee, whose death in prison is often described as a case of murder (in conversation): "My friend Vaidya Guru Dutt was with Mookerjee when he died. Mookerjee, a heart patient, had consumed a whole chicken against medical advice and this precipitated his death."

On Deendayal Upadhyaya (in conversation): "He was a mean, lowly kind of person. During one election, he called me and said, '*Doosron ke liye kaam karte ho, kabhi hamare liye bhi to kaam karo* ['You work for others, sometimes you have to do some work for us too'] — the allusion being to the canard that I was a CIA agent! I walked out without a word." As for Deendayal's fall through an open train door, another death often described in Sangh circles as a case of murder (in conversation): "Deendayal probably looked out of the moving train and his head hit a pole. That led to his death."

On Balasaheb Deoras (in conversation): "I met him only once. I told him that Christianity and Islam are not religions but imperialist ideologies. 'That is what you say', he replied."

On K.S. Sudarshan (letter dd. March 12, 1997): "Incidentally, Sudarshanji has written a very good article in the Hindu Sangharsh Visheshank of *Panchajanya*. Do read it. He shows considerable knowledge of Hindu tradition and the character of aggressive ideologies. One wonders what happens to this knowledge when they work in the field." But later he noted (letter dd. September 11, 1997): "I had a better opinion about Sudarshanji till I read his letter to you (latest). It seems he is no different from the herd wandering (*pravas*) across the country. I can smash all his ravings. So can you. *Bhains ke aage roye, apne nayan khoye.* ['Cry in front of a buffalo, you cry your eyes out (without provoking any reaction)', or roughly: talking to them is like talking to a wall.] Just now they are power drunk. I have been meeting some RSS rank and file. There is acute discomfort at what their leaders are doing. BJP is fully supported by the RSS leadership in crawling before Kanshi Ram. You can depend on Hindus for committing suicide."

On Dattopant Thengadi (in conversation): "He has swallowed large doses of Marxism." Moreover (letter dd. September 24, 1996): "Some years ago, Sudarshanji was staying in a summer camp of the RSS in Delhi. As usual, he rang me up and asked me to go and meet him. I had just finished my preface to *The Calcutta Quran Petition*, first edition. I took a copy of the typescript along. Thengadi was there. I have known him since 1956 when he spoke during my contest for a Lok Sabha seat from Khajuraho. He snatched the typescript from Sudarshanji and said he would read it first. A few weeks later, an article by Thengadi appeared in the *Panchajanya* praising Muhammad to the skies. It was aimed at 'fanatics' like myself. Many RSS people telephoned to Ram Swarup and myself asking us to write a reply. We refused. You cannot argue with people who have already decided what to say out of other considerations. It is a great pity that Thengadi passes as the tallest intellectual of the Sangh Parivar. At one stage I was mighty afraid that he was going to be the next Sar Sanghchalak after Balasaheb Deoras."

On K.R. Malkani (letter dd. September 24, 1996): "Malkani has been a very good friend of mine. I published his *The RSS Story* and reviewed his *Sindh Story*. Early in the 80s we met everyday in the *Organiser* office. I discovered that after meeting the Jamaat-i-Islami mullahs in jail in 1977-78, he had himself become an apologist of Islam. Now he reads only Islamic apologetics, and avoids the original sources (dogmatics and polemics). He has studiously avoided reading VOI literature. (...) Malkani has grown fast into a terrible fool. It is a pity that he along with Thengadi has become the high-priest of dialogue with Muslims. Maulana Wahiduddin, a fanatic *tablighi*, is the guru of Malkani and Nanaji Deshmukh. The road to hell is paved with good intentions."

On Nanaji Deshmukh (in conversation): "Once Nanaji invited me to meet him in his office at the Deendayal Research Institute. He wanted to know something about the history of the Sufis. When I started criticizing the Sufis, I found he was no longer interested in what I was saying."

On L.K. Advani, the only BJP leader to whom he sent copies of *Time for Stock Taking* and *Bharatiya Janata Party vis-ā-vis Hindu Resurgence* (in conversation): "Advani once remarked to me: 'You never ask anything from me.' Advani has a sharp memory. On one occasion, we were interrupted in our conversation. When we next met, Advani instantly remembered where we had broken off and resumed the conversation."

On Uma Bharati (in conversation): "Uma Bharati thinks no end of herself. Once we happened to be together in a meeting but she studiously looked the other way. Then someone mentioned that I had once contested for the Lok Sabha from Khajuraho [then her own constituency]. She probably thought I was important and immediately turned towards me."

On the Sangh Parivar (in conversation): "I once had occasion to address a gathering of RSS workers. They showed no emotion or reaction. I felt I was speaking to a wall." Worse (letter dd. September 24, 1996): "Ram Swarup says that in the Sangh Parivar there is now a will to believe in the beauties of Islam. If Islam is that good, there is no problem and you do not have to do anything about it. Rationalization for mental sloth and much indifference, if not something worse."

Moreover (letter dd. January 1, 1997): "I wonder why the RSS meetings do not ever take up any ideological issue. The other day there was news that the Minorities Commission has recognized the Jains as a non-Hindu minority. No one from the Sangh Parivar has reacted. It was the same story when the Ramakrishna Mission did the same. Sudarshanji was all sympathy for the RKM when Ram Swarup mentioned the subject to him at a dinner in my house. Article 30 is being made an excuse for walking out of the Hindu fold."

The petty personal hostilities further poisoned the atmosphere, e.g. (letter dd. September 12, 1997): "Many RSS people call me a CIA agent, others say that I am minting money. I will not be able to do anything if I cared for canards." To mention some names (letter dd. May 29, 1998): "M.G. Vaidya is not alone in being hostile. The RSS in general shows the same attitude. Sudarshanji who always telephoned whenever he was in Delhi has been silent for months. The other day, an article by a writer was turned down because it carried a quote from Sita Ram Goel. Devendra Swarup denounces me as *Hindu Dharma ka thekedar* ['contractor of Hinduism']."

Finally (over the telephone in September 1998): "The Sangh Parivar will not accept me as one of their own. They will appropriate me after my death." I had written an article on Sitaji on the occasion of his 77th birthday and sent it to *Organiser*. Initially, editor Seshadri Chari was reluctant to publish the article as he felt it almost read like an obituary. However, when I told Chari the above-mentioned feelings of Sitaji on the matter, he said: "In that case, we will certainly publish the article." The article was duly published in the Deepavali Special issue of October 18, 1998, together with Sitaji's earlier paper *Ideological Defence of Hindu Society*.

8.5. On Voice of India

On editing (letter dd. February 14, 1997): "Correcting people's English is a back-breaking job." Sitaji's English was so impeccable and his mastery over the language so complete that one could not but marvel at his language while being swept by the power of his argument. Incidentally, while Sitaji's English writings are largely hard-hitting, his Hindi can only be described as *madhur*, honey-sweet; the latter compliment was once paid by Jayaprakash Narayan.

Not everyone has such language skills, unfortunately: "I have not had a good experience of translations of Voice of India publications." (in conversation)

On Voice of India's role in the Ayodhya debate: "The evidence for a Ram Temple at the disputed site in Ayodhya that was submitted to the Government of India by the Hindu side was put together in the VOI office." (in conversation)

On Voice of India's rapport with the Hindu public (letter dd. June 9, 1994): "We [Ram Swarup and Sitaji] are happy not so much because VOI publications have taken the information to the right quarters but because the younger generation is coming forward to defend the Hindu heritage. This is the story everywhere. Hindu editors cannot publicize the Hindu point of view without at the same time giving publicity to Islam and Christianity. I wonder when Hindus will have a Hindu press."

On its limitations (letter dd. August 22, 1996): "Voice of India can do no more than what it is doing because it has no office of its own, no staff, no money worth the name. It is manned by me alone. I read, write, correct proofs, look after despatches, and am keeping accounts. We cannot get involved in the book trade. Booksellers in India are a pretty lousy lot (most of them). I can now work only for 6-7 hours compared to 14-15 earlier. I have nothing else to do. I am virtually a recluse. The only advantage is that I have not a worry in the world."

On its personal dimension (in conversation): "I am planning to organize a get-together of all VOI authors." Alas, this was not to be.

On the media response (letter dd. September 11, 1997): "I used to send all our publications for review in the mainstream papers. None of them was ever reviewed." However (letter dd. May, 29, 1998): "I tried all sorts of people and all papers for reviews long ago. I drew a blank. In any case reviews do not give us readers. Our books sell very well. The larger Hindu society is awake in spite of the Sangh Parivar."

On Ram Swarup (letter dd. November 1, 1996): "Ram Swarup has been the darling of the Sangh Parivar and still is. And Ram Swarup and I have never agreed on two subjects: 1) Mahatma Gandhi whom my instinct has always rejected as a disaster for Hindus; Ram Swarup is full of him; 2) the Sangh Parivar. I rejected it as a Hindu movement when I heard Golwalkar, with my own ears, praising Muhammad and Islam to the skies and denouncing Muslims. I have known the bigwigs of the Sangh Parivar from very close quarters. It is only recently that Ram Swarup has started getting disenchanted."

Occasionally he displayed some irritation with Ram Swarup's temperament and the resultant differences in approach and opinion. Once I had a conversation over dinner with both of them. I recall Sitaji's disapproving remark about how "nowadays, this fad of eating non-vegetarian is on the rise"; both were strict vegetarians. Anyway, at one point, Sitaji was criticizing the Sangh Parivar, when Ram Swarup left the room ostensibly for some work. Sitaji commented: "Ram Swarup will pretend he has not heard anything." And when I asked how we could get the ban on Ram Swarup's *Understanding Islam through Hadis* lifted, he said: "Ram Swarup wants others to fight his battles."

In spite of this, he continued to acknowledge his mentor's irreplaceable merits. This is how he reported Ram Swarup's passing away (letter dd. December 28, 1998): "Our beloved Ram Swarup expired on 26th December in the afternoon while sleeping. He suffered no illness." But his death was no ordinary death: "I do not grieve over Ram Swarup's passing away. The Ram Swarup who mattered in my and the nation's life is not dead. Only the *namarupa* has become *avyakta*." (i.e. his "name-and-form has become non-manifested", letter dd. January 22, 1999)

On Harsh Narain, a scrupulous historian and one of the rare Hindu scholars well-versed in Arabic as well as Persian (in conversation): "He is no more. Where will we get such a scholar?" I had inquired about Prof. Harsh Narain, not aware that he had passed away. I can still remember Sitaji shaking his head mournfully when he made that remark.

When I requested him to grant me his permission to suggest his name for the *Dr. Hedgewar Pragnya Puraskar* awarded by the Burra Bazar Kumarsabha Pustakalaya, Kolkata, he replied (letter dd. November 1, 1996): "Please spare me the humiliation of receiving *Hedgewar Puraskar*. I will have to refuse the honour. The Burra Bazar people of the Sangh still regard me as an American agent. I find it hard to forgive the Calcutta Marwaris the way they treated me."

On Shrikant Talageri (in conversation): "He is a great scholar. If you want to give the Hedgewar Puraskar to someone, let it be Talageri."

On his own life expectancy (letter dd. September 9, 1998): "I will be 77 on 16 October this year. So my career as a writer does not have much of a future." Even more pointedly (letter dd. September 15, 1998): "I shall be 77 on 16 October. It seems my days are drawing to an end. I surrender to Govind." But then, in a final flash of resolve and optimism (in conversation): "Koenraad Elst has become like a son to me. Last time he came here, he started photographing me in various moods, clearly on the assumption that it might be his last chance. I told him: 'I will not die so soon. I am going to live for 120 years as per the Hindu tradition.'"

8.6. Farewell

Towards the end, Sitaji had become a recluse. He had become virtually bedridden. Letters addressed to him would be answered by his son or assistant. With my father-in-law Sharad Mehendaley, I had co-translated Suhas Majumdar's *Jihad: The Islamic Concept of Permanent War* into Marathi. The book was being published by Bharatiya Vichar Sadhana, an RSS-affiliated publishing house in Pune. On May 12, 2003, I wrote a letter to him seeking his permission to have this translation published and inquired about Suhas Majumdar (or his kin) so that they could be given their copyright. I also mentioned to him that 25,000 copies of this translation had been booked pre-publication (post-publication, a further 10,000 copies have been sold). We had dedicated the translation to Ram Swarup and Sitaji as "our humble *guru dakshina* to these two latter-day rishis who, through the medium of Voice of India and writings elsewhere, inspired countless Hindus like us to view and critically study predatory ideologies like Christianity, Islam and Communism through a Hindu perspective".

On May 22, 2003, I received the following e-mail from Sitaji's son Pradeep Goel: "Many thanks for your kind letter dated 12 May addressed to my father Sita Ram Goel. I read the letter to my father and reply on his behalf. Sri Suhas Majumdar is no more. There is no copyright; you may not mention it on the book. We do not know any of his brothers but he had no children. Similarly, other books published by Voice of India also have no copyright. My father wants the message carried by our publications to reach as far and wide as possible. My father has not moved out of the house since last 2 years. He had LVF problem in March 2001. He is busy reading the Ramayana and the Mahabharata."

After the publication, I had posted a few copies to Sitaji and had planned to visit Delhi and hand over some copies in person. Alas, my plan underwent a change at the last moment and I could not have his final *darshan*. Though we all knew that his end was near, the communication of his death shocked us. Verily, Sitaji was the Bhishma Pitamaha of Hindu scholars, a Bhishma who fought for Truth.

(Dr. Shreerang Godbole is a medical doctor practising in Pune.)

9. Goel leaves behind unsung research

Prafull Goradia

Sita Ram Goel, who passed away on December 3, had made path-breaking research whose importance has remained largely unsung. Alexander Cunningham, the founder-director of the Archaeological Survey of India, and a few of his colleagues had discovered several temples that had been desecrated and turned into mosques. But, as officers of the ASI, their mission was archaeology in general and not specific to the places of worship. No one took up the specific task until Goel embarked upon it and catalogued thousands of converted and recycled temples.

The subject is often dismissed as obscurantist. Condemned as recalling historical wrongs merely as an excuse for seeking revenge. The old places of worship, it is alleged, have no progressive value and are therefore best forgotten. The parallel often quoted is of similar happenings in Europe. It is argued that hundreds of churches were converted to mosques and, in turn, a large number of masjids were changed into chapels, cathedrals, et al.

An outstanding example quoted is that of the Hagia Sophia cathedral in Istanbul, which is now a mosque. Another prominent instance mentioned is that at Sevilla in Spain, where the Almohad Masjid was remodelled into a cathedral bell tower. The comparison, however, is unfair because unlike Christians, the Hindus have no tradition of converting members of other religions nor has it been the Hindu practice to desecrate masjids or churches and turn them into temples. In other words, what in Europe amounts to reciprocal aggression, has been one-sided oppression in India.

For some two decades, most of the print media blacked out

what Mr. Sita Ram Goel wrote, presumably on the pretext that what he wrote might create communal ill feeling. Although what he researched and wrote was based on evidence and facts. He had no political pretensions; he was a scholar in search of truth. What amounted to a media boycott was, therefore, quite uncanny.

One explanation for this prejudice could be that it was the post-Independence policy of the ASI as well as self-styled secular leaders to conceal rather than reveal discovery. There were two glaring examples. The first one was the Rudramahalaya complex at Siddhpur, Gujarat, in the 1970s, where artefacts like the Nandi bull, etc., having been excavated, were buried back. This was reported at length in the fourth annual report of the National Minorities Commission. The second instance was in 1991 at Vidisha, near Bhopal, when due to heavy rainfall a wall collapsed and exposed a large number of idols under the apron of the Bijamandal masjid. Soon thereafter, the District Magistrate as well as the local ASI officer were transferred.

The series of central laws passed since independence reflect the policy of conceal rather than reveal, put back rather than bring out. The culmination came in 1991 when The Places of Worship (Special Provisions) Act was passed by Parliament. It declared that the character of any place of worship that existed on August 15, 1947, could not be changed. The only exception was the Ram Janmabhoomi; all the other temples turned mosques had to stay put for all time, according to this law.

To sum up, the media has silenced rather than articulated. The Education and later the HRD Ministry followed the policy of maintaining the unfortunate status quo. Ironically, even those who believe in the cause of discovery, have been more quiet than active. It is not merely a religious or an inter-community controversy. The issue also involves the more secular ethics. Is it not basically immoral to retain in one's possession property known to be loot?

The converted or recycled masjids — that require no further proof of their forcible dispossession by the conquerors — should surely be returned to the people to whom they belong. It is agreed that the present generation of Muslims has nothing to do with this plunder. They are not responsible but surely their sense of decency would lead them to give back the loot and plunder of their forefathers to the rightful owners? Unfortunately, instead, they insist on treating them as property disputes which only the courts of law can adjudicate. And, in their opinion, the courts do not have much option since the Muslim community has enjoyed adverse possession for several centuries.

(Published in *The Pioneer*, Delhi, 12 January 2004; Mr. Prafull Goradia is an entrepreneur and former BJP office-bearer who in 2004 founded a new pro-Hindu party using the old name Jan Sangh.)

10. Rights and Writing

Subhash Kak

10.1. Personal memories

I first met Sita Ramji in 1993, but I don't remember the circumstances under which I was introduced to him. My father had passed away in Hawaii in July, and I was in India briefly in August to take part in the funeral rites. On this trip I gave some public lectures in Delhi and perhaps we met at one of these lectures.

A few years earlier I had written a review of Colin Renfrew's much-discussed book *Archaeology and Language* for the *Times of India.* This was perhaps the first intimation in India that the Aryan Invasion Theory (AIT), on which standard histories of Indian civilization have been based for decades, was being questioned by archaeologists in the West. Naturally, the review had generated much interest and this is how Sita Ramji had heard of me.

Ideas about early Indian history continue to play an important role in political ideology of contemporary India. On the one side are the left and Dravidian parties, which believe that invading Aryans from the northwest pushed the Dravidians to south India and India's caste divisions are a consequence of that encounter. Even the development of Hinduism is seen through this anthropological lens. This view is essentially that of the colonial historians developed over a hundred years ago.

On the other side are the nationalist parties, which believe that the Aryan languages are native to India. These groups cite the early astronomical dates in the Vedas, noting these texts are rooted firmly in the Indian geographical region. But leftist scholars consider such evidence suspect, politically motivated, and chauvinistic.

The work of archaeologists and historians of science has concluded that there is no material evidence for any large scale migrations into India over the period of 4500–800 BC, implicitly supporting the traditional view of Indian history. The left has responded by conceding that there were probably no invasions; rather, there were many small scale migrations by Aryans who, through a process of cultural dominance, imposed their language on North-Indians.

The drama of text-book revisions, both during the NDA and the current UPA governments, is essentially a struggle to impose one or the other of these viewpoints. In any other country, such a fight would have been fought in the pages of academic journals; but in India, where the government decides what *history is,* it is a political matter.

When we met, it was a period of much uncertainty and passion in India. The Ramajanmabhumi movement had led to the demolition of the Babri structure in Ayodhya a few months earlier. There was a feeling among the nationalists that the current impasse was a consequence of the internalization by Indians of the colonial approach to Indian history and polity. They felt that this view was not supported by the Indian tradition itself, and had no basis in fact; therefore, it needed to be corrected. It was believed that although the colonial view was an instrument of the British Raj, it had been, after independence, slowly internalized by India's own elite. According to this view, India had no science, and Indian history must be seen as a continuing struggle between fractured racial and social groups.

At one level the fight in India was really not over the disputed structure in Ayodhya, but over the very soul of India. Although the media presented it as a conflict between the Hindu nationalists and minorities, it was a contest between the nationalists and the colonial mindset of the Indian elites for the history of India.

Traditional historians in India had never accepted the AIT, but they had no power in the academia. Sita Ramji and Ram Swarupji realized that the attacks on the AIT in the West meant that perhaps the time had come to free history of Indian culture from its colonial moorings. They had also heard of my work on the astronomy of the Vedic period and my analysis of the Harappan script (also known as Indus or Sarasvati script) that supported the idea of continuity in Indian culture. They were particularly pleased that my work had appeared in several peer-reviewed journals in the West. They greeted me very warmly when we met in Sita Ramji's office at Ansari Road in Delhi.

Sita Ramji offered to publish my essays on India as well as my work on Vedic astronomy, and these books appeared in print within a few months. We were to meet several times on that trip to sort out matters regarding the publication and we also met at the many public lectures I gave that year and on my subsequent visits to India.

I was most impressed with Sita Ramji's intellect and clarity of thought. He was one of the first to see the dangers that lay in the adoption of the Soviet model of economic growth. But the idea of socialism was very popular with India's intellectual class in the fifties and sixties, therefore, Sita Ramji, together with Ram Swarup, became lonely figures on the Indian intellectual scene. They were visionaries who saw trends of history years before anyone else noticed them. In India, they also pointed to the hypocrisy in public life as a consequence of the continual parroting of the slogan of "secularism" by politicians and academics. Thus, they argued that Article 30 of the Indian Constitution, which was interpreted to mean that only minority religions had the right to run their educational institutions, was leading to a fragmentation of the Hindu community with several groups approaching the Courts to be declared as non-Hindu.

These writings were perhaps instrumental in getting a section of the middle class to turn away from the Congress party in favour of the Bharatiya Janata Party. In this sense, they were prophets of the fundamental changes that were to hit the Indian polity in the beginning of the nineties.

10.2. Progress in the Aryan invasion debate

Ram Swarup and Sita Ram Goel passed away before research in genetics, which provides new independent evidence against the AIT, became generally accepted. In an important book titled *The Real Eve: Modern Man's Journey out of Africa* (Carroll and Graf Publishers, New York 2003), the prominent Oxford University scholar Stephen Oppenheimer has synthesized the available genetic evidence together with climatology and archeology, with conclusions which have bearing on the debate about the early population of India. This work has received great attention in the West, and it will also interest Indians tremendously.

Much of Oppenheimer's theory is based on recent advances in studies of mitochondrial DNA, inherited through the mother, and Y chromosomes, inherited by males from the father. Oppenheimer makes the case that whereas Africa is the cradle of all mankind, India is the cradle of all non-African peoples. Man left Africa approximately 90,000 years ago, heading east along the Indian Ocean, and established settlements in India. It was only during a break in glacial activity 50,000 years ago, when deserts turned into grasslands, that people left India and headed northwest into the Russian steppes and on into Eastern Europe, as well as northeast through China and over the now submerged Bering Strait into the Americas.

In their migration to India, African people carried the mitochondrial DNA strain L3 and Y chromosome line M168 across the southern Red Sea across the southern part of the Arabian Peninsula. On the maternal side the mtDNA strain L3 split into two daughters, which Oppenheimer labels Nasreen and Manju. While Manju was definitely born in India, the birthplace of Nasreen is tentatively placed by him in southern

Iran or Baluchistan. One Manju subclan in India is as old as 73,000 years, whereas European man goes back to less than 50,000 years.

Considering the paternal side, Oppenheimer sees M168 as having three sons, of whom Seth was the most important one. Seth, in turn, had five sons which are named by him as Jahangir, H, I, G and Krishna. Born in India, Krishna is the ancestor of the peoples of East Asia, Central Asia, Oceania and West Eurasia (through the M17 mutation). This is what Oppenheimer says about M17:

> *South Asia is logically the ultimate origin of M17 and his ancestors; and sure enough we find highest rates and greatest diversity of the M17 line in Pakistan, India, and eastern Iran, and low rates in the Caucasus. M17 is not only more diverse in South Asia than in Central Asia but diversity characterizes its presence in isolated tribal groups in the south, thus undermining any theory of M17 as a marker of a "male Aryan Invasion of India".* (p.152)
>
> *Study of the geographical distribution and the diversity of genetic branches and stems again suggests that Ruslan, along with his son M17, arose early in South Asia, somewhere near India, and subsequently spread not only south-east to Australia but also north, directly to Central Asia, before splitting east and west into Europe and East Asia.* (p.153)

Oppenheimer argues that the Eurocentric view of ancient history is also incorrect. For example, Europeans didn't invent art, because the Australian aborigines developed their own unique artistic culture in complete isolation. Indian rock art is also extremely ancient, going back to over 40,000 BC, so perhaps art as a part of culture had arisen in Africa itself. Similarly, agriculture didn't arise in the Fertile Crescent; Southeast Asia had already domesticated many plants by that time.

Oppenheimer concludes with two *extraordinary conclusions*: "First, that the Europeans' genetic homeland was originally in South Asia in the Pakistan/Gulf region over

50,000 years ago; and second, that the Europeans' ancestors followed at least two widely separated routes to arrive, ultimately, in the same cold but rich garden. The earliest of these routes was the Fertile Crescent. The second early route from South Asia to Europe may have been up the Indus into Kashmir and on to Central Asia, where perhaps more than 40,000 years ago hunters first started bringing down game as large as mammoths." (pp.153-154)

This synthesis of genetic evidence makes it possible to understand the divide between the North- and the South-Indian languages. It appears that the Dravidian languages are more ancient, and the Aryan languages *evolved in India* over thousands of years before migrations took them to central Asia and westward to Europe. The proto-Dravidian languages had also, through the ocean route, reached Northeast Asia, explaining the connections between the Dravidian family and the Korean and Japanese languages.

Perhaps this new understanding will encourage Indian politicians to get away from the polemics of who the *original* inhabitants of India are, since that should not matter one way or the other in the governance of the country. Indian politics has long been plagued by the Aryan invasion narrative, which was created by English scholars of the 19th century; it is fitting that another Englishman, Stephen Oppenheimer, should announce its demise.

10.3. Indian Writing

As a tribute to Sita Ramji, I summarize the argument about the continuity in Indian writing from the Harappan script onwards. The evolution and origin of writing was a subject very dear to his heart and he avidly followed reports of "decipherment" of the Indus script.

It is generally recognized that modern Indian scripts, such as Devanagari, Telugu, Tamil and Bengali, are less than two thousand years old; and that they sprang from Brahmi, which, in turn, is at least 2,500 years old. Early writings of Brahmi, discovered in Sri Lanka, have been dated tentatively to about 500 BC. The more commonly known Brahmi records belong to the reign of the Mauryan king Ashoka (250 BC). The Indus script was used widely during 2600–1900 BC. Its starting has been traced back to 3300 BC and its use continued sporadically into the late centuries of the second millennium BC.

The Brahmi script is the parent not only of the Indian scripts but also of most other Asian scripts. It also influenced the development of the Japanese and the Korean scripts.

We know that writing was used in India prior to 500 BC. Written characters are mentioned in the Chhandogya and the Taittiriya Upanishad, and the Aitareya Aranyaka refers to the distinction between the various consonant classes. The voluminous Vedic texts also contain hints of writing in them. For example, Rigveda 10.71.4 says:

> *utā́ tvah pā́shyan nā́ dadarsha vaā́cam utā́ tvah shrnvā́n nā́ shrnoty enaam*
> One man has never seen Vak, yet he sees; one man has hearing but has never heard her.

Since *Vak* is personified speech, it suggests knowledge or writing. Another verse (RV 10.62.7) mentions cows being marked by the sign of "8". The Atharvaveda (19.72) speaks of taking the Veda out of a chest (*kosha*), and although it may be a metaphor for knowledge coming out of a treasure-house, it could equally have been meant in a literal sense.

The traditional date for the Rigveda is about 3000 BC, with the later Vedic texts and the Brahmanas coming a few centuries later. The Aranyakas, Upanishads and the Sutras are, in this view, dated to the 2nd and early 1st millennia. The astronomical evidence in the texts is in accord with this view. Furthermore, the currently accepted date of 1900 BC for the drying up of the Sarasvati river, hailed as the mightiest river of the Vedic age with its course ranging from the mountain to the sea, implies that the Vedas are definitely prior to this date. It is also significant that the Brahmana texts speak of the drying up of the Sarasvati as a recent event. This brings the Vedas to the period of the use of the Indus script in India. It is also significant that the geography of the Harappan region corresponds to the geography of the Rigveda.

Even if one accepted the colonial chronology of ancient India, the period of the Rigveda corresponds to the later period of the Harappan culture. This means that the Indus script is likely to have been used to write Sanskrit and other languages spoken in the 3rd millennium India, just as Brahmi was used to represent North- and South-Indian languages 2,500 years ago.

Although there was great emphasis on memorizing the Veda, this does not mean that writing was unknown in the early Vedic age. The subsidiary subjects of prosody and grammar that were central to the Vedic experience could not have arisen without writing. This view is further supported by the organization of the Rigveda, which is according to a precise numerical plan.

There are many competing theories about the nature of the Indus script. The main difficulty with "proving" any decipherment is that the texts are very short, very rarely having more than ten characters. For a proposed decipherment to be scientifically established, one needs texts that are at least 25 characters long, and such texts do not exist.

Some historians believe that Brahmi is derived from one of the West Asian scripts and, indeed, there are interesting similarities between their characters for several signs. On the other hand, there is a remarkable continuity between the structures of Indus and Brahmi. Since a script can be used to write a variety of languages — even unrelated ones —, the question of structural relationship is particularly interesting.

Indus and Brahmi connections become evident when one considers the most commonly occurring letters of the two scripts. In a series of articles in *Cryptologia*, I examined these connections for similarity in form, case endings for inscriptions, and the sign for "ten".[1] The parallels are extraordinary and the probability that they arose by chance is extremely small. To see these parallels it is absolutely essential to examine seals from the historical period, as was done by Kiran Kumar Thaplyal in a very important book.[2] Since the technical arguments related to the relationship between the two scripts are beyond the scope of this article, let me only reproduce the ten most likely letters from the two scripts (*Tables 1 and 2, see page 128*).

Notice that the three most commonly occurring letters in both the scripts are the "jar", the "fish", and the "man". The number of matches in the ten signs is 7; the probability of this happening by chance is less than 10^{-12}. It is also remarkable that the "fish" sign is used as a symbol for "10" in the Indus (used without the gills; such use was determined by a statistical analysis) and the Brahmi scripts, although the Brahmi "fish" for "10" is shown sideways.

As for case endings, when we examine early Brahmi seals, we find that most of them are either dative or genitive, i.e. "for So-and-So" or "So-and-So's". In Sanskrit, the most common ending for the dative grammatical form is "-ai" (as in *tasmai*, or *tasyai*) and the most common ending for the genitive grammatical form is "-as", "-sya", or "-am" (as in *Ramas, Ramasya, -abhyam*). This means that the most common case endings in Brahmi letters are "arrow" (for "ai"), and "-s", "-sya" and "m". The most common ending letters in the Indus script are the "jar" that we have identified as "-s", the "fish" sign that we have seen it as "m", and an "arrow" sign! This reinforces the view that the Brahmi script is derived from the Indus script.

---

[1] Subhash Kak: "A frequency analysis of the Indus script", *Cryptologia* # 12, 1988, pp.129-143; "Indus and Brahmi: further connections", *Cryptologia* # 14, 1990, pp.169-183; "An Indus-Sarasvati signboard", *Cryptologia* # 20, 1996, pp.275-279. See also S. Kak: "Indus writing", *Mankind Quarterly* # 30, 1989, pp.113-118; S. Kak: "Evolution of early writing in India", *Indian Journal of History of Science* # 29, 1994, pp.375-388; and S. Kak: "A note on Harappan writing", *Adyar Library Bulletin* # 66, Chennai 2002, pp.79-85.

[2] K.K. Thaplyal: *Studies in Ancient Indian Seals*, Lucknow 1971.

Table 1: Ten most common Brahmi letters in rank order and with percentage

Rank	1	2	3	4	5	6	7	8	9	10
Brahmi sign	𑀲	𑀫	𑀢	𑀦	𑀧	𑀬	𑀯	𑀭	𑀤	𑀘
Value	s	m	t	n	p	y	v	r	d	c
Percentage	12.6	11.2	8.6	7.9	6.9	6.5	5.1	4.6	4.2	4.0

Table 2: Ten most common Indus signs (Mahadevan Concordance)

Rank	1	2	3	4	5	6	7	8	9	10
Indus sign										
Frequency	2245	1254	837	459	411	406	343	292	256	243

Regarding the similarities between Brahmi and early Semitic scripts, it should be noted that Indic kingdoms, in which Sanskrit names were used, were prominent in West Asia in the second millennium BC. Just like in the Vedic system, the Ugaritics, a people closely related to the Phoenicians and the Hebrews, had 33 gods. Also, it is a remarkable coincidence that *Yahvah*, the name of God in the Judaic tradition, occurs as an epithet for Agni in the Rigveda a total of 21 times (*yahva* in RV 10.110; *yahvah* in RV 3.1, 3.5, 4.5, 4.7, 4.58, 5.1, 7.6, 7.8, 9.75, 10.11; *yahvam* in RV 1.36; 3.3; 4.5; 5.16; 8.13; 10.92; *yahvasya* in RV 3.2 and 3.28). Indus ideas on writing may thus have, through the agency of the powerful Mitanni kingdom of Syria, been influential in the various Semitic traditions of the second and first millennia BC.

If one accepts the derivation of the Brahmi from Indus, and recognizes that the Brahmi and Semitic scripts are related, then the only conclusion open is that the chronologically earlier Indus script is the parent of both. The Mitannis could very well have been the agents responsible for the spread of Indus-like writing in West Asia.

(Prof. Subhash Kak teaches computer science at Louisiana State University, USA, and has published extensively on the history of science in India.)

11. Sita Ram Goel taught his people their history

Saradindu Mukherji

11.1. Sita Ram Goel as I knew him

I first heard about Sita Ramji from my uncle, the late Sri Abhas Kumar Chatterjee. He had just returned from a stint at Queen Elizabeth House, Oxford University, after completing a Fellowship there, and written an article in the *Indian Express* about Father Tieffenthaler's testimony on the history of the Ramjanmabhoomi temple at Ayodhya. Knowing my interest in such matters, he wrote to me that if I was interested in doing some substantial academic work, it was time I got in touch with Sita Ram Goel, who would "initiate me into the movement". I was wondering who this gentleman was and how come that, living in Delhi, I knew nothing about him. Those were the days of the Ayodhya movement and there was an earnest desire on everyone's part to contribute to this movement of national regeneration.

Hesitatingly, I rung up Sita Ramji. After some preliminary conversation, he said he would come to my place and talk to me. After a few days, he came along with some of the books written by him, and some other publications. The conversation was very interesting and enjoyable and he said that he was not looking for buyers but for readers. I had never heard anything like this from an author/publisher like this before. After he left, the same evening, I started reading his *How I Became a Hindu*. Once I started reading it, I could not take a break except to have my dinner. By the time I finished reading, it was past midnight and I had tears in my eyes. I had realized by then that Sita Ramji was a rare genius the like of whom one does not come across very often. Later on, when

Prof. Subhash Kak from the University of Louisiana told me that he considered this book a classic, I had no hesitation in concurring.

Sita Ramji was more than a scholar: he was a rare intellectual-ideologue of a movement. When he introduced me to Ram Swarupji, it was another revelation to me. Here was another great man, another scholar of outstanding depth and originality. Sita Ramji considered Ram Swarup a thinker next only to Sri Aurobindo in terms of his originality of ideas. Only a great man like him could see the greatness in others.

He was indeed a scholar extraordinary, an intellectual giant. I felt he had probably read more Bengali literature than I had. He knew Sanskrit, Hindi, Gujarati, English, Urdu and Persian very well and so he could read most of the sources in the original. He had studied Hinduism, Buddhism, Sikhism, pre-Christian Paganism, Christianity, Islam and other religious systems thoroughly, as well as various other subjects, and more surprisingly, he remembered most of it. Having learnt Sanskrit very late in life, he could cite appropriate shlokas to explain many situations. Similarly he could delve into the past to give some relevant explanation of the contemporary problems. Often he wrote to the "eminent" state-funded intellectuals and leading journalists to point out the wrong version of facts they were presenting. They rarely responded, obviously not having the intellectual honesty to admit their colossal ignorance nor the courage to go against the received truth which suited their political and career prospects.

No wonder, Sita Ramji considered most of the "eminent" academics (especially social scientists) as semi-educated. He perhaps rightly believed that the really brilliant minds were actually to be found outside the university system. He could not tolerate ignorance and bad writing. When I look back on his range of scholarship and uncanny ability to predict socio-political developments, my reading was that some of the really prominent scholars that one has come across would not be worth even ten percent of his calibre. And if we remember the outstanding contribution of Voice of India scholars like Shrikant Talageri, Koenraad Elst and a host of others, we know what his impact was.

Sitaramji's academic standards and his integrity as a human being were of the highest order. He always insisted that scholars should be very sure of the sources they cite. This, of course, we professional historians learn early in our training, and it is a different matter that even people who are taught those things eventually smother evidence which does not suit their ideological line or career prospects. Sitaramji would never tolerate this attitude. What he wanted was that scholars should not hesitate to tell the truth. One must go by the evidence one has. That was, he said, the fundamental difference between a scholar and a propagandist. In the process, he warned, one would encounter many problems but not be scared off by them.

That is why he was always full of praise for Abhas Chatterjee, for his consistency in principles, his courage and utter disdain for power and position, and of course, his academic brilliance. He and Ram Swarup did not like it when Chatterjee resigned from the Indian Administrative Service at the age of 49. They felt that the time was not appropriate. When Chatterjee's *Concept of Hindu Nation* came out, both of them felt that this was a major contribution. Sita Ramji always maintained that the sacrifice made by Chatterjee was rare in Hindu society.

He had a tremendous capacity to judge men and movements and consistently maintained that a genuine Hindu/nationalist movement was yet to emerge in India. Thus, he had no illusions about the BJP-led government of 1998-2004, which we discussed in 2003 when I had been asked by the BJP appointees in the NCERT to write one of the new history textbooks. From his sick bed he told me that I might be writing the book for the NCERT but chances were quite strong that it might not be published. And effectively, my text was discarded for reasons that I could have expected the preceding Marxist establishment to cite, but not a Hindu or nationalist one. Not that I did not anticipate this possibility but he could predict things with devastating accuracy.

Those who have read even a fraction of what he wrote, or who met him for even fifteen minutes, would know what an encyclopedic mind he had. Most important, and where he scored over all others, were his encouraging words, the useful tips he gave, and the assurance of all kinds of support to an author. He was building up a team where only merit mattered and where the ideology of national/Hindu resurgence was not compromised.

A man of very simple habits though he could afford every comfort of life, he maintained a Spartan life-style. He could speak effortlessly on diverse subjects relating to history, society and people, moving rapidly through the corridors of time. Those who had seen him totally engrossed in preparing the index for the books would know the profound scholarship that went into it. It is he who showed us that reading an index prepared by him was sometimes as educative as reading the original text.

One could go on and on talking about many facets of this rare personality, the anecdotes, the little-known facts of history and the very original interpretation that he offered. Not that we always agreed, e.g. we had very different views on Rammohan Roy's position regarding Christianity or on the merits of Anwar Sheikh's theses regarding Islam, but this never led to any misunderstanding. He believed that without knowledge no society or movement can progress, and his regret was that very few people were interested in knowledge. He worked selflessly without aspiring for any personal gain and this is why he never compromised on the basics, as some people tend to do. No wonder, he could draw some of the most selfless and brilliant minds into his Herculean mission.

11.2. A case study in politicized history

In Sita Ram Goel's footsteps, let us try our hand at countering a small instance of history manipulation. The *Ananda Bazar Patrika* of Kolkata (15 July 2004) carried an article titled *"Mata binimoyer mukto ganotantroei uttorener path, batlalen Amartya"* ("Exchange of opinions as practised in liberal democracy is the way to progress, says Amartya"). Nobel laureate Prof. Amartya Sen had reportedly lauded the exchange of free opinion as one of the most important attributes and benefits of the democratic system. He had emphasized that "deliberation" was the most characteristic feature of "deliberative democracy". One would readily agree with this observation, well known and very much accepted by people except for the Marxists and Islamists whose worldview Prof. Sen habitually propagates. Among the historical references he cited to give some flesh to his thesis, Sen mentioned this: "To widen the path for economic development, one has to expand the democratic system, which provides for greater liberalization of political rights. That has been our heritage for long. Moghul Emperor Akbar tried this exchange of opinion in the 16th century when in Europe, dissenters like Giordano Bruno were being burnt to death."

While agreeing with the first part of the statement, one does not find an iota of evidence to show that Akbar (1542-1605) was a trendsetter for a democratic polity in India. This is an outlandish claim. The example Sen cites from 16th-century European history to prove a lamentable lack of accommodative spirit, innovative ideas or idealism in the socio-political realms in Europe is also wrong. Conversely, his rosy presentation of the Moghul polity appears to be equally mistaken, misleading and possibly mischievous.

If occasional feats of tolerance and open-mindedness can be cited for a few of the Moghul emperors, these were not representative of a general evolution towards the spirit and practice of democracy. The opposite is true for Europe in the same period, where acts of tyranny and persecution were symptomatic of the struggle of authoritarian and obscurantist forces against a rising tide of enlightenment, tolerance and freedom. Yet, Sen's purpose is to portray the 16th-century administration of Akbar as the one area of sunshine and the starting point of Indian democracy, with distant Europe still continuing to rot in the Dark Ages.

In reality, the modern democratic polity with its intellectual freedom was already on the horizon in some European states and struggling to become the norm. The Netherlands broke free from Spanish Catholic rule, set up a Republic and instituted toleration of religious dissent. In Great Britain, the Tudor partnership with the Parliaments (1485-1603) paved the way for the latter's phenomenal success later on. In fact, renowned historians of British constitutional history have rejected the older thesis of Tudor despotism because they found that despite the House of Commons' elitist character and limited powers, it did accustom the Crown to deliberative interaction with the people. Very few Islamic countries have this much of people's participation in policy-making even today, and the Moghul empire certainly didn't have it.

The halt called by Henry VIII (r.1509-1548) when an unauthorized "Amicable Loan" was levied by the Parliament in 1525, as he apprehended a rebellion, indirectly proves the gradual growth of a certain anti-authoritarian mindset in early 16th-century England. In 1543, the Speaker of the House of Commons first claimed for it "the right to freedom of speech"; this, one must accept, is the cornerstone of democracy. And Henry VIII did not stop him. In late Elizabethan England, there were many instances of differences between the Queen and the Parliament but no attempt was made to abolish it or threaten the vocal members into submission.

The fragmentation of Christianity by Protestantism initially led to bloody conflict but it undeniably contributed to the rise of accomodative pluralism as well, and even to the promotion of popular sovereignty and the rule of law. In fact, as G.E. Aylmer has shown, "Protestantism was on the whole allied to the cause of parliamentary democracy and the rule of law, Catholicism to that of foreign intervention and absolute monarchy. In particular the radical wing of English Protestantism, the Puritan movement having found itself increasingly at odds with the Crown and the bishops, had, as early as the 1570s and 1580s, used the House of Commons as an alternative platform from which to campaign for further religious changes."[1]

Yes, there were executions of critical minds like Giordano Bruno or Thomas More, but the century of Leonardo da Vinci and William Shakespeare can hardly be considered an age of darkness, can it? And closer to Amartya Sen's own field, the religious and intellectual churning also led to new ideas on socio-economic relations. Thus, Oxford scholar Robert Crowley's edition of *Piers Plowman* is considered a classic of social criticism, yet he belonged to that unenlightened 16th-century Europe. It is Crowley who wrote: "If the possessioners would consider themselves to be but stewards and not lords over their possessions, this oppression would soon be redressed." How surprising that Amartya Sen, who has studied and taught in the UK, should be missing out on this.

If Prof. Sen had cared to be objective, he could not have maintained his outlandish hypothesis that humane policies and ideas of freedom had come to India as a gift of the Moghul invaders. As a personal beneficiary of the liberal-rationalist tradition of Europe, he could hardly have denied it credit where it is due, later on in his distinguished academic career, an act of ingratitude that is not exactly edifying. And as a child of the Bengal Renaissance (admittedly in its fading phase), he could not have been promoting, by assertion or omission, the uncharitable thesis that the native Kafirs of Hindustan had no worthwhile contribution to the making of democratic India.

---

[1]G.E. Aylmer: *A Short History of 17th-Century England*, Mentor Book, New York, 1963, pp.63-64.

11.3. Falsely claiming merits for Islam

If Prof. Sen had taken a broader historical view, he would have realized the absurdity of his claims for the Moghul empire as the pioneer of democracy. He must be aware of the overwhelming grip of military strongmen and religious obscurantists in the parts of Akbar's erstwhile empire which most identify with their Moghul heritage: Pakistan, the self-declared successor state of the Moghul empire, and her prodigal daughter Bangladesh. These countries have a shocking record of undemocratic politics, religious intolerance and blatant persecution of minorities, apparently the bedrock of their civilizing mission. Why could these countries not absorb and retain those strands which Akbar, according to Prof. Sen, had gifted to Indic civilization? I suggest that it is, firstly, because Akbar never pursued a political ideal even remotely resembling what Sen erroneously claims to be his legacy. Secondly, the Islamic ethos, far from being conducive to secularism and peaceful co-existence between communities, is actually hostile to it.

As for Akbar's open mind, Sen must be referring to his interfaith meetings in the *Ibadat Khana* (House of Worship) at Fatehpur Sikri, to the *Din-i-Ilahi* (the unitarian "godly religion") and *Sulh-i-kul* ("universal peace"). One may accept that for a Muslim ruler, the fact of his dialogues on religious issues with people from other faiths (how many times?) and his abolition of the *Jizyah* were novel, but nothing more need be seen in that. There is no need to blow it out of proportion. Then the question is: how many followers actually joined his *Din-i-Ilahi*? And who were they? How many *momin*s and how many *kafir*s were there in that congregation? What was its impact? Did it really influence the general public and particularly the Muslims? Only after we have a satisfactory answer to these questions, could we begin to accept the claim of Akbar's contribution to the emergence of a genuine liberal ambience in religious matters.

Even if Akbar emerges triumphant in this religious arena, it would be absurd to trace the concept of parliamentary democracy to these religious discussions, as Prof. Sen wants the gullible to do. There was no provision and space for *"jonomuktir khetra"* (Sen's liberalization of political rights for the people) in Akbar's world-view. Without anything even remotely resembling a Tudor parliament with its steady advancement, nor any innovative ideational force such as Puritanism, a few meetings on religious matters without any deviation from the fundamentals of Islamic theology can not be taken as a significant departure from the authoritarian praxis of Akbar's Muslim empire. No social scientist worth his salt can invent facts of history, but Prof. Sen tries his best with all the clout a Nobel Laureate has.

Moreover, as against Prof. Sen's "seminal" contribution to the further glorification of the Nehruvian icon Akbar, some extant data undermine the liberal reputation of even this most enlightened among Muslim rulers. They show that Akbar was less than consistently liberal and "secular", and that he even lapsed into intolerance and ruthlessness once in a while. In the classical introductions to this period of history,[2] one can find demythologizing facts such as these:

1. Akbar showed only limited zeal in actually enforcing his more liberal decrees, which his lieutenants tended not to implement. Thus, having ordered the abolition of Jizyah in 1564, another order had to be issued after ten years to enforce it. Hussain Khan, the Governor of Lahore, ordered Hindus "to stick patches on their shoulders so that no Muslim could be put to the indignity of showing them honour by mistake, nor did he allow Hindus to

[2]R.C. Majumdar, H.C. Raychaudhuri and K.K. Datta, *An Advanced History of India*, Part II, Macmillan, London, 1963, p.434; and in Sri Ram Sharma, *Religious Policy of the Mughal Emperors*, Asia Publ., Bombay 1962, pp.19-20; K.S. Lal: *Theory and Practice of Muslim State of India*, Aditya Prakashan, Delhi 1999, pp.37-40.

saddle their horses", — exemplifying the *Zimma* regime (permanent humiliation and disenfranchisement of non-Muslim subjects) of which the Jizyah was a part. Badaoni tells us that it was customary to "search out and kill heretics" (mainly Shias), not to mention non-Muslims, as late as 1574. Other contemporary sources such as the *Akbar Nama* and the *Ain-i-Akbari* confirm that at least prior to 1593, there had been conversions of Hindus to Islam by force.

2. Akbar was unsecular as well as unchivalrous in his treatment of non-Muslim captives. Upon being captured, the father of Himu (Akbar's main Hindu military adversary) was offered a choice between death and conversion to Islam. In 1581, the Portuguese captives at Surat were also given this choice between conversion and death.
3. While attacking Chitor, Akbar called himself a *ghazi*, i.e. one who kills unbelievers in *jihad*. The mayhem that he caused was typical jihadi style. Thirty thousand poor peasants were killed in the fort of Chitor. A number of Rajput women committed suicide by setting themselves on fire (*jauhar*), preferring death to abduction and rape by Akbar's men. Apparently these directly affected contemporaries hadn't heard of Akbar's liberal reputation.
4. Even iconoclastic zeal did not disappear under Akbar. During an attack on the Hindu state of Kangra, a Hindu temple was wantonly desecrated. Akbar's official Bayazid converted a Hindu temple into a Muslim school. Jaina idols in Gujarat were vandalized. In a letter to Abdullah Khan Uzbek in 1586, Akbar declared himself a Muslim and boasted that on account of his conquests, Islam had spread to other territories where it had not been heard of before, and the temples of the unbelievers had been converted into mosques.

5. Akbar declared that the institutes of the Prophet and the revelation of God "have always been my guides". His allegiance to Islam rather than to secularism or to some new unitarian religion is confirmed by the fact that his children by Hindu wives were all given Arabic names and brought up as Muslims.

While the historians to whom I refer do concede the "change of mind and heart" which Akbar showed later in life, their explanation for this welcome deviation from pure Islam is hardly the one that Sen believes or wants us to believe. Rather, "one reason is the most prominent — Akbar's association with Hindu scholars".[3] So there you have it: pluralism and freedom of thought are a gift of Hinduism, where they had existed for literally thousands of years before Akbar's reign, and not of Islam nor even of any personal new insight by Akbar.

But lecturing in Kolkata, that too in a meeting called by the Marxist government and allied "progressive intellectuals", Sen just had to propagate the secularist party line. This author once asked Prof. Sen why he was avoiding the real issue when he was talking of the Hindu-Muslim divide, i.e. why he was not asking whether Islam believes in secularism, whether Islam believes in religious toleration, whether Islam believes in the peaceful co-existence of communities. Instead of replying, Sen blurted out that he was "listening to a pre-Partition speech!"[4] It seems that a decade and a Nobel Prize later, he still refuses to come down to earth and face uncomfortable facts.

Logically, it should seem odd that peddlers of "scientific socialism" like Amartya Sen are so often found praising or supporting the Islamist forces of obscurantism. As Ram Swarup once pointed out, the common denominator is

[3]K.S. Lal: *Muslim State*, p.33.

[4]Vide Saradindu Mukherji: "A Lesson for the Progressives", *The Pioneer*, 28 Feb. 1993.

authoritarianism, that object of fascination and attractor of the loyalties of so many modern progressives. Sen's enthusiasm for authoritarian systems is a matter of record; he prefers them over the freedom that India offers. During a recent lecture in Hong Kong, he praised Maoist China's Cultural Revolution and the medical care by "barefoot doctors" which it had provided to the masses. He contrasted Maoist China favourably with his own Nehruvian, socialist-leaning but democratic India, and attributed the diminishing gap between India and China in life expectancy (from China's 14 years' lead in 1979 to a 7 years' lead now, obviously due to India's increasingly successful health care) to China's abandonment of the Maoist model. Fortunately, a former barefoot doctor, Shan Weijian, was present in the audience to give a first-hand account: "I observed with my own eyes the total absence of medicine in some parts of China. The system was totally unsustainable. *We used to admire India.* If they had made the system optional, nobody would have opted for it."[5] But so far, Amartya Sen is not yet on record as recanting his pro-authoritarian and anti-Indian position.

11.4. Denying the merits of Hinduism

Nehruvian secularism's sins of commission typically go hand in hand with sins of omission. Lies about the beauties of Islam get their full effect against a background of silence about the merits of Hindu civilization. While talking of India's heritage, Prof. Sen could not go any further back in India's past than the age of Akbar, though the preceding millennia contain numerous examples when Indians more than "tried" a free "exchange of opinion". For him the history of India suddenly begins in the medieval age. Like many Nehruvians, he has an unwavering fixation with Akbar as the starting point for a real breakthrough in India's political and intellectual history.

---

[5]"An 'Annie Hall' Moment", *WSJ.com Opinion Journal*, 21 Feb. 2005; emphasis added.

Prof. Sen refuses to see the obvious, indeed the universally accepted explanation: the traditional Hindu spirit of accommodation and toleration is the foundation of our pluralistic democracy, with Anglo-Saxon parliamentary institutions providing the mechanism.[6] His willful ignorance is neither shocking nor surprising. For him, the pre-Islamic age in Indian history is an unacceptable *jahiliya*, an "age of foolishness", as Muslims disparagingly call any history preceding the revelation of the Quran through Mohammed.

Even methodologically there is a flaw. Those who deal with the history and sociology of idea, whether intellectual trends or socio-economic changes, would know that there are no watertight compartments in the domain of ideas. It is futile and unacademic to look for an undisputed date, event and personality for the grand beginning of a general trend or movement or its termination in such matters. Real revolutions in the sense of clean breaks with the past or with the pre-existing conditions are unlikely and rare.

If democracy failed in Pakistan, in spite of Anglo-American pressure repeatedly forcing new attempts at its restoration, it is at least in part because against the country's Islamist background, a successful democracy would indeed have been a revolution. Too radical a revolution for the past-oriented and closed mentality underlying the whole Pakistani project. Conversely, if democracy has succeeded in India, this is because it required no great discontinuity with the existing native way of life and freedom.

(Prof. Saradindu Mukherji teaches modern history at Hansraj College, Delhi University, and has published on Bangladesh and on rural development problems in various countries.)

---

[6]Vide Saradindu Mukherji: "Tradition and innovation in post-colonial South Asia: a case for contemporary India", paper presented at the World Conference: *Dialogue Among Civilisations: Key to a Safe Future*, 23-26 April 2003, Warsaw.

12. Remembering a Karmayogi

Virendra Parekh

12.1. Our one meeting

"How old are you?" Sitaramji asked me. "Forty." "You are younger than my younger son", he said affectionately.

Thus began my first and only meeting with Sitaramji in November 1993. I was on my way to Manali along with my family and had happily foregone sightseeing in Delhi in order to be able to meet him. As a bonus, Sitaramji had offered to take me to Ram Swarupji.

For years, his writings had just mesmerized me. Even a few paragraphs were enough to bring out his originality of approach (more about it later), incisive analysis, fiery style and a stubborn refusal to be tamed by considerations of political correctness imposed by the Mulla-Marxist-Missionary-Macaulayite combine. If style is the man, then the picture that Sitaramji's writings threw up was that of a sterling patriot who happened to be a great scholar and a fearless fighter. *Brahmakshatriya* is the only word that comes to the mind to describe him.

However, what put him in a class apart from angry pamphleteers was his reverence for truth, a breadth of vision combined with an eye for detail and accuracy, and a willingness to go wherever his search for truth led him. If he had only contempt for Indian secularists, he had no burning desire to be counted among the officially recognized champions of *Bharatiyata*. He was a seeker of truth, not a camp follower. He would not spare Hindu kings for their myopia, disunity and strategic failures. He would praise Gandhiji for arousing Hindu society by stirring its heart like the Savarkars and Hedgewars never could, because his commitment was to the ideal of truth, goodness and beauty, not to any individual or group.

Our conversation was brief and informal, but Sitaramji did make a few perceptive remarks. "Where *Brahmins* are blind, *Kshatriyas* are lame", he said. "Intellectuals (Brahmins) are the eyes of the society, and the ruling class its arm. Hindu society, which does not lack in numbers, valour or devotion to its culture, is kicked around in its own land, because Hindu intellectuals lack vision", he explained.

He referred to the fateful decision of the Vijayanagar King Ramaraya to have two battalions of Muslim archers who could shoot from the horseback. In the critical battle of Rakshasi-Tangadi, widely though erroneously known as the battle of Talikota (1565), these battalions deserted their employer and joined the invaders. Ramaraya lost the battle and his life. The great Hindu kingdom of Vijayanagar which had kept the saffron flag aflutter in the South for over two centuries, suffered a terrible blow from which it could never recover. "Look at the irony, Parekh. In this land of Lord Ram and Arjun, the idea of having our own archers did not occur to the king", commented Sitaramji.

He went on to say that there should be a *Catalogue of National Mistakes* which must be taught to all children in the schools with a view to avoiding their repetition. History which does not provide an insight into our weaknesses and mistakes, which is merely a source of false pride through glorification of a mythical past, is no history at all. Secularists would readily accept this, but their definition of India and Indianness would be suspect.

Sitaramji drove me from his residence in Shakti Nagar to Maharani Bagh where Ram Swarupji was staying. It was one more act of kind affection from a great person who had over the years replied to each of my letters, enlightened me by answering every question I asked, communicated his candid views on several issues, and sent me for free all the publications of Voice of India, some of them beyond my means. My meeting with Ram Swarupji was brief, about an hour. I told him that measured against the depth and vastness of his knowledge, he had written very little. He smiled and said that that may be true in some sense, but that he did not like to be repetitive.

Around 9 p.m., Sitaramji dropped me at the hotel where my family and friends were waiting for me. I could not have asked for more. My purpose of coming to Delhi was fulfilled.

12.2. His mission

During our conversation, Ram Swarupji had made an important point about the work of Voice of India. It deserves greater attention.

For long, Hinduism has been defined for Hindus by its enemies. They told us that Brahmins were a class of deceitful exploiters and oppressors, that Sanskrit was a dead language, that Hinduism was a mumbo-jumbo of silly superstitions, puerile priestcraft and meaningless mysticism, and that the caste system was the root of all evils afflicting Indian society. They even taught us that the Vedic Aryans had come to India from outside (so why cavil at Muslim or Christian invaders?), that the history of India was actually a series of India's conquests by one invader after another.

Even their praise was motivated. The missionaries and Mullahs always praise Hindu society for its tolerance and generosity (something that they have never shown to their rival creeds) and expect the Hindus to look the other way when they themselves malign Hinduism and convert its weaker sections through force, fraud and allurements. The missionaries always praise Hindus for their religiosity, but never for their religion. The Pope praises Hinduism for its secondaries, while hiding his contempt for its primaries.

The enemies of Hinduism floated false notions about their own creeds, too. We were told that Islam is a religion of peace and brotherhood; that Christianity has nothing but love and mercy for non-believers, that Marxism has the master key to the "ascent of mankind from the kingdom of necessity to the kingdom of freedom." The greater tragedy is that the Hindus have gone along with this con game, slavishly or foolishly. What the enemies of Hinduism found wrong with us, we found wrong with ourselves. Even today, few Hindus can see through these mischievous canards. Hindus feel flattered by the motivated praise of their tolerance by the missionaries, little realizing that it is a ploy for their moral disarmament against a ruthless, systematic onslaught on their culture and tradition; that it is akin to a sermon on detachment and renunciation by a pickpocket while he is relieving you of your wallet.

Centuries of cultural and political enslavement have led Hindus to look at themselves and others through the tinted spectacles forged by the inveterate enemies of their religion and culture. Voice of India, said Sitaramji, wanted Hindus to use their own eyes for looking at themselves and at others. All its efforts were directed at equipping them for doing so.

The means of achieving this end was a detailed and objective first-hand study of the rival ideologies (Islam, Christianity and Marxism) from their primary sources. It meant a study of their scriptures, their sources of inspiration, their worldview, their objectives and methods and their historical record. It also meant studying Indian history from primary sources and interpreting it, on the basis of undisputable and recorded facts, from the perspective of Indians rather than that of invaders and conquerors.

Perhaps for the first time in its long and chequered history did Hindu society take up this Herculean task. Ordinary Hindus had long regarded Islam as a barbarism masquerading as religion, at least for non-Muslims. They had not regarded Christian missionaries as anything more than wily, cunning, arrogant fanatics who were hand in gloves with India's foreign masters. And for all their skills in sophisticated slander and manipulation of the mind, the Communists have not been able to expand their influence beyond the two corners (Bengal/Tripura and Kerala) of India.

However, Hindu scholars had by and large neglected to examine critically the tall claims made by these ideologies. This was at par with the failure of the Hindu rulers to keep abreast of developments in the neighbouring lands, even those developments that had a direct bearing on national security. The consequences of both these failures have been heavy. The myopic refusal of the Hindu rulers to look beyond their nose led to the political enslavement of the country, whereas the failure of the Hindu scholars to examine critically the doctrines of Islam and Christianity, not to speak of Communism, left the ideological field open to the enemies of Hinduism. Whatever they said about their own creeds went uncontested.

Sitaramji and Ram Swarupji moved in to fill this vital gap. In the nineteenth century, Swami Dayanand Sarawati, founder of the Arya Samaj, had subjected the Quran and the Bible to the test of traditional Hindu polemics. Before him, Brahmins from Tamilnadu had asked a few pertinent questions of Christian missionaries. But the task before the duo was truly daunting. As Sitaramji wrote to me in a personal letter: "My heart sinks when I think of the organizational, financial and political resources at the command of our adversaries. Voice of India is not even a drop in the ocean."

Sitaramji went about his lifework in the spirit of a true *Karmayogi*. Calculations of personal cost and benefit never mattered to him. His detachment (*anasakti*) afforded him tenacity, fearlessness and independence of judgement. He sat at the feet of great masters like Vyasa, Valmiki, the Buddha, Vivekananda and Aurobindo and recaptured a vision of India that was dazzling in its brilliance. This vision defined for him the mission of Voice of India.

12.3. National vision

As Sitaramji himself pointed out, his vision of India is nothing new. It is only a restatement in modern language, in a modern setting, of the ancient Vedic vision as unfolded in the Vedas, in the Upanishads, in the Jainagama, in the Tripitaka, in the Ramayana and the Mahabharata, in the Puranas, in the Dharmashastras and in the latter-day poetry of saints and *siddhas*. We have had countless spokesmen of that Vision throughout our history.

The first dimension of that vision is that India is the land of Sanatana Dharma. As Sri Aurobindo said in his Uttarpara Speech, India would rise with the rise of Sanatana Dharma, India would sink if Sanatana Dharma sank and India would die if it were at all possible for Sanatana Dharma to die.

The second dimension of that vision is that of a vast and variegated culture. According to *adhara* and *adhikara*, various sections of our population, various segments of our society, various regions of our country, developed their own culture, their own art, their own literature. It is a vast fabric, this art and literature. But its spirit is the spirit of Sanatana Dharma. It is informed by Sanatana Dharma in all its details.

The third dimension of that vision was that this great society, the society which we describe as Hindu Society today, was reared on the basis of spirituality and a great culture created by Sanatana Dharma. The Hindu social system, epitomized in the phrase *Varnashramadharma*, has degenerated under the onslaught of foreign invasions and is the subject of severe criticism today. It was originally, and it has been for centuries, a harmony model which enabled people of various abilities and inclinations to live together as an organic whole.

As Dr. S. Radhakrishnan pointed out, the *Varnavyavastha* was founded on two ideals: firstly, society should be based on cooperation and accommodation, not competition and exclusion; secondly, the highest place in society should go to the men of learning and character, not to the men of wealth and power. As for *Ashrama Dharma*, the division of life into four stages of *Brahmacharya* (period of celibacy and learning), *Grhasthya* (period of householding), *Vanaprastha* (period of retirement) and *Sannyasa* (period of renunciation), indicates that this life is a pilgrimage to the eternal life through different stages. Finally, for all its weaknesses and ills, Varnashramadharma has saved Hindu society from destruction — the destruction which overtook so many societies outside India at the hands of Christianity, Islam and Communism.

The fourth dimension of that National Vision is that the history of India is the history of the Hindu society, of Hindu culture, of Hindu spirituality. In short, it is the history of the Hindu nation and not the history of foreign invaders as we are being taught today.

And the last dimension which India's great men have stressed, which they have affirmed again and again, is that this land of *Bharatvarsha* is one indivisible whole; that it is the cradle of Hindu society, of Hindu culture, of Hindu spirituality; that it is the homeland of the Hindu nation. Other communities are welcome to live in this land provided they come to terms with Hindu society and Hindu culture. Today, *Bharatvarsha* stands divided into several countries such as India, Pakistan, Bangladesh and Afghanistan, which are not only politically but also culturally hostile to each other; and we seem to have become reconciled to that division. But the Vision that was given to us by our great men was that of *Bharatvarsha* as an indivisible whole, not only geographically but also culturally.

It was from this perspective that Sitaramji judged ideologies like Islam, Christianity, Communism and their united front, which in India is called secularism, as well as Indian history and contemporary developments. Thus, about the demolition of the Babri Masjid, he wrote to me in a personal letter: "My only grievance is that the Hindus had to do it surreptitiously.

(...) I never thought that the Hindus would assert themselves or that the Communist empire would disintegrate. I have fought for both. I am fulfilled."

One has only to look around to realize how far we have moved away from this pristine vision of India shining in its natural glory. We are taught that even today's truncated India is a multi-religious, multi-racial, multi-lingual, multi-cultural and multi- many-other-things entity struggling to evolve some principle of unity that can hold together its disparate components; that it is a nation in the making, to use a phrase dear to the secularist elite. Indian history has been massively perverted. Stalinist activists masquerading as historians have thoroughly and systematically distorted and falsified every period of Indian history with the malicious intention of cleansing it of all Hindu influences, to negate every dimension of the national vision outlined above. The very idea of India is adulterated to suit the designs of invading ideologies.

Sitaramji made it his lifework to defend this idea of India, this national vision as it has existed through millennia. He has set out the problem and its solution in the books *Hindu Society Under Siege* and *Defence of Hindu Society*. His books relating to Indian history (*Story of Islamic Imperialism in India*; *Heroic Hindu Resistance to Muslim Invaders*; and *Muslim Separatism, Causes and Consequences*) convincingly nail the secularist propaganda. In *Perversion of India's Political Parlance*, he traced and exposed the secularist sleight of hand whereby Muslim communalism became respectable as "secularism" while Indian nationalism was reviled as "communalism".

When he handled the works of others, Sitaramji brought out the depth, perspective and relevance of the original work in bold relief. His publication of *The Calcutta Quran Petition*, the *Niyogi Committee Report on the Activities of Christian Missionaries*, and, to some extent, *Catholic Ashrams: Sannyasins or Swindlers?* provides examples of this.

His two major contributions, *Hindu Temples: What Happened to Them* (vol. I & II) and *History of Hindu-Christian Encounters* are classics of original research and will stand the test of time.

Sitaramji's works (and VoI publications in general) are characterized by a depth and an intellectual honesty that are rare in secularist writings on Hindutva. The views and arguments of the other side are rendered faithfully and then answered cogently by setting out an alternative perspective backed by facts and reasoning. Ancient India had this tradition of scholarly debate. It is said of Shankara, the great philosopher, that he formulated the arguments of his opponents better than they themselves could. Indeed, these are elementary features of public debate in a civilized society, but Indian debate on issues like (what passes for) secularism, the cultural content of Indian nationalism, the nature of Indian society, the interpretation of Indian history and the role and direction of the Indian State leaves much to be desired on this count.

Much of Hindutva writing is characterized by whining and self-pity, dwelling on the atrocities and injustices heaped on Hindus by others. Sitaramji carried the battle to the enemy camp, taking on the adversaries in a frontal attack. Instead of calling himself secular and others pseudo-secular, as the BJP is doing, he discussed secularism (of the Indian variety) threadbare and showed that it was far from being a noble idea. Instead of presenting Hinduism as a monotheistic religion, he showed that monotheism as extolled in the Abrahamic religions was a monstrous idea responsible for a great deal of strife and bloodshed in the name of God.

12.4. Critique of India's secularism

Sitaramji's critique of what passes for secularism here is epitomized in the title of his book *India's Secularism: New Name for National Subversion*. Jawaharlal Nehru, who had not used the term in his pre-Independence writings or speeches, picked up a prestigious word from Western political parlance and made it mean the opposite of what it meant in the West.

In the West, secularism stood for rationalism, universalism and humanism. In India, it is a united front of all anti-Hindu ideologies: Islam, Christianity and Communism. Each of these is an intolerant, aggressive and violent ideology. Each of them aims at conquest of the world by rooting out other religions. Each of them has a history soaked in the blood of the innocent. All over the world, they are enemies of one another; but in India, they are always found on the same side against their common enemy: Hinduism. In the West, secularism was directed against Christianity, which spurned reason, suspected science, punished doubt and claimed absolute monopoly of truth in all matters, secular and spiritual. In India, secularism is ranged against Hinduism which respects reason and experience, which imposes no belief system but enjoins every one to realize the spiritual truths in the cave of his heart through his own effort in his own way.

It is the ultimate irony of Indian politics that those who masterminded this subversion of the national psyche have positioned themselves as guardians of democracy and secularism in the country, and that votaries of authoritarian ideologies lecture the Hindus on the virtues of pluralism. Hindu society, which is the national society, which has borne the brunt of all foreign invasions and fought all freedom struggles, is driven into a corner and made to shout that it is secular, that it regards Islam and Christianity as noble religions, that it regards Islamic heroes as its own.

In pre-Independence days, the Muslim minority had a veto on what was national. Only that leader, that party, that programme was national, which was approved by the Muslim leaders. The rest were, by definition, communal. In the post-Independence period, the same game is played in the name of secularism: only that leader, party, organization, or programme is secular, which is approved by Muslim leaders. Whatever they disapprove is, for that very reason, communal.

Sitaramji showed that this deliberate and malicious perversion of thought has thoroughly distorted the national perspective. Love for one's country and its world-renowned ancient culture has been turned into a cardinal sin. Foreign invaders and tyrants have become lawful rulers while national heroes are downgraded as petty rebels fighting for personal gain. The catchword "secularism" provides a smokescreen behind which several types of imperialism — Islamic, Christian, Communist and Consumerist — are stealing a march over Hinduism.

Sitaramji urged Hindu intellectuals to see through this con game perpetrated on them by the residues of imperialist ideologies with the help of a self-alienated denationalized elite, and to counter it by conducting the public debate in the proper language. Such a language, he said, would substitute "Indian nationalism" for "Hindu communalism"; and "national subversion" for "secularism"; and "Islam" for "Muslim communalism" or "Islamic fundamentalism".

12.5. Two traditions of worship

A major contribution of Sitaramji and other VoI scholars, especially Ram Swarup and David Frawley, is a clear enunciation of two types of religious traditions. One may be called the Biblical or Abrahamic tradition and the other, Vedic or Indic tradition.

The Bible-derived creeds are founded on a central figure (Jehovah, God, Allah or History) who commands the exclusive and overriding allegiance of the believers. He is jealous, cruel, and brooks no rival. He deals with his people through an intermediary, messenger, prophet, or only saviour. His teachings are contained in the Book. The Book is the sole repository of Ultimate Truth.

Thus in these creeds, there is only one Truth; there is only one way to it; the God has given it to us, the Chosen People, and us alone; it is contained in our Book and in our Book alone. Since the Book is authored by God himself, every word in it is true, excellent, immutable and binding. The Book, *al-Kitab*, is beyond the comprehension of most of even the believers, and certainly the non-believers. We must therefore heed the Church, the Priest. The faith in the Book is the overriding duty, as is the duty of making others see the light. Since this is the absolute Truth, since it alone can lead to Heaven or permanent bliss, mankind must be awakened to it for its own good at any cost in whatever way. No sacrifice is too great for holding on to it; no means are impermissible for converting others to it.

The very idea of an absolute monopoly of ultimate truth contains within it the seeds of intolerance, aggression, strife and authoritarianism. It is a charter for killing, destruction and subversion with a clean conscience. There will always be more than one claimant to this monopoly while there are bound to be others who refuse to acknowledge the authority of the Church or the Party.

The Vedic tradition, on the other hand, is founded on very different premises. The starting point of this tradition is human consciousness, which can be explored, which can be purified progressively and which can be transcended till it attains the highest heights of knowledge and creativity. At this summit, the Self becomes one with the Universe and sees all things, animate and inanimate, as its own symbols and sequences. In this vast vision, sanctity attaches not only to human life but to the whole of creation. This is the summum bonum of spiritual humanism, which has always been India's message to mankind.

The Vedic tradition teaches us that spiritual truths are not of the nature of a revelation received by a historical prophet from an extra-cosmic God or some other supernatural source. Nor are those truths contained in or confined to a Book. On the contrary, these truths lie secretly in every human heart and have always been accessible to those who seek for them. These truths are never in need of a crusade for their spread and propagation. On the contrary, these truths are self-propagating due to their own inner strength. The only defence they need is the dedication they inspire spontaneously in all those who invoke them.

Sitaramji pointed out that the Vedic tradition advises people to be busy with themselves, that is, their own moral and spiritual improvement. Several disciplines have been evolved for this purpose: *tapas* (austerity), *yoga* (meditation), *jnana* (reflection), *bhakti* (devotion), etc. A seeker can take to (*adhikara*) whichever discipline suits his *adhara* (stage of moral-spiritual preparation). There is no uniform prescription for everybody, no coercion or allurement into a belief system, and no claim of merit for aggression against others.

The Biblical tradition, on the other hand, teaches people to be busy with others. One is supposed to have become a superior human being as soon as one confesses the 'only true faith'. Thenceforward one stands qualified to 'save' others. The only training one needs thereafter is how to man a mission or military expedition, how to convert others by all available means including force and fraud, and how to kill or ruin or blacken those who refuse to come round.

The Vedic tradition has given to the world schools of Sanatana Dharma, which have practised peace among their own followers as well as towards the followers of other paths. On the other hand, the Biblical tradition has spawned criminal cults such as Christianity, Islam, Communism and Nazism, which have always produced violent conflicts as much within their own camps as with each other and the rest of mankind.

As Sitaramji pointed out, the syrupy slogan of *sarva-dharma-samabhava* glosses over the basic difference between these two traditions. This has caused an enormous amount of confusion.

12.6. Critique of Islam

The magnitude of crimes credited to Muslim monarchs by the medieval Muslim historians was beyond measure. In his book *The Story of Islamic Imperialism in India*, Sitaramji has devoted two long chapters to the magnitude of the Muslim atrocities. He showed with the help of detailed documentation that with a few exceptions, Muslim kings and commanders were monsters who stopped at no crime when it came to their Hindu subjects. He showed that there was a broad pattern to those crimes. The pattern is that of a *jihad* in which the *ghazi*s of Islam 1) invade infidel lands; 2) massacre as many infidel men, women, and children, particularly Brahmins, as they like *after* winning a victory; 3) capture the survivors to be sold as slaves; 4) plunder every place and person; 5) demolish idolatrous places of worship and build mosques in their places; and 6) defile idols which are flung into public squares or made into steps leading to mosques.

Hindus were long familiar with this "behaviour pattern patented by Islam". Sitaramji's distinct contribution was to trace this behaviour pattern to the tenets of Islam. Apologists of Islam, from Mahatma Gandhi to Mohammad Habib, regarded the atrocities committed by Muslim rulers on Hindus as aberrations and deviations from true Islam; they attributed it to greed, political compulsions, inherent barbarism of certain tribes etc.

Sitaramji showed that far from being aberrations or deviations from the true faith of Islam, these atrocities were the logical outcome of the teachings of Islam. Far from being a slur on the fair name of Islam, the behaviour of Muslim rulers towards the Hindus was the true face of Islam, it is what Islam had in store for non-believers. He showed that this is exactly the pattern 1) revealed by Allah in the Quran; 2) practised, perfected and prescribed by the Prophet in his own life-time; 3) followed by the pious Khalifas of Islam in the first 35 years of Islamic imperialism; 4) elaborated in the Hadis and hundreds of commentaries with meticulous attention to detail; 5) certified by the Ulama and the Sufis of Islam in all ages including our own; and 6) followed by all Muslim monarchs and chieftains who aspired for name and fame in this life, and houris and beardless boys hereafter.

It is, therefore, poor apologetics to blame the Islamized Turks alone of being barbarous. Islamic barbarism was shared in equal measure by all races and communities who were forced or lured into the fold of Islam — the Arabs, the Turks, the Persians, the Pathans, the Hindu converts. The conclusion is inescapable that Islam brutalizes all those who embrace it. And that is where the blame should be laid in all reason and justice.

12.7. Critique of Christianity

Sitaramji's views on Christianity are equally clear and instructive: "Hindus, from early-seventeenth-century Pandits of Tamil Nadu to Arun Shourie in the closing years of the twentieth, have spent no end of ink and breath to demolish the dogma of Christianity and denounce missionary methods. But it has hardly made any difference to the arrogance of Christian theologians and aggressiveness of Christian missionaries. That is because the dogma was never meant for discussion. It is an axiom of logic that that which has not been proved cannot and need not be disproved. Who has ever proved that the nondescript Jew who is supposed to have been crucified by a Roman governor of Judaea in AD 33 atoned for the sins of all humans for all time to come? Who has ever proved that those who accept that man as the only saviour, will ascend to a heaven of everlasting bliss, and those who do not, will burn forever in the blazing fire of hell? Nor can the proclamation or the promise or the threat be disproved. High-sounding theological blah blah notwithstanding, the fact remains that the dogma is no more than a subterfuge for forging and wielding an organizational weapon for mounting unprovoked aggression against other people. It is high time for Hindus to dismiss the dogma of Christianity with the contempt it deserves, and pay attention to the Christian missionary apparatus planted in their midst."

"The sole aim of this apparatus is to ruin Hindu society and culture, and take over the Hindu homeland. It goes on devising strategies for every situation, favourable and unfavourable. It trains and employs a large number of intellectual criminals ready to prostitute their talents in the service of their paymasters, and adept at dressing up dark designs in high-sounding language. The fact that every design is advertised as a theology in the Indian context and every criminal euphemized as an Indian theologian, should not hoodwink Hindus about the real intentions of this gangster game." (*Pseudo-Secularism, Christian Missions and Hindu Resistance*, pp.1-2)

Sitaramji said time and again that Hindu society was committing a blunder in regarding Christianity and Islam as religions at par with Sanatana Dharma. These are ideologies of power, masquerading as religions. They proceed from very different premises and have very different objectives: "Hindus are committing a grave mistake in regarding the encounter between Hinduism and Christianity as a dialogue between two religions. Christianity has never been a religion; its long history tells us that it has always been a predatory imperialism par excellence. The encounter, therefore, should be viewed as a battle between two totally opposed and mutually exclusive ways of thought and behaviour. In the language of the Gita (ch.16), it is war between *daivi* (divine) and *asuri* (demonic) *sampads* (propensities). In the mundane context of history, it can also be described as war between the Vedic and the Biblical traditions." (*op. cit.*, p.2)

On Islam, he was even more unequivocal. "Islam in India is still suffering from the high fever of self-righteousness, though lately it has shifted its claim from the 'only true religion' to the only 'human brotherhood'. Powered by petro-dollars, it is again dreaming of an empire in India. Hindus, on the other hand, have learnt no lesson from history as is evident from their slogan of *sarva-dharma-samabhava* vis-à-vis Islam, which is only a totalitarian and terrorist ideology of imperialism. And now the Hindu secularists are bent upon perverting the historical record in order to prove that Islam never intended any harm to Hindus or Hinduism!" (*Story of Islamic Imperialism*, p.87)

And he added a warning: "Will Hindu society have to pay the price again? It is highly doubtful if Hindu society will survive another determined assault from Islam, such is the mental, moral and spiritual health of this society. A society which has no self-confidence, which suffers from self-pity, which indulges in breast-beating at the behest of every Hindu-baiter, and which stands in daily need of certificates of good conduct from its sworn enemies, has not the ghost of a chance in a world which is becoming deadlier with the passing of every day. Can such a society make any creative contribution to the greater good of mankind? Let every Hindu search his heart, and seek the answer." (*ibid.*)

12.8. Focus on ideas, not people

Notice that the focus is on the ideas, not on people; it is on Islam, not Muslims; on Christianity, not Christians. In his prolific writings, Sitaramji always took care to distinguish between Islam and Muslims, between Christianity and Christians. At the end of his discussion of the two traditions of worship, he clarified that this analysis cannot be applied mechanically to all persons born and brought up in these two opposite traditions. The head and heart of a person can be smaller or larger than any thought pattern. Therefore ordinary men born and brought up in both these patterns are found to be of good as well as bad behaviour.

This distinction between ideas and people marks out VoI from many other pro-Hindu organizations. Many Hindus sincerely believe that Islam is good, but Muslims are wicked; Christianity is good, but Christians are crooked. As a result, they are baffled by the behaviour pattern of Muslim leaders or missionaries and harbour prejudices against them. The VoI approach removes prejudices against people, while providing a proper basis for understanding their behaviour: "It has long been a Hindu habit to resent the behaviour pattern of Muslims and Christians, while praising Islam and Christianity as revealed religions. (...) We are asking Hindus to reverse this process (...) to study Christianity and Islam to see for themselves that Christian and Muslim behaviour patterns follow from the belief system of Christianity and Islam." (*History of Hindu-Christian Encounters*, pp.453-454)

The whole approach to the communal problem is redefined. "Muslims are not be hated", Sitaramji said to me, "they are our own people alienated from their ancestral society and culture by a divisive doctrine masquerading as religion." Target the ideas, not the people.

It also imparts a wider dimension to the noble endeavour of VoI. By speaking up for Hinduism as an ancient, pagan religion that has survived the onslaughts of monotheistic creeds, VoI is speaking up for pagan America and Africa, and also for the pagan past of Egypt, Iraq, Persia, Arabia, Greece, Rome and Europe in general. As Ram Swarup put it in the preface to his *Hindu View of Christianity and Islam*: "Today, there is an awakening in many parts of the world. Many people are coming to know what they have gone through and what they have lost. They have also begun to realize that their present religions are impositions on them, that they once belonged to a different spiritual culture which had a different orientation and was built on a deeper and wider base. As this realization becomes more acute, many of them are trying to break form their present confines and recover their lost identity. They are also seeking a more satisfying spirituality. Probably Hinduism can help them. It has survived many physical and ideological onslaughts and it still retains in its bosom layers of spiritual traditions, intuitions and knowledge which other nations have lost; it can therefore help these nations recover their lost religious roots and identity."

12.9. Conclusion

Sitaramji was a karmayogi whose personality was a lively synthesis of *jnana* (knowledge), *karma* (action) and *bhakti* (devotion). This brave son of Hindu society took up cudgels in its defence on a frontier that was left largely unmanned for ages. He showed the difference that an individual can make with dedicated effort. In any history of the Hindu renaissance, the contribution of Sitaram Goel and Voice of India will be acknowledged in golden letters.

(Virendra Parekh is Senior Economist at Indian Merchants' Chamber, Mumbai. He writes on economic and political subjects in English and Gujarati periodicals.)

13. Sita Ram Goel, a doughty warrior for Hinduism

Baljit Rai

13.1. Personal recollections

The saga of Sita Ram Goel's (1921-2003, hereafter SRG) life eminently qualifies for a full-length biography and I am writing this piece in the fond hope that at some time in the future some scholar will undertake this job of national importance. That author will discharge the debt that Hindu society owes him for his seminal writings in defence of the Hindus, Hinduism, Hindu society and India.

Let me record at the outset that one of the best things ever to happen to me in my life was to have come in contact with SRG in 1991. I was 63 at that time and what brought us together was my first book, *Muslim Fundamentalism in the Indian Sub-continent* (1991) which someone had presented to him. Thereafter, for the next ten years, I had the privilege of being treated as a member of his family and showered with utmost affection. He was extremely kind and generous to me. Beside regularly sending me books on the subject of Hinduism, Islam, Christianity and Communism, all written by his friend and mentor Ram Swarup and by himself, he did the onerous job of preparing the index of my second book, *Demographic Aggression Against India — Muslim Avalanche from Bangladesh* (1993). He also arranged to have the book formally released at the Constitution Club, New Delhi.

On one occasion he sent me a list of publications of Voice of India with a small note on the right hand corner of the list which read: "Let me know if you need any of the titles listed here" (7-8-1995). That was SRG at his magnanimous best.

I shall remain eternally beholden to him and his memory as fervently as I owed deep gratitude to him in life. Since I knew SRG fairly well I have the right credentials to write about him and his works. My only regret is that during the last 2 or 3 years of his life, when he was not keeping good health, he become a recluse and stopped meeting people, denying them the privilege of listening to his inspiring views and his saintly company.

SRG was no great leader who would address and mesmerize huge congregations. He had little to show in his persona that would set him apart as a towering personality in a group of normal human beings. He was tall, well built and always simply dressed in kurta and loose pajama. He occasionally smoked. Once he began to talk and dilate on the subject of Islam, Christianity or any other subject, a simple-looking man would transform into an intellectual giant with peerless perceptions. He was a rationalist to the core and not in the least fanatical about anything. Firm in his convictions, he was a veritable pugilist who could not only return blow for blow but also deliver the *coup de grâce* in polemical arguments. He wielded his pen with stunning force and effect. Along with his friend Ram Swarup, he marshaled facts of history as a counterblast and released forces which struck at the very roots of the three closed ideologies of Islam, Christianity and Communism. He did not consider the former two as religions (in the sense of *dharma*) but as bloodthirsty ideologies.

SRG was an erudite scholar. Although born in a poor family, he climbed to the top of the ladder in education. His rationalism came flooding his life, which set him on the path of self-discovery and of realizing his potential as a writer. The story is told in his autobiographical booklet *How I Became a Hindu* (1982). On the subject of Islam he wrote many books, some of them really path-breaking. The list of his books on the subject of Christianity and Communism is also substantial.

Besides, he wrote numerous articles and letters and contributed papers to other books. SRG was truly a prolific writer.

All three of these ideologies were carnivorous and must have devoured untold millions of innocent people since their respective birth and rise to power. SRG, endowed with an extraordinarily perceptive mind, embarked on his life-long mission to expose the warts on the faces of these ideologies. Since each has a long history, it will not be possible to deal with all three in one article. Hence, this piece covers only the ideology of Islam which has plagued our country and the Hindus for the last 1300 years.

13.2. SRG on Islam

Among the two most important contributions of SRG to the comprehension of the centuries-old Hindu-Muslim conflict, we note first of all the clear-cut distinction that he made between Islam and Muslims. He was forthright and hard-hitting in his statement that the problem was not the Muslim but Islam itself, and that Islam is not a religion but an imperialist and violent ideology totally devoid of spiritual content. Secondly, he successfully exploded the myth that the Hindus suffered defeat after defeat at the hands of foreign invaders and that they are a cowardly people. If that were so, Hinduism would have been wiped out by the Muslims centuries ago. We shall take these two points one by one.

At the ideological level, India appears to be an absolute desert during the last 1300 years when no Hindu carried out a proper study of Islam and how blood-thirsty it is or why Muslims have been repeatedly indulging in unspeakable barbarities. Swami Dayanand (19th Century) was the first Hindu to ever study the Quran and he came to the remarkable conclusion that Prophet Muhammad considered Allah as his domestic servant who invariably obliged him (the prophet) with a verse which eminently suited him. It is this basic truth about Islam that SRG relentlessly followed to its logical ends.

He attacked and exposed its tenets and tenaciously asserted that Muslims themselves were the victims of Islam. He spared no words in denouncing the teachings of the Quran, the Hadis and the Shariat or Islamic law as elaborated in the Hidayah.

The Muslims, the world over, consider the Quran as the word of Allah (God of the Muslims only) communicated to Prophet Muhammad through Archangel Gabriel. As such it is an object of utmost reverence and veneration, and any criticism of the same in any manner or even in the mildest language can invite retribution of the direst kind. For writing against Islam, SRG received numerous threats to his life, but he was made of sterner stuff and did not hesitate to give expression to his deeply-held convictions, arrived at after studying the letter and spirit of the Quran. The Quran deals with several aspects of life but the one with which SRG was concerned the most was the concept of *Jihad*, which is an irreversible warrant of death in perpetuity against non-believers. In the words of SRG, "the doctrine of Jihad, which is the core of the Quran, deals primarily with the performance of the Muslim military machine till the time an 'infidel land' is conquered and the Muslim hold is consolidated over it by terrorizing its people through slaughter and pillage" (*Calcutta Quran Petition*, 2nd ed., p.76; 3rd ed., p.210). The irrationality of some verses relating to Jihad in the Quran is truly perplexing, as would be evident from the following highly incomplete selection:

1. "Allah is an enemy to unbelievers." (2:98)
2. "On unbelievers is the curse of Allah." (2:161)
3. "Fight against them until idolatry is no more and Allah's religion reigns supreme." (2:193).
4. "Fighting is obligatory for you, much as you dislike it. But you may hate a thing although it is good for you, and love a thing although it is bad for you. Allah knows, but you do not." (2:216).
5. "Muslims are the best of all nations." (3:110)

6. "Therefore, we stirred among them (i.e. the Christians) enmity and hatred, which shall endure till the Day of Resurrection, when Allah will declare to them all that they have done." (5:14)
7. "Unbelievers are those who declare: 'Allah is the Messiah (i.e. Christ), the son of Mary.' Say: 'Who could prevent Allah from destroying the Messiah (i.e. Christ), the son of Mary, together with his mother and all he people of the earth?" (5:17)
8. "O Believers! Do not make friends with the Jews and Christians Ö who so of you makes them his friend is one of them." (5:51)
9. "I shall cast terror into the hearts of the infidels. Strike off their heads, maim them in every limb." (8:12)
10. "Tell the unbelievers that if they mend their ways (i.e. embrace Islam) their past shall be forgiven: but if they persist in sin (i.e. idol-worshipping) let them reflect upon the fate of their forefathers." (8:38)
11. "Make war on them until idolatry is no more and Allah's religion reigns supreme." (8:39)
12. "The basest creatures in the sight of Allah are the faithless who will not believe." (8:55)
13. "O Prophet! exhort the believers to fight. If there are twenty steadfast men among you, they shall rout a thousand unbelievers, for these are devoid of understanding." (8:65)
14. "Allah and His apostle are free from obligation to the idol-worshippers. Proclaim a woeful punishment to the unbelievers." (9:3)
15. "When the sacred months are over, slay the idol-worshippers wherever you find them. Arrest them, besiege them, and lie in ambush everywhere for them. If they repent and take to prayer and pay the alms-tax, let them go their way. Allah is forgiving and merciful." (9:5)
16. "Believers! do not befriend your fathers or your

brothers if they choose unbelief in preference to faith. Wrongdoers are those that befriend them." (9:23)

17. "The unbelievers are impure." (9:28)
18. "Humiliate the non-Muslims to such an extent that they surrender and pay tribute." (9:29)
19. "O Prophet! make war on the unbelievers and the hypocrites. Be harsh with them. Their ultimate abode is Hell, a hapless journey's end." (9:73)
20. "Believers! make war on the infidels who dwell around you. Let them find harshness in you." (9:123)
21. "Garments of fire have been prepared for unbelievers. Scalding water shall be poured upon their heads, melting their skins and that which is in their bellies. They shall be lashed with red hot iron." (22:19-21)
22. "Do not yield to the unbelievers, but fight them strenuously." (25:52)
23. "Muhammad is Allah's Apostle. Those who follow him are ruthless to the unbelievers but merciful to one another. (...) Through them Allah seeks to enrage the unbelievers." (48:29)
24. "We renounce you (i.e. the idolaters): enmity and hate shall reign between us until you believe in Allah only." (60:4)
25. "O Prophet! make war on the unbelievers and the hypocrites and deal sternly with them. Hell shall be their home, evil their fate." (66:9)
26. "We shall say, 'Lay hold of him and bind him. Burn him in the fire of Hell, then fasten him with a chain seventy cubits long. For he did not believe in Allah, the Most High." (69:30-33)

A reading of the above directives from Allah leaves no doubt that so far as non-Muslims or non-believers are concerned, the Quran is not a religious book at all but a war manual and a penal code.

These verses determine the behaviour pattern of Muslim invaders and rulers as well the Muslim masses over the last 1300 years. Every Muslim invader, whether Arab, Turk or Moghul had as his clear objective to advance the cause of Islam. The invader would complete his victory with mass slaughter of the vanquished male population; the enslavement of women and children; destruction of temples and raising mosques in their place with their debris; loot; rape and rapine and forcible conversion of people to Islam. SRG has documented the historical facts, based on original sources recorded by Muslim chroniclers of the destruction of countless beautiful temples. The incentive for such wanton destruction is provided to the soldiers of Islam by the theologically prescribed 4/5th share of the enormous war booty and an unlimited number of female slaves for their sexual gratification. The remaining 1/5th is kept as ruler's share and for the state treasury. The behaviour pattern continued for centuries and lasted till the invasion of Ahmad Shah Abdali and that unmitigated curse called Tipu Sultan. This behaviour pattern underwent no fundamental change until the disappearance of Muslim rule in India.

13.3. Sufi Jihad

One important aspect of Muslim rule in India was the appearance of the so-called Sufis on the soil of India. Many Hindus nowadays are quite enamoured of Sufis, Sufism, Sufi culture, Sufi poetry and Sufi music. One can only pity such people for their abysmal ignorance about the so-called Sufi saints who in reality were cheats and the civil arm of the Islamic polity with not a single objective and ideal different from that of the armed wing. To India's everlasting misfortune the Mongols had rained death and destruction over the Muslims of central Asia and Iran and destroyed the *Dar-ul-Khilafat* at Baghdad in AD 1258. Thousands of Sufi parasites who had been living in absolute luxury and debauchery made a beeline for India where they found the climate most salubrious for their nefarious activities.

The atrocities committed by the Mongols on the Muslims had no lessons for these Sufis who continued to support the barbarities of the Jihadis against the Hindus. One such Sufi migrant who arrived in India was Khwaja Muin-ud-din Chishti about whom Prof. Aziz Ahmad, a noted scholar of Islam in India says: "In Indian Sufism anti-Hindu polemics began with Muin-ud-din Chishti. Early Sufis in the Punjab and early Chishtis devoted themselves to the task of conversion on a large scale." (SRG: *Muslim Separatism*, p.45). It is this monster whose grave is visited by Muslims and Hindus alike. He is an early Muslim version of St. Francis Xavier.

Ahmed Sirhindi (1564-1624) was another Sufi who was determinedly opposed to Akbar's accommodative policies towards the Hindus. Here are some gems of Islamic wisdom left behind for posterity by this Sufi who proclaimed himself the "Renovator of the Second Millennium of Islam". "Shariat can be fostered through the sword": that was the slogan he raised for his contemporaries. Moreover: "The cow-sacrifice in India is the noblest of Islamic practices. The Kafirs may probably agree to pay Jizya but they shall never concede to cow-sacrifice." Again: "The execution of the accursed Kafir of Gobindwal [Guru Arjun Dev tortured to death by Jehangir] is an important achievement and is the cause of the great defeat of the Hindus." (*Muslim Separatism*, p.46) Ahmad Sirhindi was not simply a fanatic but a maniac who had said that "they (non believers/Hindus) should be kept away like dogs". There is little doubt that the study of Islamic theology not only diminishes a Muslim but also transforms him into a barbarian. Centuries later, after the 1965 war between India and Pakistan, Zulfiqar Ali Bhutto (Prime Minister of Pakistan, who was later hanged) called Indians "dogs" in a debate in the Security Council of the United Nations. The Muslim mind stands permanently contaminated with the poison of Islamic theology.

This maniac was followed by many more in the subsequent years, whom SRG call the Don Quixotes of Islam. These include Shah Walliullah (1703-1761), also a Sufi; Abdul Aziz (1746-1822), son of Shah Waliullah; Syed Ahmad Barelvi (1786-1831); Mir Nasser Ali of Barasat in Bengal, better known as Titu Mir or Titu Mian (1782-1831); and Dudu Mian (1819-1860). All of them considered themselves as great Mujahids who wanted to restore the glory of Islam in the face of Maratha power, Jats, Sikhs and the East India Company, which by 1850 had become an invincible power in India. But these tin-pot Mujahids left no stone unturned in not only spreading hatred against Hindus but also inviting and coaxing the Amir of Afghanistan to invade India in the interest of Islam.

During the Mutiny of 1857, this school of Don Quixotes managed to drag the last Moghul Emperor into a failed attempt at restoring Muslim power. With his defeat and incarceration in far-off Rangoon, a long phase of Muslim aggression and barbarism, begun with the arrival of Mohammed Bin Qasim in AD 712, came to an end. From now onwards Muslims had to change their attitude and tactics towards the Hindus and in this transformation the British rulers had a major role to play. The character of Hindu-Muslim conflict changed altogether.

It was no more a conflict between Hindus and Muslims of foreign extraction but a conflict between Hindus on the one hand and Hindu converts to Islam on the other. There was also a total change in the behaviour pattern of the Muslims, most of whom did not have even a single drop of Arab, Turkish, Persian or Moghul blood in their veins. These Hindu converts to Islam were as implacably hostile to the Hindus as were the Arabs, Turks, Persians and Mughals. It must be noted that such terrible animus among the Hindu converts to Islam and their progeny against the Hindus could only be induced and sustained by an ideology like that of Islam.

13.4. Muslim strategy under British rule

In the post-Mutiny period, there was a radical transformation in the political map of India. The British had turned out be to the most powerful and the only supreme power in the country. The elite section in Muslim society, who had memories of having ruled the country for centuries, now felt utterly despondent. The British too were looking for friends in the Indian population with whose support they could strengthen their Empire in India. The Muslims and the British came closer to each other. It was a symbiotic relationship, which decreed that the British would stand by the Muslims through thick and thin while the Muslims would not join the nationalist forces which had risen against the British. Both parties remained true to their commitment except for a period of two years or so during the Khilafat movement (1920-22), when the Muslims became hostile because of the Turkish problem.

With the solid support of the British, the Muslim population frequently raised the slogan of Islam being in perpetual danger. The new strategy, which gave shape to the behaviour pattern of the Muslims, was to continuously lament the plight of the Muslims as poor and backward, being prevented from slaughtering cows on festive occasions, having to suffer Hindu processions playing music before mosques and danger to the Urdu language. These four items acquired talismanic status with which the Muslims continued to blackmail the Hindu community and the nationalists. There were countless Hindu-Muslims riots, in which the Hindus suffered terribly. Hindu blood continued to be shed by the Muslims under British rule, like during centuries of Muslim rule. This pattern of Muslim behaviour brought about not only the Partition of India but also the total destruction of Hinduism and Sikhism in Pakistan, the genocide of Hindus in Bangladesh and the "ethnic cleansing" of the Hindus from the Kashmir valley.

Since 1947 and down to the present, this behaviour pattern has proved to be no less destructive, if not more, than the one in vogue during the rule of Sultans and Moghuls.

Regarding cow-slaughter, as SRG has pointed out, the Hindus "know next to nothing about Islam. Otherwise they would have pointed out that although Islam stood for a lot of slaughter of animals as well as of human beings — the poor cow was nowhere in the picture. They would have quoted a hundred Islamic theologians who had recommended cow-slaughter not to secure heaven for the Muslims but to humiliate the accursed Hindus." (*Muslim Separatism*, p.78) So, the persistent demand of Muslims to slaughter cows was not a religious requirement, except in the sense that it was deemed meritorious to humiliate the Hindus. This is what the Hindus did not understand.

Similarly, in respect of music before mosques, SRG writes: "The Muslims needed to be told that the practice of not permitting processions to pass before a mosque had nothing to do with the peace or silence during Muslim prayers. Hindus could have quoted Caliph Umar and a hundred other treatises like the Hidayah to point out that the prohibition of non-Muslim public celebrations, religious or otherwise, was one of the twenty-two disabilities which an Islamic state had always enforced on the hated Zimmis. Hindus under Muslim rule had not been permitted to celebrate their festivals loudly even inside their homes, not to speak of celebrating them on the streets. It was just another instance of unjust privilege usurped by Muslims in the period of their political supremacy." (*Muslim Separatism*, p.79)

This Muslim behaviour pattern was a part of the psyche of not only countless ordinary Muslims but also of the elite. One such person was Maulana Azad, the so-called nationalist Muslim, who highly commended Ahmad Sirhindi because "but for these letters [written by Sirhindi], Muslim nobles would not have stood by Islam, and but for the efforts of Sheikh Ahmad, Akbar's heterodoxy would have superseded

Islam in India". This is not the place to give an exhaustive list of quotations showing the Maulana's anti-secularism, but at least we can hope the reader will be on guard the next time he is told of how Azad stands out as an enlightened nationalist merely on the strength of his opposition to the Partition. To Azad, Partition did not mean the securing of a henceforth inalienable Muslim state, as it did for Jinnah, but amounted to renouncing the prospect of a neo-Moghul empire spanning the whole subcontinent.

For a conclusive testimony, we may let the final word rest with Mahatma Gandhi, that great friend of the Muslims. In an article in *Young India* dd. 29 May 1924, Mahatma Gandhi himself had noted: "My own experience confirms that the Muslim as a rule is a bully." SRG adds: "Only he did not trace this Muslim behaviour pattern to the tenets of Islam, which continued to be a 'noble faith' for him till he himself was consumed by the flames ignited by this faith." (*Muslim Separatism*, p.97) In the ultimate analysis, Gandhi's policy of non-violence turned out to be as carnivorous as Islam, Christianity and Communism. The only difference is that while the later three consumed people of other ideologies, Gandhi's non-violence devoured Hindus only.

13.5. Hindu valour

Now we come to the second major contribution of SRG regarding Hindus being cowardly and suffering defeat after defeat at the hands of foreign invaders. There is an awful burden of cynicism being voiced by the educated section of Hindu society. They lament day in and day out that Hindus, too inept or too cowardly to put up a fight, were humbled again and again by the Muslims invaders on the battlefield. When asked to do something now, they would squirm like real cowards. What is the remedy?

First of all, the so-called liberal sections of Hindu society must remove countless cobwebs in their minds, which inhibit them from understanding the true nature of Islam as an ideology and not a religion. The point becomes clear when we hear Mahatma Gandhi complaining (*Young India*, 30 Dec. 1927) that "Islam was born in an environment where the sword was and still remains the supreme law. (...) the sword is yet too much in evidence among Mussalmans. It must be sheathed if Islam is to be what it means: peace. (...) The thirteen hundred years of imperialistic expansion have made Mussalmans fighters as a class. They are therefore aggressive. Bullying is the natural excrescence of an aggressive spirit. The Hindu has an age-old civilization. He is essentially non-violent. (...) Predominance of non-violent spirit has restricted the use of arms to a small minority. (...) Not knowing their [= arms'] use nor having an aptitude for them, they [= Hindus] have become docile to the point of timidity or cowardice."

Thirteen hundred years of Muslim invaders' relentless struggle against the unbelievers in India has been described thus by Will Durant in his famous book *The Story of Civilization*: "The Islamic conquest of India is probably the bloodiest story in history. It is a discouraging tale, for its evident moral is that civilization is a precious good, whose delicate complex of order and freedom can at any time be overthrown by barbarians invading from outside or multiplying within." So, the record of the invaders is well-known. But how about the defenders of India and her civilization? Did the Hindu never defend his land?

Before we answer this question, it is advisable to compare the remarkable expansion of Islam in the lands east or west of Arabia with its long march against India. The prophet of Islam died in AD 632. Within the next eighty years, Arab armies rapidly overran Palestine and Syria (AD 636-637), the Sassanid empire of Persia including Iraq, Iran and Khorasan (AD 637 ff.), Turkish-speaking territories of Central Asia (AD 650 ff.), Egypt (AD 640-41), then North Africa and then even Spain (AD 709). Within eleven years of the death of the prophet the boundaries of the Caliphate touched the frontiers of India. Territorial expansion of Islam also led to equally rapid Islamization of people of different creeds and races living in the conquered lands and their total assimilation within the Islamic fold. But the record of the progress of Arab armies towards India, not only in the corresponding period but even in later centuries has been dismal and demoralizing for the Muslim commanders, many of whom were killed. For example, between AD 661-680, Caliph Muawiyah sent six expeditions and all were repulsed.

The first Arab expedition that had a semblance of success in Sind was led by Mohammad Bin Qasim, who ransacked several towns and became master of Sind and Multan by AD 713. But he had to face severe resistance from the Hindus. One incident that showed the utter contempt of the Hindus for the Islamic invaders then and throughout the succeeding centuries must be recorded here. This was when king Dahir was killed in the battle of Rawar in AD 712. When the battle was lost, Dahir's queen saw her doom inevitable. She assembled all the women in the fort and addressed them thus (as reported in the chronicle *Chachnama*): "God forbid that we should owe our liberty to those casteless cow-eaters. Our honour would be lost. Our respite is at an end and there is nowhere any hope of escape. Let us collect wood, cotton and oil, for I think we should burn ourselves and go to meet our husbands. If any wish to save herself, she may." Then: "They entered into a house where they burnt themselves in the fire of *jauhar*, thereby vindicating the honour of their race." (related in K.S. Lal: *Legacy of Muslim Rule in India*, p.89)

There were several such *jauhar*s in the history of India when Hindu women burnt themselves alive to save their honour from Muslim predators. The latest such collective honour suicide was performed by dauntless and brave women in the village Thoha Khalsa (District Rawalpindi, Pakistan) in March 1947. As G.D. Khosla relates (*Stern Reckoning*, p.112): "Almost every village in the Rawalpindi district where non-Muslims lived was attacked and plundered in this manner and Hindus and Sikhs were murdered and subjected to indescribable barbarities. In Thola Khalsa some Sikh women were thrown into a well, others jumped in of their own free will (all glory to them) to save themselves from being raped."

Readers may note that the time span between the two rape-avoiding suicides is 1235 years, and how the dreaded Islamic methods had remained unchanged over the centuries. Is Gandhi wrong when he says, "the sword is yet too much in evidence among Mussalmans. It must be sheathed..."? The stark reality and the lesson that history teaches is that faithful Muslims will never sheath their sword. But Hindu resistance is no less a match for the Muslim sword and violence.

Regarding the history of Hindu heroism between the first Muslim invasion and the establishment of the Delhi Sultanate (636-1206), and commenting on Dr. Ram Gopal Misra's relevant monograph *Indian Resistance to Early Muslim Invaders Upto AD 1206* (Anu Books, Meerut 1983), SRG put it this way: "Dr. Misra is one of those few historians who have helped Hindu society not only to recover the national perspective on Indian History but also to resurrect the heroic image of *Hindu personality*. In giving a blow-by-blow account of how Hindus fought tenaciously and for a long time for every inch of their homeland in the face of an inveterate enemy inspired by a diabolical creed, he has brought out in bold relief not only the fact that Hindus were second to none when it came to making sacrifices for their motherland but also the fact that Hindus were fighting in defence of something which they valued above their very lives. 'The early successes of Islam', he writes, 'were against religions which had lost their hold on the minds of the people. But in India the Hindu way of life, symbolized by high moral values of tolerance, truthfulness and justice was very much the part and parcel of the multitude's mental and material being. These eternal and moral values of life which constitute the core of Hinduism were to sustain it in the next five centuries of Muslim (1206-1757) and another two centuries of British rule

(1757-1947). *The conclusion, therefore, seems inescapable that much of the decline in social and moral values of Hindu society is the result and not the cause of their foreign subjugations.*'" (*Heroic Hindu Resistance*, pp.6-7, emphasis SRG's)

After the establishment of Muslim rule in Delhi and other parts of India, the freedom struggle continued under resistance leaders springing up in all parts of India: Maharana Pratap in Rajasthan, Hakka and Bukka in the South, Chhatrapati Shivaji and the Peshwas in Maharashtra, Banda Bairagi and Ranjit Singh in Panjab, Chhatrasal in Bundelkhand, Lachit Barphukan in Assam, and many others. By the mid-18th century, Hindu resistance had broken the back of the Moghul empire and but for the British intrusion, India would have reverted to native rule. These facts of history provide ample proof that Hindus were certainly no cowards and Islam had to face resistance at every step.

However, this is not to suggest that the Hindus came out of the combat with Islam unscathed. Far from it, for as SRG observes, "it is in this context that Dr. Misra's searching analysis of the causes of our defeat at the end of the 12th century acquires an immense importance. The struggle between Islamic imperialism and Indian resistance, military as well as socio-cultural, was grim and long-drawn-out, lasting as it did over 570 years. The new contest is not likely to last that long due to the changed character of warfare. It is true that we battled against Islamic imperialism for another 550 years and defeated it in the final round in the middle of the 18th century. But it is also true that the losses we suffered in terms of territory (Afghanistan, Seistan, Makran), population, social disintegration and spiritual corruption were simply staggering. By the middle of the 20th century Islam succeeded in consolidating the gains it had made during more than a thousand years' aggression against India. On the other hand, we have come out of the latest contest more confused than ever before, so much so that while a highly humanitarian national culture gets condemned as a narrow and militant communalism, an ideology of totalitarian terror gets registered as a religion, a closed and theocratic creed struts about as secularism, and a fanatic fraternity addicted to frequent rounds of violence passes for a 'poor and persecuted minority'. The situation is far from reassuring." (*Heroic Hindu Resistance*, p.39)

13.6. Hindu losses in the 20th century

Hindus suffered the greatest loss in terms of territory and numbers in the 20th century, which opened with the following exhortation to Muslims: "Ye Mussalmans, arise, awake! Do not read in the same schools with the Hindus. Do not touch any article manufactured by the Hindus. Do not give any employment to the Hindus. Do not accept any degrading office under a Hindu. You are ignorant, but if you acquire knowledge you can send all Hindus to *Jahannam* (Hell). You form the majority of the population in this province. The Hindu has no wealth of his own and has made himself rich only by despoiling you of your wealth. If you become sufficiently enlightened, the Hindus will starve and soon become Mohammedans." (quoted in *Muslim Separatism*, p.87) This exhortation was contained in the *Lal Ishtahar* (Red Pamphlet), which was distributed all over Bengal in the wake of first Muslim League meeting in Dhaka in 1906. In the subsequent decades the Muslims unleashed unprecedented violence against the Hindus.

In the 20th century, Hinduism was destroyed root and branch in 1/4th of India, and residual India too was left battered, bruised and bleeding. Among the highlights of the nerve-shattering Muslim violence against the Hindus, we may mention the Moplah slaughter of thousands of Hindus (1921); the Kohat riots against Hindus and Sikhs (1924; the murder of Swami Shraddhanand (1926); the murder of Mahashay Rajpal (1928); the Dhaka riots against Hindus (1928); the great Calcutta killing (August 1945); genocide of Hindus in

Noakhali (November 1946); genocide of Hindus and Sikhs in West Pakistan (1947); continuous terror against Hindus in East Pakistan/Bangladesh (August 1946 till today); countless communal riots in India, almost always started by the Muslims (1966 till today); a million Hindus slaughtered in East Pakistan by the Pakistani army (1971); proxy war in J&K unleashed by Pakistan (1989 till today); massacre and ethnic cleansing of the Kashmiri Pandits (1989-91); serial blasts in Bombay killing hundreds of people (12 March 1993); a bomb blast in Calcutta killing scores of people (15 March 1993); numerous blasts by Islamic terrorists in South India targeting BJP and RSS and killing scores of their members (1992-99), including an attempt on L.K. Advani's life in Coimbatore which killed forty BJP supporters (1998); Muslim terrorist attacks on the Red Fort in Delhi, the Kashmir State Parliament, the Indian Union Parliament, twice the Raghunath Temple in Jammu, the train from Ayodhya in Godhra and the Swaminarayan Temple in Ahmedabad (1991-92). In recent years, Pakistan has stepped up its proxy war by extending its support to non-Islamic terror groups as well, esp. in the Northeast, with Bangladesh providing refuge and training grounds. Shifting from one frontline to another, Islamic terrorism continues unabated.

What are the chances of Hindu-Muslim rapprochement? In my opinion, none at all. Hindus may like to live in peace but the Muslims have different ideas. In the 1920s, Khwaja Hasan Nizami, a reputed Sufi (frequently quoted by secularists as claiming that Rama and Krishna were "prophets of Allah"), published a book, *Fatami Dawat-i-Islam*, in which he advocated all means, fair and foul, to convert Hindus to Islam. He advised the Mullahs to concentrate on Hindu untouchables and convert them *en masse* so that the Muslims could achieve parity of population with the Hindus. This diabolical scheme got leaked out and was frustrated by Swami Shraddhanand by means of his *Shuddhi* Movement.

But that doesn't mean the Islamic forces have given up: "And now we have the same scheme resurrected before us by the Islamic Centre in London in a still more ambitious form. The aim of achieving parity with the Hindus has been abandoned in favour of full islamization of India. The Islamic fraternity in India has welcomed the scheme with open arms. Jama't-i-Islami is the most fanatic constituent of this fraternity. There are many more individuals and organizations operating under different guises. In any case, the scheme is pushed ahead vigorously with the aid of petro-dollars. (...) The full contours of the conspiracy were revealed by Javed Ansari in the December 1981 number of *Arabia: The Islamic Review*, published by the Islamic Press Agency, London." (*Muslim Separatism*, p.114) With such treacherous activity aimed at the annihilation of Hindus and Hinduism, how can there ever be peaceful relations between the two communities? SRG warned the Hindus of this Islamic Manifesto and a disaster staring them in the face if they do not wake up.

13.7. Conclusion

SRG's lifelong efforts and achievements have to be recorded in letters of gold. We like-minded people should join hands to not only vigorously propagate his views but to set up a *Sita Ram Goel Foundation* to carry on the work started by him. I salute and pay homage to the memory of Sita Ram Goel, the brave warrior and sentinel of Hinduism.

(Baljit Rai is a retired IPS officer from Chandigarh.)

14. Intellectual kshatriya par excellence

Navaratna S. Rajaram

14.1. First acquaintance

What follows is a personal account of a fruitful relationship by a grateful author. I got to know of Sita Ram Goel in 1993, a few months after I had returned to India from the United States where I had been living for more than twenty years. Remarkably enough it came about through Leftist circles. The well-known feminist sociologist Devaki Jain passed on to him a transcript of my lecture on the Aryan invasion theory that had I given her father, the late M.A. Srinivasan. (He was a family friend of ours, particularly close to my late grandfather Navaratna Rama Rao.) Goel then contacted me, asking if he could publish it as a Voice of India booklet. I agreed and sent him another transcript — of a lecture given at the Bharatiya Vidya Bhavan in Chennai. He published these as a small book, *Aryan Invasion of India: The Myth and the Truth* (1993). He was later to publish several of my books on the same theme including *The Politics of History* (1995) and *Vedic Aryans and the Origins of Civilization* (1997/2001), the latter with David Frawley.

At that time I knew nothing about Sita Ram (as Devaki Jain always referred to him, and I will too, and not as Sita as many others did). He sent me several Voice of India and Aditya publications on history and politics, which I found interesting, as did my late father. My father, Navaratna Srinivasa Rao, had spoken very admiringly of Sita Ram Goel. My reaction at the time was probably not very different from that of most people of my background — a western educated Indian with commitment to Hindu civilization but with a somewhat condescending attitude towards Indian intellectuals.

Fortunately, I had recently come to know David Frawley (Vamadeva Shastri), exchanging ideas with him on several areas, especially ancient history. This had forced me to recognize the spiritual underpinnings of ancient civilizations and to look at India and her civilization with a more open mind. Still, it took me a while to recognize that Sita Ram and Ram Swarup had introduced a profoundly new way of studying world religions and political ideologies from a Yogic perspective.

In my own work, since I never practised Yoga or meditation, I followed a secular-objective approach that was probably a variation of Sankhya. My first effort in the direction was a talk on secularism that I gave at a seminar in Bangalore. I sent an expanded version of its transcript to Sita Ram, feeling that it might be of interest to him. To my surprise, he called me immediately and said that both he and Ram Swarup liked it and felt it should be published. Voice of India brought it out as a small book with the title *Secularism: The New Mask of Fundamentalism* (1995). I was surprised by the wide and largely favorable reception it got and the many reviews, including one by Jaswant Singh, later a Union Minister. It was translated into other languages and also excerpted in several publications. I can only suppose that it filled a vacuum.

14.2. The Aryan invasion debate

It was also in 1993 that Shrikant Talageri's book *Aryan Invasion Theory: A Reappraisal* came out through Aditya Prakashan. I had seen a highly laudatory article on it by the late Girilal Jain in *The Times of India.* I wanted a copy, but was having difficulty getting it. If my memory serves me right, this was shortly before I got to know Sita Ram. But soon after he got in touch with me about my articles, he sent me a copy of it along with three books by K.D. Sethna on ancient India. I had heard of Sethna, but had a typically condescending attitude towards him — until I read his *Karpasa* (1981), one of the books sent by Sita Ram. It left me flabbergasted, for his conclusion based on Indian and Sumerian records was exactly the same as my own based on the ancient mathematical texts of India, Babylonia and Egypt: chronologically the Harappan civilization overlapped with the Sutra period of the later Vedic Age. Only, Sethna had reached it a decade before I did. But importantly, we now had two totally independent derivations of a fundamental chronological equation. Frawley and I gave it the name Harappa-Sutra-Sumeria equation. Following this, we dedicated our book *Vedic Aryans* to Sethna, calling him the *Bhishma Pitamaha* of ancient Indian history.

There is now a third derivation of this equation, thanks to Natwar Jha and his readings of the Harappan seals — both the symbolism and the script. But Sethna's breakthrough was crucial, because it gave me confidence in my own derivation knowing that it was not a flash in the pan but a fundamental relationship that had independent support. It was crucial also in determining the language of the Harappan writing, independently of the decipherment.

I did not know Sita Ram very long, only about a decade. Nor did I see him often, first because I rarely traveled to Delhi in those days, and later, when my visits to Delhi became more frequent, he was bed-ridden much of the time. It was an ordeal for him even to speak on the phone. Earlier, when he was in better health, we used to communicate fairly regularly both by mail and by telephone. Later, it was mostly by e-mail.

One of the more memorable phone calls I received from Sita Ram was in January of 1997. I had just given a talk on Natwar Jha's decipherment of the Indus (Harappan) script, having recently learnt about it from a review article in *The Hindu.* When I sent a copy of the talk to Sita Ram, he called me immediately and asked me what I planned to do with it. I told him I had contacted Jha with a proposal for a jointly authored book, but had reservations about finding a competent publisher because of the technically demanding nature of the work. I did not know any publisher or editor in India or anywhere else who could handle it. He told me not to worry and go ahead with the book; he would take care of it. Thanks to Sita Ram, *The Deciphered Indus Script* by N. Jha and N.S. Rajaram came out through Aditya Prakashan in March 2000.

It received wide notice, but what I was not prepared for was the fierce reaction, not only from the usual 'secularist' historians in India, but more especially from some Indologists in the West. Having had my academic career in mathematical sciences and technology, I had no idea of the ferocity with which humanities scholars fight to save their positions. Our book, arguably written in a provocative style, dealt a body blow to their whole academic edifice built over a century and based on the Aryan invasion theory and the Vedic-Harappan dichotomy. Careers and reputations were at stake, especially in the West already reeling under what has been termed "downsizing of the humanities" at the universities.

In the circumstances, it was perhaps natural to get a hostile response, but what took us by surprise were the personal attacks in the media. The lead was taken by a relatively obscure Sanskrit professor at Harvard, who charged that our claim relating to the presence of the horse in Harappan remains had been fabricated though it had nothing to do with our decipherment and was limited to a couple of partial footnotes, as we pointed out in a series of letters and articles in *The Hindu*. (The argument, for those who might be interested, was that horses were unknown in India until the invading Aryans brought them from Central Asia or Eurasia. Therefore horses could not have existed in Harappan remains. This has been demolished by archaeology and also by the fact that the horse described in the Vedas is the native Indian breed, anatomically quite different from the Central Asian.)

In the midst of all this turmoil, Sita Ram's attitude was interesting. While others were worried that attacks from such a prestigious source might do serious damage to our work, Sita Ram took the opposite view. He saw, rightly, that the very ferocity of the attacks showed that our adversaries were feeling threatened and told me not to get worried. There were hints (called 'suggestions') from several quarters indicating that the attacks would stop if we were to retract our decipherment. Shrikant Talageri called me several times, expressing concern. When he called Sita Ram, fearing I might yield to pressure, Sita Ram told him not to worry, that I was strong enough to weather the storm. I was much gratified by this expression of support.

14.3. The politics of history

It was a similar story when I was nominated to the ICHR (Indian Council of Historical Research) by the HRD Minister Murli Manohar Joshi. I had no inkling of it, and would have tried to dissuade the Government from nominating me, as I don't like to serve on committees of any kind. Two years earlier, I had turned down a similar appointment on a committee related to the Archaeological Survey of India. I learnt of the ICHR nomination only when some friends in Delhi called me to inform me that the *Hindustan Times* had devoted several reports to it, including an editorial (later, at least one more) attacking my nomination. Several friends called me to support my nomination, insisting that I should accept the nomination and use it as an opportunity to change the climate in the History establishment. But I had already decided against it and tried my best to explain my reasons for not accepting it. Sita Ram again saw my side and felt that I should not have anything to do with government organizations. In fact, he had cautioned me against it even before my decision became public. Later developments in the ICHR have vindicated it.

One of the great benefits of my relationship with Sita Ram has been the friendship of scholars that it brought me. Thanks to him I came to know Shrikant Talageri, Bhagwan Singh, Arun Shourie, Koenraad Elst — and above all, the late Ram Swarup. One of my cherished memories is of translating a few articles from French at Ram Swarup's request, shortly before his death. These have been widely reprinted though mostly without acknowledgement. (May I request Indian authors and publishers to be more meticulous in acknowledging sources? I say this not out of any personal pique, but only because it will be of service to the reader in tracing a source.) I hope it was not a one-way street, for I too brought some distinguished authors to his attention, notably David Frawley and Natwar Jha.

In addition to my books on history, Sita Ram published a few of my books on Christianity and Islam, most recently *Profiles in Deception: Ayodhya and the Dead Sea Scrolls* (2000). It happens to be the first study of the Dead Sea Scrolls by anyone outside the Judaeo-Christian tradition published in India. (My earlier book on the Dead Sea Scrolls had appeared in England.) I was preoccupied with other things at the time, especially my work on the Harappan script with Jha, and would probably not have written it but for Sita Ram's persistent encouragement. More recently, he drew my attention to the work on *dhimmitude* by Bat Ye'or, which led to my writing columns on it that became widely known.

I mention this only to point out that Sita Ram Goel has been as important through his pioneering publishing work as through his scholarship and writing. In fact, I regard him as the most original serious publisher in India. His work, writing and publishing has led to the creation of the most important school of thought in the Indian humanities today, the Hindutva School in all its diversity. In this regard, his publishing house Voice of India has been more like a research centre and think-tank than a commercial house. While the Marxists and the anti-Hindu 'secularists' are running for cover, desperately clinging to what is left of their perks and positions (their influence is all but gone), many of the positions advocated by Sri Goel are moving into the mainstream. He was twenty years ahead of his time.

Though the English language media continues to shun his name, his influence is proving to be significant and growing. Discussion of *jihad* is now all the rage, often found in the front pages of newspapers, but no one mentions two important books published by Voice of India — Suhas Majumdar's *Jihad: The Islamic Doctrine of Permanent War* and Goel's own *The Calcutta Quran Petition*. The latter is probably the best introduction available on the theory and practice of Islam, compiled by drawing upon both Islamic scripture and history. It is the same story when it comes to ancient history. The Aryan invasion theory is on its last legs, its only support coming from Christian missionaries and Communists — now practically one and the same — yet Voice of India and Aditya Prakashan (founded by his son, Pradeep Goel) have published more scholarly works refuting the Aryan invasion and proposing alternatives than all other publishers in the world put together.

While the media is beginning to recognize the contribution of several Voice of India authors like David Frawley, Koenraad Elst, Shrikant Talageri and this writer, it continues its policy of ignoring Sita Ram Goel. When Elst's *Decolonizing the Hindu Mind* came out, a national weekly did a feature on Koenraad Elst as a major voice of Hindutva but said not a word about Sita Ram or his publications, without which Elst (and a few others) might have remained in obscurity. It is time that the media, the English-language media in particular, dropped its petty prejudices and recognized his contribution.

14.4. "Intellectual kshatriya"

As a writer, Sita Ram Goel is best known for his incisive and uncompromising analysis of Islam, Christianity and Communism as political ideologies and of their impact on Indian history. His range of knowledge, however, was much wider. I already noted his initiative in recognizing the importance of *dhimmitude* (Ram Swarup had also noted it earlier as *zimmitude*, but that was ahead of its time). Another example: in 1996, when I acquainted him with the work I was doing with Natwar Jha on the decipherment of the Indus script, he immediately grasped its significance. He went on to point out that like the Indus script, Gurumukhi was also written without vowels. This led Jha and me to explore the origins of northwestern scripts, particularly Landa and Morea, which were once in use in areas where the Indus script was widely distributed. I can only contrast this with the illiterate but pretentious response of some "eminent" academics in India and abroad.

This brings up another facet of Sita Ram's character: though obviously aware of his own worth, he freely acknowledged the contribution of others. He had worked closely with the late Ram Swarup, and the following statement made at a lecture bears eloquent testimony to Sri Goel's generosity and modesty: "In fact, it would have been in the fitness of things if the speaker today had been Ram Swarup, because whatever I have written and whatever I have to say today really comes from him. He gives me the seed-ideas which sprout into my articles (...) He gives me the framework of my thought. Only the language is mine. The language also would have been much better if it was his own. My language becomes sharp at times; it annoys people. He has a way of saying things in a firm but polite manner, which discipline I have never been able to acquire."

Many would disagree with this self-assessment — that his insights came from Ram Swarup while he did little more than give them shape. My experience is that Sita Ram contributed many insights, like the one relating to the Indus script I already mentioned. The second part of his statement, with regard to his language, comes from the experience of some who accuse him of being abrasive. But in the overall scheme of things, in the light of his magnificent contribution, it is at the most a minor irritant. I sometimes feel that he made his task of gaining support for his views unnecessarily difficult because of his way of expressing dissent, and some people's excessive sensitivity to it. Happily, there are now winds of change and the ideas he propounded and propagated are proving their worth. It is time that the people of India, the media in particular, gave him his due.

I owe him personal gratitude not only because he published my books, but even more, for being the medium for some memorable friendships, especially of the late Ram Swarup. In a sense it spoilt me. The quality of editorial work at Aditya and Voice of India was so exceptional that I was unprepared for the general mediocrity prevalent among other Indian publishers. It takes some getting used to.

Sita Ram Goel was a prolific writer. It is not easy to pick one or two of his books as his most significant. Nonetheless I would recommend *The Calcutta Quran Petition* and his monumental two-volume compilation, *Hindu Temples: What Happened to Them*. Written in finely chiseled English (his Hindi being no less distinguished) with scrupulous attention to facts and sources, they are indispensable to every serious student of India. A collection of his writings should be compiled and prescribed as a text for all students of history. The Government also should recognize his contribution by a suitable award and institute scholarships in his name. (Sita Ram objected when I suggested it, but I feel it should be pursued by a private foundation if not the government.)

In the passing of Sita Ram Goel, India lost a scholar, writer, publisher, and creator and mentor of a vigorous school of thought rooted in Sanatana Dharma. It is not easy to describe this many-sided man, but the phrase *intellectual kshatriya*, to my knowledge first used by David Frawley, appears appropriate. How are we to describe an intellectual kshatriya? Fortunately Sri Aurobindo has already done it for us: "[Such a person] should be absolutely unsparing in (...) attack on whatever obstructs the growth of the nation, and never be afraid to call a spade a spade. Excessive good nature will never do (...) in serious politics. Respect of persons must always give way to truth and conscience (...) What India needs especially at this moment is aggressive virtues, the spirit of soaring idealism, bold creation, fearless resistance, courageous attack; of the passive tamasic inertia we already have too much." I can think of no better epitaph for Sita Ram Goel.

(Dr. Rajaram is a retired professor of Mathematics in American universities and a former consultant with NASA; now based in Bangalore, he writes on factual and methodological issues in ancient and contemporary Indian history.)

15. The ideological battle

B.K. Rao

15.1. Assessing the enemy as he really is

An ideological battle has to be waged in order to avoid the other battle, the physical battle. Societies failing to fight an ideological battle and refusing to repel ideological aggression invite physical aggression sooner or later. If ideological aggression is not stopped, a society gets taken for granted and physical aggression follows. This is a law of Nature.

We did not fight against the ideological aggression of the Muslim League. The latter was later on joined by the Communist Party of India (CPI), which collected facts and figures to give respectability to the ideological aggression from Islam. I know it personally because I was myself a Communist at that time. And we know what happened. Physical aggression followed. The country was partitioned. Millions were rendered homeless, millions were killed.

So, if we want to save our society from physical aggression, from physical clashes, from street riots, from bloodshed, we should take up this ideological battle immediately. But we have to be equipped in order to fight this battle. We have to know our own Hindu society, our own Hindu culture, our own Hindu history, our own Sanatana Dharma. We have also to know Islam and Christianity and Communism from their own sources, from the horse's mouth. We should not have any private versions of these alien ideologies. We should know them as they are in themselves, as expounded by their own spokesmen.

We Hindus have a bad habit, a suicidal habit, of finding in our own traditions, in our own scriptures, whatever the alien ideologies claim for themselves. We try to find Christianity in our scriptures, we try to find Islam in our scriptures, we try to find Communism in our scriptures. This is a very bad habit. We must know the enemy as he is, otherwise the ideological battle is not really joined.

15.2. The "Sita" surprise

"You wait a little", Sri Ram Swarup told me, "Sita will be coming."

I was meeting Sri Ram Swarup for the first time. My father, Sri M.A. Venkata Rao, had taken me to Sri Ram Swarup's residence, next to Multan Dayanand Arya Vidyalaya High School, at Sir Gangaram Hospital Road in Delhi. My father and some other intellectuals and journalists were then working together for the *Society for the Defence of Freedom in Asia* (SDFA), which had been initiated under Sri Ram Swarup's inspiration. Their pamphleteering and journalistic work was to expose the nefarious activities of the Communists in India and their political and economic links with the Soviet Union. While the leftists claimed that the Soviet state was a "heaven on earth", others described it as the "Soviet slave empire".

I knew next to nothing about Sri Ram Swarup's personal life at my first meeting with him. Being an "eligible bachelor", I was anticipating interesting possibilities, guessing that "Sita" was perhaps Sri Ram Swarup's daughter! And suddenly "Sita" arrived, a tall and lean man, agile and in his prime, wearing white khadi kurta and pajama. So, this was the "Sita surprise" I had that evening.

Later, I learnt that Sri Ram Swarup was a bachelor and a yogi, that he was an honours graduate in Economics and that he had played an active role in the freedom struggle. In college Sri Ram Swarup had been one year senior to Sri Sita Ram Goel.

It was winter in Delhi and I had come from Bombay to see the first India International Industrial Exhibition, among other things. The exhibition was on at what is now Pragati Maidan. The only permanent structure there at that time was a specially designed gate. The rest were temporary structures to house the exhibits and the states' emporia.

15.3. Philosophical background

Soon after my graduation in Bangalore — a Bachelor of Arts with History, Economics and Politics as my subjects — I went to Bombay (it was not yet Mumbai in 1953) to join the Libertarian Social Institute as a Research Assistant. There were two other researchers. One was Sri K.D. Valicha, who had considerable literary talent and later became a professor in English Literature. The other was Sri B.S. Sanyal, who was building an academic career in Philosophy. He was effervescent with philosophical ideas and ever formulating definitions. He later authored the work *Hindu Ideology Made Simple*.

Dr. Sanyal, who had studied European philosophy, was developing Kantian epistemology. I was a keen student of the Anglo-Hegelian school of idealism as developed by Bradley and Bosanquet. My father, who taught philosophy at the Maharani's College, Bangalore, until he resigned his job due to university politics, called this Anglo-Hegelian system a "concrete idealism". I have had several philosophical discussions with my father and preferred calling my position a Natural Idealism, as expounded by Robert Adamson in his *Development of Modern Philosophy* (William Blackwood & Sons, Edinburgh and London 1909). Adamson's basic idea, or *mûla-mantra*, is that all distinctions are within the felt unity of experience. With this idea it is easy to accommodate both science and rationalism and integrate them with Sanatana Dharma.

My father, Prof. Venkata Rao, who studied under Dr. Radhakrishnan in Mysore University, called himself a returned Macaulayan. By this he meant that the depth and range of

Vedantic thought could be better appreciated if the Macaulayans studied and understood the idealism of the British thinkers. European idealism is derived from Plato and Plato is part of the universal mystic tradition. According to Alfred North Whitehead, the history of European philosophy can be described as footnotes on Plato.

Mr. Sanyal and myself applied our minds to using my father's way of thinking for making a comparative study of religions. We concluded that while the Christian clergy and the Muslim Maulvis had suppressed mystics and Sufis, the Indian spiritual tradition had placed sages and mystics at the top of the religious hierarchy. Each individual spiritual aspirant was guided to meeting God face to face, as it were. This direct contact with God was called *aparoksha jñâna* or non-proxy knowledge. This experience would confirm the validity of the scriptures like the Vedas and the Upanishads.

Sri Sanyal included this idea of supremacy of the mystics in religious matters in his *Hindu Ideology Made Simple*. I had reviewed this two-volume work as Sri Sanyal had sent me his books for my comments. I found Sri Sanyal's definitions rather complicated but they conformed to his philosophical style of giving complete logical definitions. This was his special contribution.

On reading the book on Hindu ideology and my review of it, Sri Ram Swarup said he had also developed this criterion of the role of mystics as the decisive factor for distinguishing Hinduism from Christianity and Islam. Sri Sita Ram said Sri Sanyal had clearly studied a lot before writing the book. He asked me what I thought about it. I said I found it abstract.

I had come to Sri Ram Swarup and Sri Sita Ram with this intellectual background, having developed my own methodology for comparing religions and ideologies. But all such thinking was described as "mere cerebration": that is how Sri Ram Swarup had dismissed Sri Sita Ram's thoughts about the merits of western thought and Marxian ideology.

Goel recalled (*How I Became a Hindu*, p.39): "One day, in my exasperation, I struck a superior attitude and said: 'We find it difficult to come to any conclusion because I have a philosophical background while you proceed merely from economic, social and political premises.' Ram Swarup enquired what I meant by philosophy and I rattled out the list which I had ready in my mind: Locke, Berkeley, Hume, Descartes, Spinoza, Leibnitz, Kant, Hegel, Schopenhauer and so on. Ram Swarup told me that at one time or the other he had studied all of them but had found them irrelevant and useless. I was surprised as well as pained. Ram Swarup explained: 'Suppose one knows this philosophical system or that. Does it make a better man out of one in any way? These systems are mere cerebrations and have little to offer towards practical purposes of life.' The word 'cerebration' got stuck in my mind, and made it impossible for me to read any abstract philosophy any more. I had been very fond of Western metaphysics and epistemology till that time."

15.4. A Higher Mode of Consciousness

After many evenings of meditations and discussions where mostly Sri Ram Swarup, Sri Sita Ram Goel, Sri Prakash Jain and myself participated, I realized that I was in the presence of yogis in whom a higher mode of consciousness was operating. I came to this understanding gradually over a period of 10 years of close contact with them. Such people are rare, but they do exist. The behaviour of such people is based on awareness of more things and events in their interdependence and interactions. Such people keep in view very long-term interests and consequences. A philosopher — lover of wisdom — is a spectator of all time and existence, as Plato would say. By "philosopher", Plato meant a yogi or a *jñâni* — knower of God.

It is a wisdom which makes the yogi compassionate in his dealings with himself, man animal and nature in general. And his spiritual consciousness makes the yogi see himself living in the whole world and the whole world in himself. As the Bhagavad Gita (6:29) says:

Sarvabhûtasthamâtmânam
sarvabhûtâni câtmani
îkshate yogayuktâtmâ
sarvatra samadarshanaha.

Or in translation: "His mind being harmonized by Yoga, he sees himself in all beings and all beings in himself; he sees the same in all." Such a consciousness becomes stable in a Yogi because he has realized God. He lives in God just as all other beings also live in God. As Krishna explains (Bh.G.6:30):

Yo mâm pashyati sarvatra
sarvam ca mayi pashyati
tasyâham na pranashyâmi
sa ca me na pranashyati.

This means: "He who sees Me everywhere and sees all in Me, never becomes lost to Me, nor do I become lost to him." These spiritual matters are not soft-headed mysticism or wishy-washy sentimentalism, though some people try to dismiss them as such. Spiritual truths have a "granitoid" quality, writes Sri Ram Swarup in his magnum opus *The Word as Revelation: Names of Gods* (p.88 of the original edition):

"A poet may use words for their softer and gentler suggestions and meanings in order to evoke a picture of mildness and delicacy and a twilight world made of dream-stuff. But at another level, words have also more stable and granitoid meanings, meanings which cannot be pulled or pushed or coaxed. These are spiritual meanings revealed to a mind which has attained to a certain level of purity, freedom and equanimity and self-status."

I developed respect for this company because they were advanced in their intellectual development, which helped me round off my own thinking on political, social and philosophical studies. Their analysis and exposition of views on several current problems had a greater depth and range than what I had myself managed to develop. Moreover, they had evolved a distinct ideological perspective based on a practical understanding of the spiritual traditions of India known as *Sanâtana Dharma*, "everlasting righteousness", meant to be lived by all mankind.

This view of life appealed to me because when I came to Delhi from Bombay I was in my late twenties and had experienced what the yogis describe as awakening of the *kundalinî shakti*. This had been induced in me by my paternal uncle Sri Mahabala Rao, who had served in the Indian Army on the Burma front. After release from the army he was working as weaving master in a textile mill in Bombay. He had spontaneously manifested yogic supernormal powers. He had not practised any *pûjâ*s or austerities in this life.

This activation of Kundalini in me took place some time in December 1956. I frequently visited my uncle during weekends and sat watching him doing his 'ad hoc' puja and meditating in front of a picture of Sri Raghavendra Swami which he had painted and got touched up by an artist. This swami was a pontiff in one of the *maths* established by Sri Madhvacharya, who had articulated the so-called dualistic interpretation of the Vedanta in opposition to Sri Shankaracharya and Sri Ramanujacharya.

Sri Raghavendra Swami is famous and popular in Karnataka, Andhra Pradesh, Maharashtra and also Tamil Nadu and Kerala because he was a yogi who decided to die on a particular day, at a particular place and time. The swami instructed his disciples and devotees to entomb him in a vrindavana which was built according to his instructions. He was alive and meditating on his favorite God-form Hayagriva when the final tombstone was placed on the vrindavana. The year was 1593 of Shalivahana Shaka Samvat, corresponding to

AD 1671. The place is Mantralaya in the Adoni district of the present Andhra Pradesh. It is a place of pilgrimage all year round to devotees in India and abroad.

Such yogis continue to live in their subtle bodies and are more effective in guiding and protecting their disciples and devotees. They work on the inner planes of consciousness.

15.5. Rationalism vs. Communism

Our task at the Libertarian Social Institute was to find ways to promote equality of opportunity for citizens by planning through the market and preventing monopolies. But the state is to be limited to formulating policies and monitoring implementation in addition to maintaining law and order. Libertarianism also warns against the formation of a criminal-politician nexus. All this is to prevent the formation of a totalitarian state. It is a strong antagonist of Communism of the Marxian variety.

The Libertarian Social Institute was set up and run by the R.L. Foundation, a trust formed by a Gujarati gentleman, Ranchchoddas B. Lotwala, at Arya Bhuvan, Vitthalbhai Patel Road, Bombay. He owned Duncan Flour Mills in Bombay, a house in London and a farm house at Deolali near Bombay. He had his own horse and a four-wheeled coach in which he went about in the cantonment area.

He was one of the many industrialists and businessmen who participated in the freedom movement in their own way by helping freedom fighters. Influenced by Swami Dayanand Saraswati, he had named his two-storey mansion Arya Bhuvan. To record his protest against the caste system he arranged a mass feeding event for out-caste people and ate his meal along with them. The Gujarati bania leaders excommunicated him for violating their caste taboo. But Lotwala, who was told to do *prâyashchitta*, i.e. atone for having committed a sin, refused to relent and remained proudly excommunicated.

Lotwala told me he was one of the earliest followers of Mahatma Gandhi to contribute money for setting up the Sabarmati Ashram. He also told me that he had paid funds to the Communist leaders to sustain industrial workers during strikes. Mr. Lotwala's regret was that some Communist party leaders did not return the books they had borrowed from him.

Lotwala was more than 80 years old during the late 1950s. If he had shaved off the crop of hair on his head, he would have looked like Gandhiji. He even had Mickey Mouse ears like Gandhiji (whom Sarojini Naidu had nicknamed Mickey Mouse). His major concern was that while the Muslims had an ideology which they strongly adhered to, Hindus had neither an ideology nor a central organization to fight for their interests. Any day Pakistan could subjugate India. Therefore he advised me to read *Satyârtha Prakâsh* (Light of Truth) by Swami Dayananda and also to study the Quran of Islam, which advocates a ruthless fight or *jihâd* against the non-believers and "idolaters". Lotwala called himself an atheist. He told me once that actually he was an agnostic, but since psychologically it was difficult to remain an agnostic, he called himself an atheist when taking a stand in public affairs.

And this Lotwala was in touch with Sri Ram Swarup and Sri Philip Spratt, who had come to India in 1926 as the topmost Comintern agent to organize the Communist Party of India. Spratt became the chief accused in the Meerut Conspiracy case of 1929 but later on turned against Communism after reading Mahatma Gandhi. At some stage, probably when Trotsky was assassinated, Lotwala also became an anti-Communist. He presented a copy of Ram Swarup's *Gandhism and Communism* to me, the first edition from Jyotsna Prakashan, Delhi, dated January 1955 and priced at 12 Annas.

Spratt was then Assistant Editor of *Mysindia* weekly edited and published by Sri Devendra Nath Hosali at Mahatma Gandhi Road, Bangalore. Spratt published about a dozen articles of mine in his weekly, presenting different aspects of

Libertarian analysis and solutions to ideological problems. In addition I read papers at his seminars and conventions between December 1953 and August 1958.

At a seminar held in Bangalore in December 1957 and organized by Sri Minoo R. Masani's *Democratic Research Service*, I read a paper titled "Democracy and the Social Sciences". It was prepared after I had read Dr. Karl Popper's books *The Open Society and its Enemies* and *The Poverty of Historicism*. Before me, the first paper was by Spratt and the second by Sri M.A. Venkata Rao. My paper dealt with Popper's analysis of scientific method — which seeks to falsify a theory in order to test its validity — and his criticism of the Marxian claim to "scientifically predict" historical events.

15.6. Rationalism, science and religion

At the fifth All-India Convention of Indian Rationalists, held in Bombay in December 1956, I read a paper titled "Reason and Rationalism". I was representing the Libertarian Social Institute, which stood for rationalism and humanism.

In my paper I had taken the position that European rationalism emerged out of the conflict between the priests and the scientists. Rationalism still carries with it the vestiges of the birth-pangs of science and often suffers from an anti-religion complex of uncertain rationality. The popular notion of the Rationalist is that he is a materialist, atheist or agnostic — whatever that might mean.

The last part of this paper of mine was printed as an article in Spratt's *Mysindia* under the heading Reason and Rationalism. The Rationalists, I had argued, are confused about two distinct investigations: (a) the socio-political history of priesthood; and (b) the metaphysics of mysticism. The validity of the statements of the priests should be treated as independent of the motives that prompt them. The test for the "religious" statement poses two questions for each statement: (a) does the relation asserted between man and his environment contradict any well established human experience? and (b) does the religious statement explain facts otherwise inexplicable? The ultimate question, therefore, is: "Do science and mysticism contradict each other?"

No!

There are scientists who respect mysticism and mystics who respect science. Albert Einstein was a mystical scientist: "The most beautiful and most profound emotion we can experience is the sensation of the mystical. It is the sower of all true science. My religion consists of a humble admiration of the illimitable Superior Spirit who reveals himself in the slight details we are able to perceive with our frail and feeble minds. That deeply emotional conviction of the presence of a superior reasoning power, which is revealed in the incomprehensible universe, forms my idea of God." (quoted by Lincoln Barnett: *The Universe and Dr. Einstein*, Mentor ed., 1955, pp.117-18)

The Upanishadic mystic can be scientific about mysticism: "There are two knowledges to be known — as indeed the knowers of Brahman are wont to say: a higher (*para*) and also a lower (*apara*)", says the Mundaka Upanishad. In the Chhandogya, we find an elaborate list of the then known sciences — belonging to the lower knowledge — including mathematics, logic, science of rulership and the fine arts, as well as knowledge about "wind and space, water and heat, gods and men, beasts and birds, grass and trees, animals together with worms, flies and ants, right and wrong, true and false, good and bad, pleasant and unpleasant, food and drink, this world and yonder".

All this, we are told, one understands with understanding or discursive reasoning: "He who reverences understanding as Brahma — he, verily, attains the worlds of understanding (*vijñâna*) and knowledge (*jñâna*). As far as understanding goes, so far he has unlimited freedom, he who reverences understanding as Brahman." When the student enquires if there be something more than understanding, the answer is: "There is, assuredly, more than understanding."

From this I concluded that both science and mysticism are valid but fragmentary experiences. Each needs the other for correction and completion. All experience is the meeting point of two variables — the subjective series and the objective series. When we standardize the subjective variables and experiment with the objective variables and formulate the results, we get the sciences. When we keep the objective series constant and experiment with the subjective variables and formulate the results, we get the religions. The sciences give us the possible ways of altering the environment — including the human organism — and the religions give us the possible ways of altering our attitudes to the environment.

But the man-in-the-world has experience of both science and mysticism. When we capture in imagination both science and mysticism and criticize each in the light of the other and formulate the result, we get a philosophical rationalism.

I concluded my paper by saying that when we examine the adequacy of any concept to communicate its corresponding experience, it is rational criticism. "Thus, then, it must be said that, in a sense, there is no ultimate criterion to which we can appeal as testing the worth of the general notions by the help of which we interpret our experiences. Experience alone is the criterion." (Robert Adamson: *Development of Modern Philosophy*, vol. II, pp.216-17)

When I went to Bangalore on a few days' leave, I asked Spratt what he thought about my articles he had published. He said: "You are trying to build a system of your own. Write about applying it in Indian conditions."

A couple of months after my return to Bombay, in August 1958, Lotwala closed down his Libertarian Institute. Sri Sanyal went away to become a teacher somewhere in Africa. Sri Valicha joined as lecturer in some college in Bombay. I came to Delhi and joined the *Organiser* weekly to work as a sub-editor under editor K.R. Malkani.

15.7. Discipleship under *Rishi* Ram Swarup

For residence, I got a place in a two-persons-per-room in the Sabba Rao Mess, Karol Bagh, just twenty minutes by walk from where Sri Ram Swarup lived at that time. The Society for the Defence of Freedom in Asia had been wound up, but some friends of Sri Ram Swarup used to meet at his place in the evening. There was no fixed time or day for these meetings, where current topics were discussed and meditation was practised. Sri Sita Ram Goel, Sri Prakash Chandra Jain and myself were frequent visitors. Saints and Sufis also visited Sri Ram Swarup on rare occasions whenever they visited Delhi. Sufi Ghulam Nabi Bani used to come here during winter. His business at Srinagar, Kashmir, was making beds and quilts, so he came in winter to buy materials from the Jama Masjid area in old Delhi. Since Prakash Jain's house was at Nayi Sadak near the Masjid, the Sufi used to visit his family also. He become a family friend of the Jains. Another visitor was Sri Anirvanji. He was also mostly a once-a-year visitor. His distinguishing mark was a tall white cap — about twice as high as the Gandhi cap or Congress cap. The cap tapered slightly towards the top.

The Sufis introduced the simple woolen overcoat which was commonly used in Kashmir. It was like a long kurta — extending to about one foot below the knee. Both Sri Ram Swarup and Sri Sita Ramji wore one over their cotton kurta-pajama or kurta-dhoti. The Sufiji was a matriculate or so. He was childlike in simplicity. But he had the capacity to read minds and otherwise know about events and people. He carried a *japamâlâ*.

Once, he told us, he wanted to know what kind of people the Communists are. He meditated about them and saw a vision. People went to a well to quench their thirst. But the Sufi saw that it was poisoned water. "Run away, don't drink this water. There are snakes in the well!", he warned them. That was the way he understood things.

Once Sri Ram Swarup sent me to meet Sri Anirvanji who had come to Delhi and was camping in a friend's place at Sujan Singh park near India Gate. Sri Ram Swarup had given me a letter to hand over to Anirvanji, informing him that the Kundalini Shakti had been activated in me and that I should be advised on the matter. Anirvanji told me, after seeing the letter, that whatever force had been working would leave some permanent benefit on myself, like flood waters leaving some fresh fertile soil on the river banks. He did not tell me what I should do about it.

Both my intellectual background and yogic tendencies inclined me to becoming a close friend — rather a disciple — of Sri Ram Swarup and Sri Sita Ram Goel. Thus I became a frequent visitor at Sri Ram Swarup's *barsâtî* residence and participated in discussions and meditations. It was during one of these meetings that Sri Sita Ram Goel was shown the Mother Goddess. Though I was also there, I did not know what he had experienced. I came to know the details later from his autobiographical booklet *How I Became a Hindu* (p.54).

During the 1950s, Sri Ram Swarup and Sri Sita Ram Goel were growing towards some positive counterview to Communism and similar ideologies. Anti-Communism by itself was no counter-ideology. Having wound up the Society for Defence of Freedom in Asia, Sri Ram Swarup was now seeking for the deeper psychological and spiritual reasons underneath the prevalent political, social and cultural clashes usually explained in terms of external forces and intellectual ideas. The clashes, Sri Ram Swarup had now come to understand, were "projections of psychic situations in which the members of a society chose to stay. His judgements had now acquired a depth which I frequently found it difficult to fathom", writes Sri Sita Ram in his autobiography (p.50).

15.8. About Nehru and secularism

During this period, a positive vision in defence of Hindu Society was being formulated. It was at this time that Sri Sita

Ram wrote several articles in the *Organiser* weekly under the editorship of Sri K.R. Malkani. The much-discussed and controversial series was *In Defence of Comrade Krishna Menon*. Sri Sita Ram's argument was that Sri Menon was faithfully implementing Prime Minister Nehru's policies. Sri Nehru was not being "wrongly advised" as critics used to say. They did not have the guts to say that Sri Nehru was himself a fellow-traveller who wanted to play second fiddle to Soviet foreign policy in international politics. He also wanted to hand over power to the Communists in India. So he placed them in important positions inside the Congress Party and in public institutions.

Nehruvian "secularism" was a perverted notion, according to Sri Sita Ram: "I have no use for a secularism which treats Hinduism as just another religion, and puts it on a par with Islam and Christianity. For me this concept of secularism is a gross perversion of the concept which arose in the modern West as a revolt against Christianity and which should mean, in the Indian context, a revolt against Islam as well. The other concept of secularism, *Sarva-dharma-sama-bhâva*, was formulated by Mahatma Gandhi in order to cure Islam and Christianity of their aggressive self-righteousness, and stop them from effecting conversions from the Hindu fold. This second concept was abandoned when the constitution of India conceded to Islam and Christianity the right to convert as a fundamental right." (*How I Became a Hindu*, p.57).

How the leftist agents of the Soviet slave empire have perverted India's political parlance has been detailed in Sri Sita Ram's booklet *Perversion of India's Political Parlance*. He had warned the people then (p.55) that "the prevalent political parlance will paralyze this country unless it is replaced by the language of Indian nationalism. It has already transformed all sorts of traitors into patriots, and all sorts of parasites into public servants. It provides a smokescreen behind which several types of imperialism — Islamic, Christian, Communist, and Consumerist — are stealing a march."

15.9. Global Perspective of Sanatana Dharma

It was during the transition from anti-Communism to Sanatana Dharma or Hinduism that I had joined Sri Ram Swarup and Sri Sita Ram Goel and imbibed their thoughts and vision. They highlighted the universal principles of Sanatana Dharma which could be, and should be, adopted by people all over the world. Dharma was not a creed to be foisted on the world by force and fraud, but a profound understanding of man in the world who could evolve into a superman if he adopted the Life Divine as the supreme *purushârtha* or human value. The impact of the transcendent spirit on terrestrial man could bring about the required transformation of human consciousness.

Hinduism had built the traditions and preserved the institutions to nurture man through a spiritual humanism: "*Sanâtana Dharma*, which is known as Hinduism at present, is not only a religion but also a whole civilization which has flourished in this country for ages untold, and which is struggling to come into its own again after a prolonged encounter with several sorts of predatory imperialism." (*How I Became a Hindu*, p.57)

The spiritual infrastructure of Sanatana Dharma and its difference from creedal religions was well brought out in one of the Saturday meetings which Sri Sita Ram and others used to attend at the Connaught Place shop where Sri Gurudatta Vaidya had practised Ayurvedic medicine and where his son was now in charge of the patients. Sri Guru Dutt was an Arya Samaji, more than twenty years senior to Sri Sita Ram. He was a noted Hindi novelist and exponent of Hindu culture. "He had been a vigilant witness to a long cultural and political history since the twenties of this 20th century. He had also developed a systematic critique of events and personalities in his own ideological perspective", writes Sri Sita Ramji (*How I Became a Hindu*, p.51). His formula of Sanatana Dharma was:

Chitta Chittantar,
Loka Lokantar,
Janma Janmantar, and
Yuga Yugantar;

which means there are "many levels of consciousness, many worlds, many lives and many durations of time" for the soul to live in.

When the soul is at one level of consciousness, it is living in one world or system of experience. It also lives through many life sequences to gather experience and it lasts vast periods of time, called *Yugas* and *Kalpas* in Sanskrit, each of which is counted in millions of years. The souls come out into the world when Brahma breathes them out, as it were, and go back into Brahma when he breathes them back into himself so there is no world anywhere. And this goes on for all eternity, called the days and nights of Brahma.

On returning home from the Saturday meetings at Guru Dutt's, where I merely listened attentively, I used to type out the summaries of the day's discussion as I remembered them. Sri Prakash Jain was a frequent participant in these group discussions and he would read my summaries to verify that I had covered the points well. What follows is an exposition of the discussion on the comparative study of religions dd. February 29, 1964.

The Bible-derived religions — Judaism, Christianity and Islam — have these things in common:

1. They believe in a transcendent God who created the cosmos out of nothing. To communicate with His creatures, God sends His messenger, the prophet. Due to his special role, this prophet is different from and superior to all men who cannot themselves aspire to the state of prophethood. Faith in the prophet is therefore indispensable for salvation. There is only one life in which one has to hear the message of God and strive to live according to the beliefs inculcated by the prophet.

2. There are many prophets who successively reveal the message of God, but there is one final prophet who gives out the complete message for all time and for all people — to the Jews that final prophet is Moses, to the Christians he is Jesus Christ and to the Muslims he is Hazrat Mohammad.
3. The creatures lower than man have no soul to be saved. Woman has no soul either.
4. On the Day of Judgement, at the dissolution of creation, the dead will be revived and either be rewarded with eternal heaven or condemned to eternal hell.
5. The prophets and the message have a specific historic date assigned to them.

In contrast, the Vedantic realism of Sanatana Dharma believes God himself became the cosmos and He is both transcendent and immanent. No special exclusive prophet is necessary to reveal the eternal truths of God: they can be seen, after proper discipline through *sâdhana*, by any man in any place at any time. Woman too has a soul and therefore she can see God and the eternal truths by turning the mind inwards.

There are many lives in which the fruits of the *sâdhana* of previous lives are preserved and enriched. The process of rebirths is governed by the law of Karma — a spiritual law governing the action and reaction of the activities of the soul in all the worlds.

The soul is the microcosm of the macrocosm and is ultimately one with God Himself. The outer world is the projection of consciousness and reflects its nature. At different times different aspects of the soul are manifested outside in the world, characterizing the four *yugas*. Irrespective of the outer yuga, one can live in any one yuga inwardly, by allowing the principles dominant in the chosen yuga to dominate one's consciousness. God is absolute and is infinite at every point and can be realized in a myriad ways, but the ultimate unity with God will give the realization of all the other pathways to God as well.

(B.K. Rao is a philosopher who has made his living as a journalist for the *Organiser* and the *United News of India*, Delhi.)

16. A hero of our time

Shankar Sharan

Wake up, folks, wake up! As intimidated as you are by the fear of going against the stream and looking racist *[c.q. communal]* you don't understand or don't want to understand that a Reverse Crusade is on the march. As blinded as you are by the myopia and the stupidity of the Politically Correct, you don't realize or don't want to realize that a war of religion is being carried out. A war they call Jihad. A war which is conducted to destroy our civilization, our way of living and dying, of praying or not praying, of eating and drinking and dressing and studying and enjoying life. As numbed as you are by the propaganda of the falsehood, you don't put or do not want to put in your mind that if we do not defend ourselves, if we do not fight, the Jihad will win. It will win, yes, and destroy the world that somehow or other we have been able to build.

Oriana Fallaci, *The Rage and the Pride*

Violence does not live alone and is not capable of living alone: it is necessarily interwoven with falsehood. Between them lies the most intimate, the deepest of natural bonds. Violence finds its only refuge in falsehood, falsehood its only support in violence. Any man who has once acclaimed violence as his *method* must inexorably choose falsehood as his *principle.*

Aleksandr Solzhenitsyn, *Nobel Lecture on Literature*

16.1. Democratic variations on totalitarianism

Writing against the current in a democratic society poses problems of a different kind than in a totalitarian system. Pondering at the range and depth of writings of Ram Swarup (1920-1998) and Sita Ram Goel (1921-2003), and the approach of our academia and media towards them, gives an inkling of the problem.

In a totalitarian political system — Fascist, Communist or Islamist — a non-conformist writer can hardly publish a thing. Even writing in private is a dangerous venture. But in a country with complete freedom of speech, with a 'politically correct' intellectual ambiance, an inconvenient author can be silently buried in indifference. Not even most open-minded readers would know of his existence. Speaking of the Soviet case, Solzhenitsyn had observed that "the environment is dense and sticky: it is incredibly difficult to make even the smallest movements because it immediately takes the environment with them". In contrast, the atmosphere in democratic countries is "like a rarified gas, or almost a vacuum: there it is easy to wave one's arms, jump, run, turn somersaults — but it all has no effect on anybody else, everyone else is doing exactly the same in a chaotic manner".[1]

Without understanding this difference we can never comprehend why even fifty years' original work of this rare duo — Ram Swarup and Sita Ram Goel — hardly left a mark on the intellectual scene of our country. Both died unsung. It is not a small measure of the regrettable situation that even a solitary biographical sketch of each of them came from a Belgian scholar, Koenraad Elst. No Bharatiya scholar, journalist or student wrote one. Not in their lifetime, nor after their passing away. In December 2003, our media could not even take note of the demise of Sita Ram Goel. The chief reason for this unfortunate state of affairs is that their work remained largely unknown to the general public of our country. Both were original and non-conformist thinkers. Our governments as well as the academic class felt quite at ease in ignoring them. The media happily followed suit.

There was a time in the Soviet Union when Aleksandr Solzhenitsyn was vilified. His works were considered

[1]Frank Crepeau and Alan Jacob: "An interview with Alexander Solzhenitsyn" (23 August 1973), in Leopold Labedz (Ed.), *Solzhenitsyn: A Documentary Record* (Penguin, Middlesex 1974), p.335.

"concoction", "betrayal", "disease" and what have you. Even in the *Soviet Literary Encyclopedia* of 1973 his name found no place at all (this, after he was already world-famous with *Ivan Danisovich* and the Nobel Prize). He simply did not exist. In this country, a very similar attitude was applied towards Ram Swarup and Sita Ram Goel as far as our academic class is concerned. Goel found no mention in intellectual debates and writings on issues he published for decades. If by exception someone mentioned him, he was scornfully dismissed as "communal". Hence unwanted, irrelevant.

It is a mark of the pathetic condition of our social sciences that after the demise of the Soviet Union and the opening up of the Soviet and East European archives, our Marxist professors were not dragged to coal for their propagandistic writings masquerading as scholarly ones. Nothing happened by way of re-examining their highly distorted writings in history, political science or economics. On the contrary, they are still ruling the roost. By corollary, even after the demise of the Communist systems, Sita Ram Goel and Ram Swarup are not accorded their due place in the scholarly arena for their realistic, incisive and far-sighted analyses of Communism. Maybe after the advent of a Saudi Gorbachev it will be done.

16.2. India's stifling opinion climate

Ram Swarup and Sita Ram Goel wrote on Communism, Marxism, Maoism, Islam, Christianity and Hindutva. In this country all these are politically sensitive subjects. As is well-known, to the first four issues it is considered politically correct to be respectful, even reverential. As for the last one, it is best to disregard it, if not mock it openly. Reasons are various for this pitiable situation in this otherwise intellectually rich country. A misconception regarding the Islamic mentality on the part of the national leaders since 1920s was one. Having the very first Prime Minister heavily enamoured of Marxism and Islam was another. It has to be understood that the founding moments of any institution, law or system invariably become crucial to set the tone and standards for a long time to come. For a free Bharat the period of, say, 1947-56 was such a founding one for our so many intellectual or socio-political traditions laid down by the left-and-Islam-leaning first Prime Minister.

English becoming the intellectual language of the country, even after freedom from British rule, was the third reason. It summarily and effectively excluded more than 95% of the population from participating in influential intellectual exercises. Thus a possible corrective to ideologically marred theories, propositions etc. was foreclosed. English ensured that even if a Bharatiya citizen is wise, experienced, knowledgeable and articulate, he or she can do nothing to check or persuade an erring intellectual or a whole intellectual group, unless he can do it in English. (Besides he must also hold a high chair to be heard.) Discourse in any language other than English in this country, howsoever rich and invaluable, simply does not touch the influential and decision-making classes. This way, intellectual pursuits became an undeclared monopoly of a very very few who, even if grossly erring, ignorant or misguided on a matter in hand, could still set the standards for the entire country to follow. History writing and the NCERT's text-books since its beginning are a case in point.

The rest of the population simply came to accept, in naïve belief, like the Soviet citizens of yore, that whatever is emanating from the high chairs of a Council, Academy, Commission, University, Centre or Ministry is certainly better informed. "They must know better who speak and write in English", became the common, if disastrous, sentiment among the Bharatiya public. In the subjects mentioned above, alas! that never was the case. The philosophy, understanding and experiences of the common Bhartiya masses were vastly different from those of the English-wielding intellectual elite about, say, the ways of socio-economic change or the Islamic character. Yet they could do nothing, thanks to the monopoly of English in matters academic or policy, to correct the academic and political decision-makers. This restrictive role of English in free Bharat is hardly considered in analyzing why such a "politically correct" intellectual atmosphere came to rule here.

In such a politically correct intellectual environment Ram Swarup and Sita Ram Goel jointly represented a diametrically opposite view. The dominant political and intellectual classes naturally detested this. It is, therefore, not surprising that the duo's rich contribution was wholly ignored. Both started publishing their critical works with the advent of freedom in 1947. Here it is outside of our purview to compare the parallel views of the duo and those of the ruling intellectual-political classes of our country. Suffice it to say that time has proved most of the analyses of Ram Swarup and Sita Ram Goel right. Of the nature and role of Marxism-Leninism, the Soviet system, Maoist practice, Communist economies etc., it is now conclusively evident that whatever our first Prime Minister and the left-leaning economists and social scientists believed for decades (some still do) were indeed mere superstitions. This is why none of the leftist professors even recalls those superstitions any more. All of them silently changed their colours. After the Soviet collapse they became "liberals" overnight. All "Marxist" historians became "secular" instead.

As for the Islamic problem, anyone can judge the far-sighted analyses the duo presented till the end. Life has shown, decade after decade, that from Mahatma Gandhi to Atal Bihari Vajpayee, every leader or preacher has seriously erred, with very tragic consequences, in assessing the Islamic problem. Wishes were not horses. Every concession, every leniency, all hosannas to Islam did never bring a single positive result. As Sita Ram Goel put so succinctly, in one of his last contributions (*Time for Stock-Taking*, p.ii):

> "A study of Hindu-Muslim relations since the foundation of the Indian national Congress in 1885 tells us that Muslims have been making demands — ideological, political, territorial — and

Hindus conceding them all along. Yet the Muslim problem remains with us in as acute a form as ever. With the advent of petro-dollars and the emergence of V.P. Singh, Laloo Prasad, Mulayam Singh and Kanshi Ram on the political scene, Muslims have become as aggressive and intransigent as in the pre-partition period."

16.3. The problem with Islam

To understand the nature of the problems we are facing today on this score, and also to value the scholarly contribution of the Ram Swarup and Sita Ram Goel, it would be helpful to see what some other gifted observers have concluded the world over. Oriana Fallaci, whom Milan Kundera calls the ideal of the 20th century journalism, has been saying this for the last twenty-five years. She is a remarkable writer inured to living with all races and habits and beliefs, accustomed to opposing any fascism and any intolerance, without any taboos.

She is indignant towards all those who did not smell the bad smell of a war to come and who tolerated the abuses that "the sons of Allah" were committing in Europe with their terrorism. Her straight reasoning: "What logic is there in respecting those who do not respect us? What dignity is there in defending their culture or supposed culture when they show contempt for ours?" She puts the likes of Osama bin Laden on a par with Hitler and Stalin, firmly arguing that fascism is not an ideology, but a behaviour pattern. She warns that the fight with this fascism "will be very tough. Unless we Europeans stop shitting in our pants and playing the double-game with the enemy, giving up our dignity. An opinion I respectfully offer to the Pope too."[2]

Do we comprehend what Fallaci is stating? Most of the members of our intellectual class would not. Let alone fighting a war, even on the intellectual plane, they tend not even

---

[2]Oriana Fallaci: *The Rage and the Pride*, Rizzoli International, New York 2002, p.85; p.81.

to see the international phenomenon. As if every disaster perpetrated by the sons of Allah in any corner of the world is a mere accident and not the manifestation of a single ideology. Question: why do some people remain unfazed even by violence of such magnitudes as Bamiyan, 9/11, Godhra or dozens of Nandimarg in Kashmir? They readily try to explain away such violence blaming some "primary" cause and thus shield the barbaric perpetrators. But the very same people hysterically cry "fascism" on even an ordinary statement that the Ayodhya temple movement is a matter of national sentiment. Why such double standards? Political correctness is not the whole answer. Love for one's own comfort, ignorance and laziness also play the part for many a people.

As Solzhenitsyn aptly said concerning the condemnation of nuclear tests conducted by France and China: the double standards were "not only because of moral squint, but simply out of cowardice. Because from an expedition into the Chinese desert or to the Chinese coast nobody would return — and they know it." The same is true of keeping silence on everything Islamic, fascism or terrorism, while crying hoarse about even non-acts of "Hindu fascism". As the great author wrote: "They only protest when there is no danger to life, when the opponent can be expected to give in and when there is no risk of being condemned by 'leftist circles' (it is always better, of course, to protest with them)." This is even more true about the noisy secularists of Bharat.

Besides, we take for the greater, more painful violence not that which is in fact greater but that which lies close to our predilections or ourselves. So we have different scales of values for wickedness and punishment. According to one, killing of an innocent-looking terrorist (Ishrat Jahan for instance) or a missionary indulging in illegal proselytizing activities (Graham Staines) shatters the imagination and fills the newspaper columns with rage. While according to another, systematic cleansing of Hindus from the territory of Kashmir, Assam and Nagaland, burning an entire train coach with Hindu pilgrims in Godhra, mushrooming of Islamic terrorist dens in border areas of West Bengal (the Marxist Chief Minister admitted this, with no follow-up action), Bihar and UP, — all this is nothing to make a fuss about. No condemnation, no seminar, no books, no documentation and, of course, no campaigns along the lines of "fight against saffronization".

Whenever an Islamic assault becomes impossible to ignore and at least our editorial classes feel compelled to write something of a criticism, they never forget to mention "Hindu extremism" in the same paragraph. It is a pure fiction, an added insult to meek Hindus who have been at the receiving end all along for centuries. No one speaks for them with force, with extra-constitutional methods. Hence no question of a Hindu "extremism". But in editorials Islamic violence is never condemned alone, it is willfully clubbed with a Hindu counterpart. This artificial balancing flies in the face of hard, horrible facts. There has never been a single act on the part of the Sangh Parivar which can even remotely match, either in words or deeds, those of Islamic brotherhood: Lashkar-e-Toiba, Student Islamic Movement of Bharat (SIMI), Deendar Anjuman, Hizb-ul-Mujahideen, Tablighi Jamaat *et al.* Yet the politically correct editorial and academic classes of this country present Hindu "extremism" and Islamic terrorism on a par. Worse: for some, the former is the cause of the latter. Hence all the fight is against "saffronization" (of three or four text-books, that's all!) and none against 'Islamization' of every possible thing — land, people, culture, dress, food, language, thought and mannerisms.

What kinds of scales are used in this kind of artificial balancing of Islamic intolerance with an imaginary Hindu counterpart? The first unit on one scale may be ten, but the first unit on another scale may be ten to the sixth power, that is, one million. And can the conclusion of observers, that "both here and there the first unit has been reached", be explained only by their ignorance or by a hardening of the brain? It is high time our politically correct understood these two non-comparable scales of valuation of the volume and moral meanings of events. It is impossible to accept the ideology of Osama bin Laden as even remotely comparable to that of VHP ideologue Pravin Togadia. One is causing a *"une grande peur"* (a great fear) all over the Western world and the non-Islamic Eastern world. While the other causes nothing, because it merely express the frustration of common Hindus. An angry Hindu at best draws a derisive laugh among the Islamic brotherhood steeped in unimaginable violence. Unimaginable both in methods and scale.

If we want to understand Islam in perspective, there is no better guide than Ram Swarup and Sita Ram Goel. Yes, not even Bernard Lewis or Daniel Pipes has done it as perfectly as the duo did; their work is marred by their West-centric approach, ignoring the role Islam played in Bharat and the difficult Hindu struggle with it for centuries. Oriana Fallaci has presented the scenario very well on the empirical plane. Addressing those who remained indifferent or illusioned on the Talibani destruction of the millenary Buddha statues in Bamiyan, she asked: "Who is next, now that the 'idols' of Bamiyan have been blown up like twin towers? The other Unfaithful who pray to Vishnu or Shiva, Brahma, Krishna, Annapurna? (...) Do they hate only the Christians and Buddhists, those voracious sons of Allah, or do they aim to subjugate our whole planet?" Unfortunately, there are still very few scholars in the West to delve into the issue on a realistic plane. As for the Bharatiya scholars and journalists, very few of them have bothered to ask this kind of question. On the contrary, in its continuous anti-Hindu intellectual manufacture project, the *Times of India* tried to explain the destruction by claiming that "the Taliban wanted to draw the attention of the world, so they destroyed the statues." That is, nothing Islamic about the destruction!

It is no exaggeration to say that on the philosophical and historical planes, Ram Swarup and Sita Ram Goel presented a superior analysis of the Islamic malady. To realize all this we must first know exactly and thoroughly whatever has been happening all these decades in every corner of the world — from Afghanistan to Sudan, from Palestine to Pakistan, from Malaysia to Iran, from Egypt to Iraq, from Algeria to Senegal, from Syria to Kenya, from Libya to Chad, from Lebanon to Morocco, from Indonesia to Yemen, from Saudi Arabia to Somalia. But, considering the dictatorships and lack of a free press, can we know *all* that has been happening in the Islamic world, even for the 20th century alone? It seems the Islamic world would require a hundred Solzhenitsyns to unearth all the crimes against humanity on its own citizens perpetrated in the name of Islam. Only then can one comprehend the hollowness of artificial balancing of "both Hindu and Muslim" communalism/extremism, which is a routine mindless practice in our country. In practice it is nothing but a profound help to Islamic *jihadi* politics and terrorism targeting Bharat.

16.4. How to speak of Islamic terrorism

The phenomenon of Islamic terrorism in its modern phase arose in the late 1960s. Beginning with September 1970, "Arab terrorism" came to be known in the entire world. No academic or journalist, howsoever politically correct, could then imagine balancing that terrorism with anything else. It was original and Islamic. Balancing it with some US, Israeli or Hindu deeds is a much later invention. After the beginning of the Euro-Arab dialogue in 1975, and dubious agreements thereafter, petrodollars came to be poured into the Western media and academia. The money readily brought subtle and not-so-subtle messages and conditions. Only then did this kind of artificial balancing begin to appear in print. First in France, then in the whole of Europe and in American universities. Today from the Harvard University to the London School of Economics to the Jawaharlal Nehru University, and from the *New York Times* to the *Economist* and the *Times of India*, there are any number of scholars and hacks who compete with each other to explain that anything but Islam is responsible for the acts of Islamic terrorism.[3] That Islam is nothing but basically a religion of peace and brotherhood. And woe betide those who dare contradict this!

That exactly was the refrain of our left-secular hacks and professors towards Ram Swarup and Sita Ram Goel. Keeping the eyes wide shut towards the Islamic nature of so many international problems — violence, terrorism, intolerance — has made the West more vulnerable. It is not the problems attached to gaining insight that made it difficult for the West, but lack of a desire to say the right thing. The same can be affirmed even more assertively about our own country, for we especially prefer the comfortable to the difficult. Though it has also to do with the traditional Hindu character that remains concerned mostly with *swadharma* (one's own dharma)[4] and consequently has altogether neglected to study and understand various *paradharmas* (religions of the others), the creeds of those aggressors who, driven by permanent hostility and purpose to convert, repeatedly attacked Bharat. This careless attitude to deeply study Islam, Christian Missionaries or Communism etc. also played the part for astonishing Hindu ignorance of Islamic or Communist theory and practices. This, in turn, makes the game of the invaders, aggressors, revolutionaries and infiltrators an easy one.

However, as in Europe, here too, the spirit of Munich ("The spirit of Munich is a sickness of the will of successful people, it is the daily condition of those who have given themselves up to the thirst after prosperity at any price." — Solzhenitsyn) has been dominating the search for insight. The spirit of concessions and compromise, of cowardice and self-deception by prosperous leaders, scholars and responsible

---

[3]For an instance of "Islamic terrorist" money doing the rounds in Harvard University, see Jenna Russell: "Harvard delays decision on gift from sheikh", *Boston Globe,* 30 August 2003.

[4]For a good exposition of this concept, see Dharmapal: *Bharat ka swadharm* (Vagdevi Prakashan, Bikaner 1994, in Hindi), pp.71-72.

individuals. They all have lost the will to set limits, to be firm. This course has never in the past led to the desired results, including preservation of peace and justice. The experience of Gandhiji and the Partition is the most visible example.[5] But it seems that human emotions are stronger than even the clearest lessons of the past. Enfeebled Hindu professors, editors and leaders of Bharat paint sentimental pictures of how violence will generously allow itself to be softened up.

That is not to be. It is not without reason that of 52 Islamic countries in the world today, there is not a single one professing democracy. All are dictatorships and semi-dictatorships of one or another kind (some of them observing certain parliamentary forms all while legally oppressing dissenters and non-Islamic minorities: Iran, Bangladesh, Turkey, Malaysia), declaredly following Islam. Yes, coercion, intolerance, violence, conquest and propaganda are intrinsic to Islam. From the very beginning, at the place of its birth itself, it could not gain ground except by violence and treachery. So much so that the Arabs, "who had been hitherto upright and chivalrous, became a great scourge and cruel invaders and rulers. Their ethical code suffered a great decline. They began to live on the labour and sweat of others."[6] Reading the Koran and other authentic Islamic literature, one can easily discern that lying and treachery in the cause of Islam received divine approval. Any hesitation to perjure oneself in that cause is represented as weakness.

During a synod that the Vatican held in October 1999 to discuss the relations between Christians and Muslims, His

---

[5]For the West-European countries, some already claim that as a result of their appeasement policies towards the Muslim world, Islamization is now inevitable, e.g. Bat Ye'or: "Their future is *Eurabia*. Period." See "Eurabia", interview with Bat Ye'or by Jamie Glazer, *FrontPageMagazine*, 21 Sep. 2004.

[6]Ram Swarup: *Hindu View of Christianity and Islam*, Voice of India, Delhi 1993, p.38. For a detailed exposition, see the classic study by D.S. Margoliouth: *Mohammad and the Rise of Islam*, Voice of India, Delhi 1985 (1905).

Eminence monsignor Giuseppe Bernardini, archbishop in the Turkish Diocese of Smyrna, recounted how an eminent Islamic scholar had addressed a Christian-Muslim dialogue forum with placid effrontery: "By means of your democracy we shall invade you, by means of our religion we shall dominate you."[7] The meaning is quite clear. This typical treachery is on display everywhere in Europe. Islamic migrants force themselves on European people misusing the democratic, humanitarian laws of the respective countries, viciously threatening the local inhabitants with "I know my rights". The "rights" they don't have, and don't care to have, in their Islamic countries of origin. Some of the perpetrators of 9/11 were on the watch-list of the FBI and CIA, yet residing in the USA itself, they could carry out their inhuman mission because the humanitarian laws of the country allowed them the luxury to learn piloting, move around, meet and conspire, and finally to bring down the twin towers of New York. This is what the Islamic scholar meant.

But as in Bharat, so in the West: scholars, leaders and editorial classes have tried to downplay this essential fact. They fail to recognize, or don't want to recognize, that a Reverse Crusade is going on. It is forced on Europe and the USA. Yet their policy-makers are trying their best to appease the aggressors. The aggression is an ever-growing reality that the Western leaders senselessly feed and back up, witness their favourable treatment of Pakistan. Whatever the Bush administration has been looking for in Iraq to punish Saddam Hussain, it was all abundantly available on Pakistani territory. Undisguised, under the very eyes of US representatives. But instead of taking serious note of it, and appropriate action, they are offering Pakistan to be a "non-NATO ally". Which attitude is

---

[7]Quoted in Stephen Hand: "'Xenophobia' and the need for a careful definition", *Traditional Catholic Reflections and Reports*,

"the reason why those crusaders will become always more and more. They will demand more and more, they will vex and boss us more and more. Till the point of subduing us. Therefore, dealing with them is impossible. Attempting a dialogue, unthinkable. Showing indulgence, suicidal. And he or she who believes the contrary is a fool."[8]

Therefore, the fact must not to be lost sight of, even for a moment, that Islam is more an imperialist dictatorial political ideology than a religion. Besides, it brooks no reform. It severely punishes even members of its own fold, howsoever superior or honourable in knowledge and position, if they try any.

16.5. Muslims versus Islam

It is very important to note that "the Muslim population" and "Islam" are not synonymous terms. Just as Marxism-Leninism and the Soviet people were not identical. Just as criticizing Marxism-Leninism-Stalinism-Maoism was not an insult or vilification of Soviet people or Chinese people, so criticizing Islam is not 'spreading hate' against Muslims. It is a clever ploy of Islamist scholars, leaders, jihadis as well as Left-secular propagandists in Bharat that they arouse the Muslim masses against any such criticism as if it is against them. No, Muslims are in most cases as much the victims of the Imams, Ayatollahs etc. just as the common Russians and Chinese were at the hands of their Marxist masters. Therefore, this ploy of confusing the two, people and ideology, has to be fought tooth and nail.

In as much as Islam is a political ideology, with a complete social, political and juridical system of its own, it is as liable to criticism and scrutiny as any other political creed. More so as its political ambitions and juridical regulations are never confined to Muslims alone. It has clear rules, regulations and

---

[8]Oriana Fallaci: *The Rage and the Pride*, p.98-99.

directions applied to the non-Muslim masses, whether for the moment it is ruling a country or not. Thus, the political ideology of Islam directly affects the non-Muslims of the world. Therefore, not only the Muslims but the non-Muslims too have every right to criticize Islam. But the Islamic scholars and ulema using all kinds of pretexts and deceptions, depending on the concrete situation in a given country, deny this right to non-Muslims and Muslims alike.

However, as Ram Swarup said so meaningfully, once intellectual freedom is gained for the Muslim masses, the rest is only a matter of time. Most Islamic rulers and scholars perceive this very well. Which is why they are hell-bent on withholding intellectual freedom from their own "brothers in the faith", their Muslim subjects. They use violence, threats, regulations, logic and ploys to deny this. Why? The words of Solzhenitsyn quoted above, about the intimate connection between violence and deception, explain it. They also explain why violence is intrinsic to Islam. Make no mistake: Islamic violence is not a reaction to this or that deed of the West or the Jews or the Hindus. Rather, it is there because Islam has no verbal argument to offer on any point. The erstwhile Soviet scholars used to quote Marxism-Leninism like a spell on all questions. Even if it convinced none. Likewise, Islamic scholars quote from the Koran in every matter without the smallest regard for common human reason. That can hardly satisfy inquiring minds, whether non-Moslem or Moslem. That is why Islam regularly employs threats and violence to subdue non-conforming people.

If these essential points are glossed over, as they have been in Bharat throughout the 20th century by many respectable leaders and scholars, then the Islamic problem can never be understood, let alone solved. Therefore, neither theoretical illusions nor practical difficulties (read: fear) should come in the way of recognizing this problem and fighting this war. As the great living fighter writes, "In Life and in History there are moments when fear is not permitted. Moments when fear is immoral and uncivilized. And those who out of weakness or stupidity (or the habit of keeping one's foot in two shoes) avoid the obligations imposed by this war, are not only cowards: they are masochists."[9]

The same values, freedom from ignorance and freedom from fear, Ram Swarup and Sita Ram Goel tried to instill in us in their gentle yet firm way. They were intellectual warriors — heroes of our time.

(Dr. Shankar Sharan has published several books on Marxism and Soviet history and is presently a lecturer at the NCERT.)

[9]Oriana Fallaci: *The Rage and the Pride*, p.89.

17. Academic researchers versus Hindu civilization

Gautam Sen

"The Bhagavad Gita is not as nice a book as some Americans think. Throughout the Mahabharata (...) Krishna goads human beings into all sorts of murderous and self-destructive behaviours such as war. (...) The Gita is a dishonest book; it justifies war. (...) I'm a pacifist. I don't believe in 'good' wars."

(Wendy Doniger, Indologist and Professor of History of Religions at the University of Chicago: *Philadelphia Inquirer*, 19 November 2000)

17.1. Introduction

This discussion seeks to understand why Indian studies in the West (especially the US and the UK) are overwhelmingly hostile to their object of scrutiny. In the first place, ethnocentric and parochial perceptions will usually dominate when one culture critically evaluates another. And once the resulting interpretative canon becomes firmly established through common consent, prolonged practice and appropriate imprimaturs, it becomes painfully difficult to dislodge, even if it is motivated by an intellectually disingenuous political rationale. In the case of the contemporary Western critique of India, and increasingly Hinduism, its rationale and sheer perversity can be attributed to mundane political reasons and international power politics. In order to understand the dynamics of this phenomenon vis-ë-vis India and Hinduism one first needs to explain the role of the academic and researcher, the intellectual entrepreneurs of society, and their function as agents of the political objectives of society.

17.2. The intellectual entrepreneur

The growing numbers in contemporary society engaged in intellectual endeavour and the resulting institutionalization of their work underlines the role of the modern intellectual entrepreneur. This class of entrepreneurs operates in an intellectual marketplace that ultimately serves the needs of the prevailing order, i.e. groups and/or powerful societies and states. They are profoundly dependent for material rewards and status on established institutions. The lone intellectual entrepreneur engaged in the counterpart of isolated cottage production, at some remove from formal institutions and therefore somewhat alienated from the prevailing order, owing to intermittent direct interaction with society, is now exceptional. In this context, the production of contemporary intellectual output is much like any other modern economic activity.

Intellectual entrepreneurs in the contemporary world may display a superficial restlessness and rootlessness that suggests cosmopolitan allegiances, but they are in fact firmly anchored to the prevailing structures of political, economic and social power. Of course that has always been true to some degree in all societies. The comprehensive institutionalization of paid modern intellectual labour and the system of regulation, vetting by the peer review system of journal editorial boards and the editors of major publishing houses (and increasingly television) have seen off and/or constrained the upstart autodidact. These channels are the unavoidable conduits through which 'quality control' is exercised, as the famous intellectual Theodor W. Adorno himself discovered. The study of language, literature and the humanities enjoys a measure of immunity from explicit political sanction that subjects like international relations and anthropology are unable to escape. The origin of international relations as a subject was functional to great power politics after WWII and anthropology began as a colonial and imperial venture to investigate and thereby control subject peoples.

The scale of the complicity of intellectual entrepreneurs in the sordid purposes of the State is a little hard to believe because intellectual life is wrongly associated with probity and openness. There is also a tendency to accept the conventional account of past events offered in standard textbooks and journals. The best test for evaluating the extent of deception and lies is to judge the veracity of accounts about contemporary issues, since one is more likely to be aware of the truth. Such an exercise makes clear that dishonesty is the name of the game, and the scale of the lies by acts of commission and omission is simply huge. How many people, for example, realise that the British and French governments were assiduous supporters of the Milosevic regime in Yugoslavia while it was engaged in genocide? Such historical facts simply disappear from view because intellectual entrepreneurs comply with the injunctions of State policy.

The specific forces that govern the individual intellectual entrepreneur's output of analyses and ideas is a combination of the subjective (i.e. personal psychology, as Rajiv Malhotra has been arguing) and the dominant objective forces in society, beyond his control. The subjective motive intermixes with a curious amalgam of socialization, transparently evident in the conformist similarities of common genres, and shared ideas, underpinned by an inter-subjective 'language'. But any subjective freedom that endures is unceremoniously impaled on the logic of society's power-political structures and its purposes, by the mundane imperatives of access to funding and rules for achieving status. It scripts creativity and imposes conformity. Such objective stimuli create compelling wider competitive pressures on the individual to succeed and therefore intensify conformity.

The hallmark of such a social class is necessarily opportunism and "virtuous" dissidents that undoubtedly exist among them have a circumscribed impact (the Noam Chomsky-s of the world are extraordinarily rare). One should not therefore be unduly awe-struck by the views and postures adopted by this intellectual social class or impute excessively durable significance to their cogitation. Private, sentimental attachments have but a precarious place in such endeavours. It often entails the sacrifice of family life and friendships, which highlight some advantages for the unencumbered single entrepreneur, with a tenuous stake in the future. He may therefore turn out to be the most reliable archetype for achieving institutional political objectives. As a result, such intellectual endeavours exhibit, in sublimated form, the profile of successful criminality: keen awareness of and responsiveness to external stimuli and the capacity for instrumental ruthlessness because the type of work involved nurtures foresight and manipulative skills.

17.3. India as an object of entrepreneurial enquiry

It may be innocently imagined that an intellectual entrepreneur engaged in sustained study of a particular society or country must have empathy for it. On the contrary, such enquiry can take the shape of reconnoitring an enemy and indeed compound the distaste for the culture in question, which I imagine is the case with a majority of Western scholars of India. Critiques of the foundational ideas of a society and culture indicate, *ipso facto*, distaste for it. A society will always be vulnerable to the scurrilous deconstruction of its primordial beliefs because they are historical in character. Arbitrary first principles, usually mythical, are the basis for all human existence. Thus, pitiless scrutiny, without respect or empathy, towards the deeply held sacred beliefs of others, which defines their very humanity, is a sure sign of utter disregard.

"Scorched earth" techniques of "academic" investigation are typified by the disgraceful and (as it also happens) dubious scholarly methods employed by one American academic, who engaged in gross abuse of the Indian saint Ramakrishna. This arrogance originates in the mindset of a slave-owning culture, which devoted its ingenuity to digging holes in the ground to bury an unborn child in her pregnant black mother's swelling stomach, before whipping her bare buttocks. Some morally bankrupt Hindu psychoanalyst (the closest modern social science gets to witchcraft) supported this author deviously, without the courage to do so explicitly. He took out political insurance for himself by confessing that he had portrayed a fictional character inspired by Ramakrishna sympathetically, in a novel. Such scholarly discourse is equivalent to stripping someone's mother naked in public because it causes no actual bodily injury and merely violates the taboo of shame.[1]

17.4. British colonial roots of Cold War hostility towards India

The long-standing Anglo-Saxon critique of Hindu society and independent India has roots in the visceral British hatred of the educated Hindu elites of late nineteenth-century Bengal, whom they themselves had originally sponsored. The resulting confluence of British imperial interests and subsequent Muslim politics in India is too well known to require detailed recounting. The British inaugurated twentieth century *sectarian* Islamic politics in India as a counterweight to the pan-Indian and secular Congress, which was seeking basic political rights for all Indians. They also partitioned Bengal in 1905 to vent their anger against "native" protest at their oppressive and racist rule over all religious communities. An unbroken straight line can be drawn from this burgeoning British hostility towards Hindus over a hundred years ago to the constant fabrications of British journalists and editors in the print media and television about India today. These contemporary lies will one day transmute into "unassailable" archival material, cited in journals by academics to assert the superiority of their research methodology and dismiss the amateur investigator.

---

[1] Vide *http://www.sulekha.com/memberpages/profile.asp?shortcut=/rajiv_malhotra.*

The late-nineteenth-century British critique of Indians and their struggle for emancipation was to become fatefully embroiled in the anti-Communist politics of the Cold War, led by the US. As an outstanding study by C. Dasgupta (*War and Diplomacy in Kashmir 1947-48*, Sage, Delhi 2002) has demonstrated, Pakistan's importance as a base for control over the Middle East and prosecution of the Cold War against the Soviets was recognized in the late 1940s by the British. This conviction was subsequently accepted by the US and successive administrations have subscribed to this belief ever since. So sacrosanct is the relationship with Pakistan that the crime considered to be the most heinous in modern international relations, the proliferation of nuclear weapons to unstable regimes, is being accepted by resort to the most blatant lies. Significantly, Dasgupta's unpolemical, measured and scholarly book has been sunk almost without trace by the academic establishment, despite its impeccable professional pedigree, i.e. written by a Cambridge-educated diplomat.

WWII was a catastrophe for the survival of the British Empire and forced Britain's leaders to recognise that Indian independence could not be avoided, because the natives had become capable of expelling them physically, if need be. But they were anxious to ensure that independent India did not slip out of their sphere of influence completely. What they wished to leave behind was a weak federal India that would be politically divided and susceptible to external pressure, i.e. an India with a broken back. Their game plan was an India composed of sovereign princely states, jealous of their parochial prerogatives and looking abroad for guarantees, and constant domestic political strife because of Hindu-Muslim differences. For them, partition turned out to be a most unfortunate outcome, despite any initial gloating that the natives had been robbed of an intact legacy, because it resulted in the eventual expansion of Soviet influence in the Indian subcontinent. Although Pakistan has constituted a major source of distraction for India, the failure to keep their old nineteenth-century Russian adversary out of what might have been part of the British sphere of influence was judged a failure.

Thus, the sustained and multifarious assault on independent India, Hinduism and all its works by the Anglo-Saxon Indian Studies academic establishment must be viewed in the context of the profound US-led Western antagonism against Soviet Communism and wider power-political issues. As a corollary, the end of this struggle may also presage a change in the largely unsympathetic representation of India. But when the life-and-death struggle against Communism was going on, and it was exactly that, with the palpable fear of nuclear annihilation and the possibility of total defeat in the process, issues of truth and fairness became secondary. The world of Islam and Pakistan were political and military allies, possessing oil resources and run by anti-Communist Islamic dictatorships, installed in power by US intervention. By contrast, India was considered the enemy, described by the US State Department in the late 1940s as a potential imperialist threat to its interests akin to Japan during the 1930s (a canard repeated as late as 1992). It was also viewed as an unscrupulous Soviet camp follower.

This urgent power-political calculus and the attendant purposes of the US State imbued Indian Studies in the US. The purpose was to undermine India politically by de-legitimizing its cultural and religious values. The neutering of Indian culture and its civilization became an unthinking adjunct to the vindication of the Cold War imperative of projecting Pakistani verisimilitude. It fitted seamlessly into a deep-rooted and uncomprehending Abrahamic political and religious aversion towards the pagan and polytheistic. Successfully portraying India as a vicious civilization, riven by the racism of caste, which routinely burns widows (*Sati*, described recently as if it were widespread) and brides in the bargain, is a victory by default for Pakistani claims to a place in the world.

Interestingly, a search of the main influential journals[2] turned up one solitary scholarly article on "Islam in India" and over two hundred directly or indirectly related to the term "Hindu", overwhelmingly critical of either the politics of India or vehemently imputing a sectarian character to all Hindu socio-political activity. There was virtually not a single discussion of slavery in a global search of journals, presumably because it might reveal unpleasant truths about the fate of Hindus under Muslim rule. Mass enslavement has of course been the norm for Islamic conquests everywhere.

17.5. Attempts by academics to injure Hindu civilization

The "expose" of Indian Hindu "mumbo jumbo", the irrationality of its licentious and sensual religion, also serves to defuse India's significance in the public imagination. The exotic may be fascinating, but it is not a legitimate way of life recommended for emulation in the sane real world. Such a hostile portrayal cannot be accomplished by half measures that allow serious alternative sympathetic versions. Of course, a paid bureaucrat does not orchestrate such a venture from some central control centre. What is required is the generation of negative socio-cultural perceptions that form the backdrop to antagonistic political outcomes, consistent with State policy. This is achieved by influencing key academics and university departments, manned by professional scholars. The control over the principal sources of funding for academic

[2] *Journal of the American Oriental Society, Asian Survey, Journal of Asian Studies, Modern Asian Studies, Monumenta Nipponica, Pacific Affairs, Bulletin of the School of Oriental and African Studies, University of London, Harvard Journal of Asiatic Studies, Journal of Japanese Studies, Modern China, Australian Journal of Chinese Affairs, China Quarterly, Far Eastern Survey, Far Eastern Quarterly, China Journal, Bulletin of the School of Oriental Studies, University of London, News Bulletin (Institute of Pacific Relations)*, and *Memorandum (Institute of Pacific Relations, American Council).*

work and research remains crucial in this regard. And the official nature of major charitable US academic funding agencies is not a matter of serious dispute. Much of the rest follows through peer pressure, from the potent impact of validation by prestigious institutions and the celebrity academic stars that occupy senior positions within them.

It is a useful counterpoint to the idea of scholarly "objectivity" to note that such professional scholarship in the humanities is like a chameleon that can change colours radically (i.e. depiction, interpretations and associated political implications) and still remain legitimate in the view of peers. The same Ramakrishna portrayed by suspect scholarship and sleight-of-hand as a pederast could be recast, if the scholar chooses, as a "sensual" individual sublimating desire in the way recommended by the Vedanta.

The linguist and interpreter of myths has wide latitude and may display immense skill in imaginative reconstruction, but reconstructed myths do not become historical facts or provide a basis for reliable scientific inferences about contemporary societal mores and processes. Myths, ultimately, remain myths. But they can be made to appear distasteful and the civilization that produced them odd at best. Serious comment on the subject matter of comparative mythology requires scholarship and is outside the scope of the present analysis, but it may be argued that the faithful themselves are unduly sensitive to the suggestion that religious mythology is not equivalent to historical fact. The fusing of truth with fantasy or myth is an entirely legitimate universal basis of socio-cultural identity and self-perception that should not distress the faithful.

However, Wendy Doniger, who espouses the parochial and historically contingent category of Western feminism for intellectual inspiration, also wielded unashamedly to justify imperialist wars by her own native Christian country, let the cat out of the bag by confessing to disquiet over alleged Hindu fanaticism. Is this the deeper political motivation that lurks underneath allegedly lofty scholarly purposes? When a supreme interpreter of myth (Wendy Doniger), with vast evident knowledge of Hinduism and Hindu society, casually espouses the oxymoron of "Hindu fundamentalism" as a conceptual category, one's confidence in her wider scholarly competence begins to waver. Some/many Hindus may be bad people, their politics may be reprehensible, they may be extremists, violent, but the notion of religious fundamentalism, which has a very specific meaning about the relationship between literal textual interpretation and behavioural norms, does not advance the understanding of Indian society and politics.

17.6. The collaborationist Indian left and the West

Allied to the designs of US Cold War politics and its academics, an overwhelming majority of India's English speaking native scholars has been mobilized in a veritable campaign against the alleged dangers of a Hindu awakening in India. These "coolie" scholars and their assorted domestic allies wield influence disproportionate to their numbers, a counterpart of the anglicized Indian consumer who, despite numerical paucity, generates vast advertising revenues for India's English newspapers, though this too is changing as the pockets of the "untutored" bulge with cash. What are their motives?

An uncharitable view might be that India's current political dispensation is a source of deep anxiety for the English-speaking cosmopolitans because the untutored (and unwashed?) traditional denizens of India's provincial towns have wrested political control of mainstream politics from them. All sorts of political alliances are therefore afoot, not least with sectarian Islam, the only reliable bloc vote in India unequivocally opposed to the growing voice of the Hindu majority in Indian politics. The disadvantaged marginal Hindu groups are proving unreliable because they are insufficiently exercised by the equity of committed religious stake-holders in Indian politics to wish to disrupt India Inc. itself; their leaders merely want to supplant others in order to usurp a larger share of the spoils for themselves.

A more charitable interpretation is that, if you believe in the class struggle and seek revolutionary change to liberate the masses, horizontal societal, as opposed to vertical class, divisions among toiling Indians of different religious communities have to be opposed, by whatever means necessary. The Chinese Communists have been undermining this already improbable reverie of late by unleashing the full force of the coercive apparatus of their State on unpaid workers who dare to strike and who even commit suicide in public displays of despair. That apparently embarrasses the workers' government, which begins to look increasingly familiar as a classic example of fascism, ruthlessly directing a corporate society and all apparatuses of State power through a political party, without any public accountability or hint of apology.

Be that as it may, a few lies, subterfuges and resort to the help of international sympathizers for such a noble cause, which is permitted by revolutionary theory anyway, is hardly criminal. The idea that some of these international academic sympathizers might enjoy cordial ties with their own governmental agencies, which are hostile to Indian national interests, as many clearly do, is deemed an invention of the despicable Indian State, representing the oppressor classes. Never mind whom the infinitely more powerful US State and its imperial collaborators represent.

Once these certainties are established, the burden of accepting financial rewards and prestigious appointments from abroad is a cross that has to be borne courageously, for the sake of the eventual liberation of the masses from fascist oppression. The struggle stretches way back, beyond the Sangh Parivar to Indira Gandhi, nay her father. Indeed, Pandit Jawaharlal Nehru faced a more hostile international press than his daughter or the redoubtable Atal Behari Vajpayee.

However, India's English-speaking 'leftist' elites had a more ambiguous relationship vis-à-vis the Indian State under Jawaharlal Nehru, since the more elitist Indian social order of the period was consonant with their conception of their own place within it. Dissent was accordingly choreographed.

Former Indian Prime Minister Atal Behari Vajpayee's really serious infraction in the eyes of supposed "international opinion", the highest court of appeal for the reverential Indian left, was the nuclear tests of May 1998 that ensure India a position of virtual impregnability in a potential conventional military engagement on two fronts. One leftist Indian author, Sunil Khilnani, quoted in the London *Financial Times*, evidently espoused some form of bankrupt intellectual confetti, decrying Indian military adventurism and belligerence towards Pakistan, a country ruled by a military dictator and waging relentless war against democratic India.

17.8. Conclusion

The social and political churning that has been unfolding in contemporary India is, first and foremost, a nationalist phenomenon. It has occurred in the backdrop of a profound awakening of the nineteenth century that was primarily religious in character. The former exhibits many of the defects of intolerance and exclusivism intrinsic to all nationalist awakenings, but such shortcomings are neither unique nor necessarily fatal. Indeed nationalism remains an unfortunate necessity in a jealous world of predatory nation states, ever ready to extinguish the weak. The progressive sapping of the earlier religious renaissance, in the last remaining repository of a uniquely open-ended spiritual and philosophical quest, must nevertheless be a source of regret, although that setback need not be permanent.

(Dr. Gautam Sen taught international political economy at the London School of Economics & Political Science, and has published widely on development, international trade, defence economics and India. He has been an adviser to the Prime Ministers of India and Nepal and a founding life-member and national spokesmen of the Overseas Friends of the BJP UK. He is currently a member of the eminent person's group of the Indo-UK Roundtable and the director of the Gandhi-Einstein Foundation, which promotes Indo-Jewish understanding.)

18. Sita Ram Goel, memories and ideas

Shrikant Talageri

18.1. Personal memories

I first become acquainted with Sita Ram Goel, or rather with his writings, in the late nineteen-eighties. I had gone to Savarkar Sadan, near Shivaji Park in Mumbai, to buy a copy of Nathuram Godse's *May It Please Your Honour* — ironical since Sita Ram Goel was a staunch admirer of Mahatma Gandhi. (The truth is, over the years, without blinding myself to his many faults, some of which cost the nation dear, and without losing my respect for Godse either, I have also acquired great respect for Mahatma Gandhi and his life and philosophy, and their great relevance in an increasingly ruthless world. This may be difficult to understand if we think only in terms of black and white.)

As I was browsing through the other books available there, the late Balarao Savarkar, in charge of the books section at that time, showed me some of the then booklets by Sita Ram Goel and Ram Swarup, and urged me to buy them as they were excellently researched and written and inexpensively priced. Rather doubtfully, I glanced through the booklets, and then took two or three of them. I had just read, and been impressed by, H.V. Seshadri's *The Tragic Story of Partition*, and I saw that one of the booklets, *Muslim Separatism, Causes and Consequences*, seemed to be a review of that book. Another, *The Story of Islamic Imperialism in India*, also seemed interesting.

"Interesting" was an understatement. I was bowled clean over by the style and the deep systematic logic of Sita Ram Goel, till then a name not known to me. Two days later, I raced back to Savarkar Sadan and bought all the other Voice of India booklets available. And I wrote to Sita Ram Goel expressing my deep appreciation, and enclosing a draft of Rs.101/- asking for copies of other Voice of India booklets which I had not managed to find at Savarkar Sadan.

Sita Ram Goel wrote back (on 11/2/1987, a letter I have preserved to this day) thanking me for my interest and sending me 9 booklets, 7 by himself and 2 by Ram Swarup, and some valuable personal observations on the political situation.

I was so overwhelmed by the books, and particularly *The Story of Islamic Imperialism in India*, that I wrote to Sita Ram Goel asking his permission to get the book translated into Marathi and published serially in some Marathi magazine such as *Sobat*. I did not receive any reply.

In any case, I determined that whenever I wrote a book in future, it having been my ambition since childhood to be a writer when I grew up, it would be published by Sita Ram Goel and would proudly stand beside books by him and by Ram Swarup. Therefore, in 1989-90, when I took up the task of writing a book critically examining the Aryan Invasion Theory, I wrote to Sita Ram Goel asking him whether he would consider publishing it.

In his reply on 26/6/1990, Goel wrote back: "Personally, I feel that the subject is very complex and should best be left to the scholars. They will do justice in due course. But if you think you know all the arguments, for and against, and can write a scholarly study, I will consider it for publication. I make no promise... And I should make it very clear that I will not touch anything in the P.N. Oak style..."

Emboldened, I prepared and sent him the manuscript of the first three chapters, the only ones which were ready. The rest of the book, based on a project paper that I had helped in preparing for my sister on the subject when she was doing her B.Ed., evolved as I wrote.

In his letter of 26/2/1991, Goel wrote back; "I received your letter of the 20th and the typescript yesterday afternoon.

I finished reading it in the evening. Hats off. It is excellent. (...) You are the man I was looking for. Go ahead and finish the work. I will publish it."

Ecstatic, I went ahead and finished the work, and sent it by post, chapter by chapter. Finally, Sita Ram Goel invited me to Delhi in December 1992, as much to personally oversee the proofreading of the book as to meet him. And I reached Delhi on 6th December 1992. It was truly a historic day for me when I met the writer and scholar I had dreamt of meeting since more then five years. And, ironically, it was also a historic day in Indian politics: the day the Babri Masjid was demolished in Ayodhya.

During my week in Delhi, I also met two more very great writers and scholars high on my list: Ram Swarup and Koenraad Elst. However, I had almost no interaction with the former, except for noticing the extreme difference between the personalities of Ram Swarup and Sita Ram Goel: almost a difference between *lasya* and *tandava* (the graceful c.q. forceful modes in the performing arts). And, although I have since long considered him to be my most intelligent critic and most important intellectual confidante, in this particular week in Delhi I had little interaction with Koenraad Elst as well.

But I spent most of the days, when I was not proofreading, in the company of Sita Ram Goel. On the first day, he showed me around New Delhi (and it was only late evening, when we reached his home, where I was invited for dinner that day, that we found out about the event of the day in Ayodhya). The next few days were spent mostly in the office. But everyday we had many deep discussions and conversations. It was literally a week-long brain-storming session.

Sita Ram Goel had spent his life, right from the pre-1947 era, in the thick of things. And his conversations were full of anecdotes and information about political personalities ranging from Nehru to Lohia to Masani to Vajpayee, about organizations and institutions ranging from the Congress to the Communists to the Sangh Parivar, and about ideologies of every kind, with most of which he had been closely associated at some point or the other in his life. He had been an intense reader throughout his life (in English, Hindi, Urdu, Sanskrit, and I believe even Persian, Bengali, and some Gujarati and Marathi), and it was literally an avalanche of information.

It was an incredible and extremely memorable week. But, finally, it came to an end, and I returned back to Mumbai, then in the throes of the post-Babri demolition riots.

My second meeting with Sita Ram Goel was exactly a year later in December 1993. A function to release a handful of books on the Aryan Invasion Theory (by Koenraad Elst, S.S. Mishra, and myself) was organized jointly by Voice of India, The Historians Forum, and the Deendayal Research Institute in Delhi on 10/12/1993. The books were released by the then Baudhik Pramukh (now Sarsanghchalak) of the RSS, K.S. Sudarshan.

On that occasion our whole family went to Delhi for four days. We stayed in the Deendayal Research Institution, and therefore did not meet Sita Ram Goel as often and for as long as I would have preferred, but we did meet twice in the premises, and once we were all invited to dinner at his house, where there was greater scope for conversation.

After that, I met Sita Ram Goel in person only once, in April 2001. But throughout the decade, we were in close communication, by way of letters and telephone conversations. I made it a point to phone at least once a month, even if there was nothing particular to communicate. Sita Ram Goel had become practically a member of the family, a distant uncle, not only in my eyes but in the eyes of the other members of my family as well.

The last time I met him in person was on the occasion of the World Sanskrit Conference organized in Vigyan Bhavan, Delhi, by the HRD ministry of the Govt. of India. The conference was from the 5th to the 9th of April 2001, and I received an invitation and a phone call from the organizers asking me to participate in a special session on the Aryan Invasion Theory, organized as part of the conference on the second day. I decided to attend the conference for just the first two days, due to office constraints just then. My main aim was to grab the opportunity to meet Sita Ram Goel once more.

But when I phoned Sita Ram Goel to inform him about it, he actively discouraged me from doing so. These conferences, he told me, were nothing but a colossal waste of time, money and energy. They were just jamborees organized for the heck of it, or to fulfil some ulterior motives, and nothing serious ever emerged from them. It was better to concentrate on reading and writing. How right his judgement was, in this respect, I found out for myself later; but in any case, I changed my mind about attending the conference.

However, a few days later, I received an urgent phone call from Pradeep Goel. There had been a sudden deterioration in his father's health after our last conversation, to the extent that his father even apprehended that he would not live for long. And, since I had been eager to meet him once more on the pretext of the conference, Sita Ram Goel had asked his son to phone me and tell me to attend the conference after all. So I once more changed my mind, and decided to attend.

The conference was as predicted. I attended it till the afternoon session of the second day. But later I went to meet Sita Ram Goel; I was to leave Delhi the next day, on the 7th. It was a depressing sight to see the once robust Sita Ram Goel lying physically helpless in a bed suffering from continuous aches and pains and great weakness. His spirit, however, was as indomitable as ever, as I also knew from our regular phone conversations, but I could speak to him only for a short while. The rest of the time I spent talking with Pradeep Goel.

That was the last time I saw him in person, although I remained in regular touch with him, until I heard of his tragic death. It was shocking news, not because it was totally unexpected but because it was a severe blow on the personal level. Everyone in my house was overwhelmed with sorrow by the news. It was as if a close relative had expired. If the sorrow in our house was tempered, it was only because an even greater personal tragedy, the death of my own father in June 2002, had taken place earlier and its effects were still to wear off. Sita Ram Goel's death seemed an extension of the same.

While we all regarded Sita Ram Goel with great affection, I flatter myself in the belief that Sita Ram Goel likewise regarded me with similar affection. In the last few years of his life, his health had deteriorated to such an extent that he refused to meet most people and even to take their telephone calls. But he generally always accepted my phone calls and spoke till it became physically unbearable, a privilege reserved for not many people. He inquired about my family and was always ready to advise me on any point. His death has left a void in my personal life, quite apart from the undeniable and unfillable void he has left in the ideological life of India.

18.2. Ideas and ideals

Sita Ram Goel's death has left a void in the intellectual and ideological life of India:

1. He was an intellectual giant who, single-handedly, took on the powerful forces bent on destroying Hindu civilization, and exposed them in ruthless detail.
2. He enunciated a detailed blueprint for an intellectual Hindu Renaissance and for the rejuvenation of Hindu society.
3. He created Voice of India and provided leadership to all genuine Hindu thinkers, and inspired, guided, brought together, and brought the best out of all of them; and in the process created a veritable library of books covering every single aspect of Hindu, and Hindutva, ideology.

(In this context, it must be mentioned that Sita Ram Goel himself has rarely, if ever, used the word Hindutva in his writings. He always spoke of Hindu society and Sanatana Dharma. However, the List of Publications of Voice of India contains an Appeal, which specifies that "VOICE OF INDIA aims at providing an ideological defence of Hindu society and culture, through a list of publications", and this is what Hindutva, which means Hindu Nationalism, is all about.)

The comparison may seem odious, but Voice of India occupies the same position of moral authority in relation to Hindu Nationalist ideology that the Bible occupies in relation to Christian ideology, the Quran and Hadis occupy in relation to Islamic ideology, and the *Communist Manifesto* and *Das Kapital* occupy in relation to Marxist ideology. The difference, and this is a fundamental one, is that the other books and ideologies mentioned above represent imperialist tendencies and forces which worked against the ancient and traditional civilizations of the world and against humanity. Voice of India, on the other hand, represents the voice of the last and greatest of those civilizations in its struggle against those very ideologies, tendencies and forces.

The void left by Sita Ram Goel's death is of course that much less of a void in the sense that Sita Ram Goel's heritage, in the form of his writings and publications, remain to guide the future course of the Hindu struggle and Renaissance. But, the world will miss any significant further development of his heritage: I can speak for myself, at least, when I say that my own books would not only have remained unpublished, but they would not even have been written if there had not been the inspiration of his writings, and the energy of his moral presence, in the background. Many significant books by potential thinkers and writers, in the near future, will now remain unwritten.

Moreover, Sita Ram Goel has left us at the very point when his analysis and guidance was most needed: today the ideology of Hindutva faces one of the worst crises in its history. Events have brought about a situation where cynicism, disenchantment and frustration are rampant among Hindutva-minded Hindus, and Hindu issues appear irrelevant, meaningless and futile.

The reason for this is not clear to most of them: the more naïve assume it is because of the defeat of the BJP in the recent Lok Sabha elections. The truth is that Hindutva is today facing a crisis of confidence not because the BJP lost the elections in 2004, but because the BJP won the elections in 1998 and 1999 and ruled the country for six years. In six years, they have effectively succeeded in establishing and spreading an atmosphere of pure cynicism as regards Hindu issues, in completely demoralizing and demotivating genuinely Hindu-minded persons, and in transforming Hindutva itself into a sick joke.

This is a commemorative volume to Sita Ram Goel and to his creation Voice of India. It is in the fitness of things to write about his writings and ideas. But the best way to pay tribute to his writings and ideas is to read Voice of India books and understand them in detail, and to propagate the books on a war footing. Many of the articles in this volume will be presenting overviews and summaries of his writings and ideas much better than I could do: I refer particularly to the extremely comprehensive article by Virendra Parekh, of which I had the privilege of a preview.

I will therefore devote the major part of my article to a detailed elucidation of the ideology of true Hindutva as I understand it. And I will devote a last small section to the identification of an anti-Hindu force more dangerous to Hindu civilization than the forces of Islam, Christianity and Marxism, namely pseudo-Hindutva as represented by the BJP and its front organizations.

This will be my way of paying tribute to Sita Ram Goel, the Bhishma Pitamaha of Hindutva, and one of the very greatest sons of India. It is possible that many of the things I have to say may be unacceptable, not only to pseudo-Hindutvavadis, but even to many genuinely Hindutva-minded people, and staunch admirers of Voice of India books. But, I have the fullest confidence that Sita Ram Goel would have approved, and I deeply regret that I am not able to have the benefit of his guidance.

18.3. Conventional Hindutva

Hindu Nationalist ideology is generally referred to as *Hindutva* — a word coined by Veer Savarkar, and later taken up by the Hindu Mahasabha (of which Savarkar himself was twice President) and the RSS. In the last two decades, the word has become a common word in Indian politics, bandied about by the likes of the BJP and the Shiv Sena and by their political opponents. Anybody and everybody interprets the word to his own convenience, but there can be no doubt about its basic meaning: it means an ideology for the defence of Hindu society, culture and civilization.

The following is an attempt to elaborate on the ideology of Hindutva as a complete nationalist ideology from the point of view of three aspects:

A. Conventional Hindutva.
B. Cultural Nationalism.
C. Socio-Economic Nationalism.

Conventional Hindutva is what is generally understood by the term Hindutva: an ideology for the defence of Hindu society and civilization. As the word defence indicates, the first premise is that Hindu society and civilization are under attack.

Societies and civilizations have been under attack from other societies and civilizations since the beginnings of time. It is a natural corollary of the cruder or baser side of human nature, and the vicissitudes of Time and Nature have seen the demise of many a society and civilization.

But the Old Testament of the Bible for the first time introduced a new element: the destruction of societies and civilizations as a matter of religious ideology. The birth of Christianity, 2000 years ago, gave a final revolutionary touch by converting this local ideology (restricted only to

Palestine, the land "promised" by Jehovah to the Jews) into an international imperialist ideology. A few centuries later, Islam followed suit. The two, between them, laid waste most of the earlier societies and civilizations of Europe, Western and Central Asia, and North Africa.

In the mediaeval period, Christian Imperialism took on a new form as European Imperialism, and destroyed the societies and civilizations of North and South America and Australia, and did much damage (particularly political and psychological) in the rest of Africa and Asia. It was only when a similar ideology (Nazism) arose in a part of Europe itself, which sought to do to the rest of Europe what some parts of Europe had done to most of the rest of the world, that European Imperialism lost its steam. The centre of Christian Imperialism shifted to America. Today American Imperialism dominates the world with (apart from its military and economic clout) its three powerful ideological weapons: Proselytism, Capitalism and Consumerism. In the process, Christian Imperialism also laid low another rival imperialism, which had raised its head for one century, Marxist Imperialism; and it is now in the process of trying to do the same to its more long-standing rival, Islamic Imperialism.

Hindu civilization is the one civilization whose inner greatness and resilience enabled it to withstand centuries of Christian and Islamic imperialist attack. It is in fact the last major bastion of the pre-Christian civilizations of the world.

For that very reason, Hindu society is today the single major target of all these Imperialisms, which are backed by powerful international forces. As Sita Ram Goel puts it at the very beginning of his *Hindu Society Under Siege* (p.2): "The death of Hindu society is no longer an eventuality which cannot be envisaged. This great society is now besieged by the same dark and deadly forces which have overwhelmed and obliterated many earlier societies. Suffering from a loss of élan, it has become a house divided within itself. And its beneficiaries no more seem to be interested in its survival because they have fallen victims to hostile propaganda. They have developed towards it an attitude of utter indifference, if not downright contempt. Let no Hindu worth his salt remain complacent. Hindu society is in mortal danger as never before."

This fact is clear to anyone who looks around with open eyes at what is going on all around, and who is clear-sighted and level headed enough to see, and honest enough to admit, the situation. To illustrate this, let me quote Tavleen Singh, a journalist who cannot by any means be called a Hindu communalist. In this article itself, she reminds us that she is "not a Hindu", and Sita Ram Goel always considered her to be a typical secularist scribe. All the same, here ("This inner voice too needs hearing", *Indian Express*, Sunday 13/6/2004) she acknowledges:

> "...the word *Hindutva* is being used as a term of abuse... it is used mostly in pejorative terms... The debate appears no longer confined to the cloistered world of priests, or even the self-serving one of politics, it has expanded into a challenge to Hindu civilization... the wider attack on Indian civilization that this pejorative use of the word *Hindu* represents. It bothers me that I went to school and college in this country without any idea of the enormous contribution of Hindu civilization to the history of the world. It bothers me that even today our children, whether they go to state schools or expensive private ones, come out without any knowledge of their own culture or civilization... You cannot be proud of a heritage you know nothing about, and in the name of secularism, we have spent 50 years in total denial of the Hindu roots of this civilization. We have done nothing to change a colonial system of mass education founded on the principle that Indian civilization had nothing to offer... our contempt for our culture and civilization... evidence of a country that continues to be colonized to the core? Our contempt for who we are gets picked up these days by the Western press... racism [is] equated with Hindu Nationalism. For countries that gave us slavery and apartheid that really is rich, but who can blame them when we think so badly of ourselves? As for me I would like to state clearly that I believe that the Indic religions have made much less trouble

> for the world than the Semitic ones and that Hindu civilization is something I am very proud of. If that is evidence of my being 'communal', then, so my inner voice tells me, so be it."

If Hindu society and civilization are to be saved from annihilation, there is only one solution: Hindu consciousness must be aroused, a Hindu perspective and world-view must be cultivated. Hindus must be educated, on the one hand, about Hindu civilization and its rich heritage and its major contributions to the world in every field, and about the great sages, seers, saints, scholars, scientists, soldiers, artistes and statesmen, the individuals in every field who represent our past glory and heritage; and, on the other, about the forces out to destroy this civilization, about the textual sources, ideologies, histories, strategies and present activities of these forces, and about the Hindu struggles against these forces and the Hindu heroes involved in these struggles.

It is also necessary to alert Hindus to the inner weaknesses which make Hindu society susceptible to these forces, the dangers of Secularism, the self-alienation among the Hindu elites and ruling classes and their indifference to, and contempt for, their own culture and civilization, the breakdown of the defence mechanism of Hindu society, the perversion of certain Hindu values like tolerance, universalism and humanism, and the abandonment of certain other Hindu values like self-respect, rationalism and capacity for objective analysis.

Voice of India books have sought to do just this. Before Voice of India came on the scene, Hindutva discussion hovered around topics and issues which could be broadly subsumed under the headings "appeasement of minorities" and "discrimination against Hindus and Hinduism" in the Indian polity. The discussions were concerned only with the symptoms of the disease rather than with the root causes and the cure. Voice of India changed everything: it identified both the external forces as well as the internal weaknesses, and it offered the only cure: *Knowledge of the Truth.*

The only solution, according to Sita Ram Goel, was for Hindus to *know the truth* about the forces out to destroy Hindu society. Once Hindus knew the truth, the whole truth and nothing but the truth, these forces would lose their self-righteousness, their self-assurance, and their vigour and potential for damage. Hindu society, on the other hand, would recognize its own potential and would regain the self-confidence to rise up again to take its rightful place among the comity of nations.

The only solution is, therefore, to propagate Sita Ram Goel's writings and Voice of India publications, and the message and facts contained in these writings and publications, on a war footing. An awakened Hindu society will do the rest.

18.4. Cultural nationalism: environmental

Sita Ram Goel, at the very outset of his *Hindu Society Under Siege* (pp.1-2), tells us: "there are many Hindus who are legitimately proud of Hindu art, architecture, sculpture, music, painting, dance, drama, literature, linguistics, lexicography and so on. But they seldom take into account the fact that this great wealth of artistic, literary and scientific heritage will die if Hindu society which created it is no more there to preserve, protect and perpetuate it."

In my 1993 book *The Aryan Invasion Theory And Indian Nationalism*, I have pointed out in detail how conversion to Islam and Christianity creates a process of cultural de-Indianization. De-Hinduization of Indian society, therefore, will inevitably lead to the demise of Indian culture: Hindu society must survive if Indian culture is to survive.

But the reverse is also true: Indian culture must survive if Hindu society is to survive. *Hindu society would no more be Hindu society if it lost all vestiges of Indian culture or if it allowed Indian culture to die out. And Hindutva without Indian culture as its very basis is a meaningless exercise.*

Before going further, let me clarify what exactly the words "culture" and "Indian culture" mean in our discussion in this section on Cultural Nationalism.

Culture does not refer only to "values", "ethos" and "way of life", which are really vague words and which can be made to mean anything. It refers to actual concrete culture. As I put it in the 1997 VOI volume *Time for Stock Taking* (p.227), it refers to "every single aspect of India's matchlessly priceless heritage: climate and topography; flora and fauna; races and languages; music, dance and drama; arts and handicrafts; culinary arts; games and physical systems; architecture; costumes and apparels; literature and sciences..." And Indian culture refers not just to the "cultural practices springing from Vedic or Sanskritic sources, but from all other Indian sources independently of these: the practices of the Andaman islanders and the (pre-Christian) Nagas are as Hindu in the territorial sense, and Sanatana in the spiritual sense, as classical Sanskritic Hinduism".

Indian culture is the greatest and richest in the world. India (i.e. the Indian subcontinent) is the only place in the world which is rich in all the fields of culture: natural (topography, climate, flora and fauna), ethnic (races and languages), and civilizational (music, dance and drama; lore and literature; art, sculpture and handicrafts; architecture; costumes, ornaments and beauty culture; cuisine; games and physical systems; religion; philosophy; social and material sciences, etc.). Its greatness lies in both factors: the richness of its range and variety, as well as its contributions to the world, in every single field of culture.

To give just a glimpse: in climate, we have the hottest place in the world, Jacobabad (in present-day Pakistan), but also, as per the *Encyclopaedia Britannica*, we have, outside the Polar regions, "the largest area under permanent ice and snow". We have dry arid regions in the west, which receive no rainfall at all, and at the same time the area, around Cherapunji in the east, with the highest rainfall in the world. And we have, in different parts of the land, a wide range of shades of climatic conditions between these extremes. The topography of India, from the most intriguing and diverse mountain system in the world, the Himalayas, in the north, through the plains, plateaus, mountains and valleys of the peninsula down to the Andaman-Nicobar and Lakshadweep island clusters in the south, also seems to leave no topographical feature unrepresented.

India's forests and vegetation also cover every range and variety from the coniferous and deciduous types to the monsoon and tropical types to the desert and scrubland types. And India has been one of the primary contributors to the world in every kind of plant and forest product. To name only some of the most prominent ones: rice, a variety of beans, a wide range of vegetables including eggplants and a number of different types of gourds, fruits like bananas, mangoes and a range of citrus fruits, oilseeds like sesame, important woods including teak, ebony and sandalwood, spices like black pepper, cardamom, cinnamon, ginger and turmeric, dyes like madder and indigo, important materials like cotton, jute, shellac and India-rubber, a wide range of medicinal herbs, etc., etc. Moreover, being strategically situated between, and sharing in, three different ecological areas, India shares countless other important plants and products with northern and western Asia on the one hand and Southeast Asia on the other. And, as a detailed study will show, it has indigenous equivalents, or potential equivalents, for a wide range of other non-Indian plants and products.

India's fauna is the richest in the world. Robert Wolff, in the introduction to his book *Animals of Asia*, tells us that "India has more animal species than any other region of equal area in the world". But the richness is not only in comparison with regions of equal area. For example, India is the only area in the world which has all seven families of carnivora native to it.

The whole of Africa has five (no bears or procyonids), the whole of North and South America together have five (no hyaenas or viverrids), the whole of Europe has five (no hyaenas or procyonids), and, in Asia, the areas to the east and north have six (no hyaenas) and the areas to the west have six (no procyonids). Within the carnivora family of cats, India is the only area to have all six genera. The whole of Africa has four (no uncia or neofelis), North and South America together, and Europe, have four (no acinonyx, uncia or neofelis), and, in Asia, the areas to the east and north have five (no acinonyx) and the areas to the west have four (no uncia or neofelis).

In respect of snakes, India is the only area in the world to have all twelve of the recognized families, while the whole of Africa has eight, and both North and South America together have nine. Extra significant is that one of the twelve families (Uropeltidae or shield-tailed snakes) is found only in South India and Sri Lanka, so that India alone has twelve families, while the whole rest of the world put together has eleven. Of the three families of crocodilians, two (crocodiles and gavials) are found in India, one of them (gavials) exclusively in India. India is the richest area in the world in the variety of bovine species, second only to Africa in variety of antelope species, and second only to China in variety of deer species. The list is a long one. And India is not only a primary wildlife destination, it is also one of the important centres of domestication of animals. The most important of these being the domestic buffalo, the domesticated elephant, one of the two races of domestic cattle and the commercially most important bird in the world, the domestic fowl. The most ornamental bird in the world, the peacock, is also Indian.

There are three recognized races in the world (Caucasoid, Mongoloid and Negroid), and India is the only area in the world which has all three native to it: the Andaman islanders are the only true Negroids outside Africa. Sometimes, a fourth race, Australoid, is postulated (otherwise included among

Caucasoids), and we have it among the Veddas of Sri Lanka. As to languages, six of the nineteen language families in the world are found in India, three of them only in India: Dravidian, Andamanese and Burushaski. The numerically and politically most important family of languages in the world, Indo-European, originated (as I have argued in my books) in India.

18.5. Cultural nationalism: intellectual

As a civilization, India is the oldest continuous civilization still in existence. As A.L. Basham puts it in his *The Wonder That Was India*: "The ancient civilization of India differs from those of Egypt, Mesopotamia and Greece, in that its traditions have been preserved without a break down to the present day. Until the advent of the archaeologist, the peasant of Egypt or Iraq had no knowledge of the culture of his forefathers, and it is doubtful whether his Greek counterpart had any but the vaguest ideas about the glory of Periclean Athens. In each case there had been an almost complete break with the past. On the other hand... to this day legends known to the humblest Indian recall the names of shadowy chieftains who lived nearly a thousand years before Christ, and the orthodox Brahman in his daily worship repeats hymns composed even earlier. India and China have, in fact, the oldest continuous cultural traditions in the world."

India has been one of the most important centres of civilization in the world in practically every age. We need not refer here to Indian traditions of fabled kingdoms going back into the extremely remote past. Even in the perception of the world in general, and scholarly perception at present, India was always a fabled wonderland. In (at least) the third and second millenniums BC, the Indus-Sarasvati sites represented a relatively egalitarian and peaceful, highly organized, standardized and developed civilization, with many features unparalleled elsewhere. It covered a far larger area and remained constant and relatively unchanging for a far longer period (nearly a millennium) than any other civilization. In the first millennium BC, the Arthashastra depicts an extremely organized civilization which appears almost modern in many respects, and India was idealized and mythicized by writers from China to Greece. In the first millennium AD, we had the golden period of Indian civilization during the reign of the Guptas, at which point of time, according to A.L. Basham, "India was perhaps the happiest and most civilized region of the world". And in the second millennium AD, India was the desired land of dreams, in the quest for which half the world had the misfortune of being "discovered" by Europe.

And this civilization has made primary contributions to the world in every single field of culture. To begin with, religion: India is one of the two centres of origin of the major world religions, the other being West Asia. Buddhism was at one time the dominant religion not only in East and Southeast Asia, but also in Central Asia and parts of West Asia. It is increasingly being accepted as having been one of the major influences on the initial formative stages of Christianity. With Hinduism, it was the source of many religious trends (asceticism, monasticism etc.) in the past, and even today, Hindu-Buddhist philosophies are acquiring an ever-increasing following among thinkers and intellectuals all over the world. Hindu religio-philosophical concepts and terms (*guru*, *nirvana*, *karma*, etc.) have become basic components of the international spiritual lexicon.

Science and the scientific temperament are among the defining points of a civilized society, and India's contributions to the development of science in the world have been more fundamental than that of any other civilization then or since. India, to begin with, invented the zero-based decimal system, without which no significant scientific development and advancement beyond certain rudimentary levels would ever have been possible in human society. This contribution is so very important, and so well illustrates the level of scientific thought-processes in India, that it needs to be elaborated in some detail here.

To begin with, the first logical stage in the development of a numeral system in any primitive society would be the very concept of numbers (one, two, three, etc.). The second logical stage would be the representation of these numbers in pictorial form, e.g. three pictures or symbolic figures of cows and two of sheep would represent three cows and two sheep. The third logical stage would be the shifting of the concept of numbers from concrete objects to abstract ideas, e.g. by the use of a simple symbol, usually a vertical line, to represent the number one. Seven vertical lines followed by the picture or symbol of a cow would represent seven cows. As the need for using bigger and bigger numbers arose, attempts would be made to create groups, as in the common method of keeping the score by drawing up to four vertical lines to represent numbers up to four, and then a fifth line vertically across the four to represent a full hand. The fourth logical stage would be the development of a base number, usually ten, on the basis of the number of fingers on the two hands used for counting.

Egyptian civilization was at this stage of development in its numeral system, which invented specific symbols for one, ten, hundred, thousand, ten thousand, etc. So, instead of representing the number 542 with 542 vertical lines, the Egyptians represented it with five repetitions of the symbol for hundred, four of the symbol for ten, and two of the symbol for one. This still had the drawback of requiring symbols to be repeated as many as nine times; and the Greeks, who borrowed the Egyptian system, went off at a tangent, off the logical track, in their attempt to remedy this. They invented halfway symbols: additional symbols for five, fifty, five hundred, etc. The Romans, who borrowed the Greek system, went even further off the logical track: they tried to avoid even four repetitions by employing a minus principle. Thus, four, nine, forty and ninety were not IIII, VIIII, XXXX and

LXXXX, but IV, IX, XL and XC. Going off at another tangent, the Ionian Greeks, the Arabs, the Hebrews, and others, assigned numerical values to the letters of their alphabet. The numbers one to nine were represented by the first nine alphabets, the numbers ten to ninety by the next nine, and so on, creating a more concise but highly illogical numeral system of limited utility.

The fifth logical stage would be the avoidance of repetition of the base symbols by means of specific symbols to represent each number of repetitions. Chinese civilization was at this stage of development in its numeral system, which had base symbols for one, ten, hundred, thousand and ten thousand, as well as symbols for the numbers from two to nine. Thus, the Chinese represented 542 with the symbols for five, hundred, four, ten, and two, in that order. The sixth and last logical stage would be a numeral system with a rigid place system and a symbol for zero. Indian civilization reached this last and highest logical stage in its numeral system, with symbols for the numbers from one to nine and a symbol for zero, and a rigid place system, which made it possible to represent any and every number with only ten symbols.

Incidentally, the Mesopotamians and the Mayas of Central America had also hit upon their own versions of zero. But, as they had gone off the logical track in the earlier stages, their systems remained grossly unwieldy and illogical. The Mesopotamian system had an unwieldy base of sixty, but symbols only for one, ten and zero; and even a symbol to incorporate a minus principle, as in the Roman system. And the Maya system had a base of twenty, but symbols only for one, five and zero; and, to accommodate the calendar, the second base was 360 instead of 400.

India's contribution of the zero-based decimal system (and, incidentally, also of most of the basic principles in the different branches of Mathematics) represents a fundamental revolutionary landmark in the history of world science on a par with the invention of fire or the invention of the wheel. But this invention was no accident. The scientific temperament in India was so developed, that it, such a fundamental development should inevitably have taken place only in India. As Alain Daniélou puts it in his *Introduction to the Study of Musical Scales* (p.99): "The Hindu theory is not like other systems, limited to experimental data: it does not consider arbitrarily as natural certain modes or certain chords, but it takes as its starting point the general laws common to all the aspects of the world's creation..." Curt Sachs, on the same subject (in his monumental work *The Rise of Music in the Ancient World — East and West*, p.171), refers to the "naïve belief of historically untrained minds that patterns usual in the person's own time and country are 'natural'...", and contrasts it with classification in India which "starts from actual facts, but is thorough in its accomplishment regardless of practice".

It was this scientific temperament which led the ancient Indians to go deep into the study of any and every subject, and to produce detailed texts on everything, whether on religious laws, rituals and customs (the vast Vedic literature: Samhitas, Brahmanas, Kalpasutras, Dharmasutras, etc.), philosophy (the Upanishads, and the sutras, commentaries, and other texts of the six Darshanas and the Buddhist, Jain and heterodox philosophies, etc.), linguistics (Panini, Yaska, and numerous Vedic and post-Vedic texts on Grammar, Phonetics, Etymology, etc.), medicine (the Samhitas of Charaka, Sushruta, Vagbhata, etc.), administration and statecraft (Kautilya's Arthashastra, etc.), the performing arts (Bharata's Natyashastra, etc.), and every other possible art, craft, technology and science, right down to the art of making love (Vatsyayana's Kamasutra). No subject was beyond the detailed investigations of the ancient Indians. And basic texts, on any subject, themselves the culminations of long and rich traditions, were followed by detailed commentaries, and by commentaries on the commentaries. And there were well-established and regulated systems and forums all over the country for objective debates on controversial points or subjects. With all this, it is not surprising that Indian civilization should have been the source of origin of so many things.

18.6. Cultural nationalism: health, beauty, pleasure

As an illustration of India's role on the world stage, consider the performing arts, i.e. music, dance and drama. A.C. Scott writes (*The Theatre in Asia*, p.1): "It will be seen that stage practice in Asia owes a great deal to India as an ancestral source. Indian influence on dance and theatre which are one and the same in Asia was like some great subterranean river following a spreading course and forming new streams on the way". Curt Sachs tells us (*The Rise of Music in the Ancient World*, p.192) that Indian music "had a decisive part in forming the musical style of the East, of China, Korea and Japan, and... what today is called Indochina and the Malay Archipelago. There was a westward exportation, too... Indian influence on Islamic music... the system of melodic and rhythmic patterns, characteristic of the Persian, Turkish, and Arabian world, had existed in India as the ragas and talas more than a thousand years before it appeared in the sources of the Mohammedan Orient." Elsewhere, he goes into more specific details about this fundamental Indian influence on the music and dance of China and Japan (pp.139, 145), Bali (p.139), Siam (p.152), Burma (p.153), and Indonesia (pp.130-132).

Alain Daniélou tells us (*Introduction to the Study of Musical Scales*, p.99) that the Indian "theory of musical modes... seems to have been the source from which all systems of modal music originated". He goes so far as to suggest that "Greek music, like Egyptian music, most probably had its roots in Hindu music" (pp.159-160). India first recognized the division of the octave into seven notes, twelve semi-tones, and twenty-two microtones (the world has still to progress towards, and Indian music as it is practiced today has even regressed from, the microtones). India was the land of origin of a wide range of musical concepts and musical instruments, not only in respect of the musical systems of Asia, but even beyond. According to the *Guinness Book of Facts and Feats*, bagpipes (so characteristic of Scottish music), and hourglass drums (the talking drums or message drums of Africa), originated in India. The present classification of musical instruments into four classes (idiophonic, membranophonic, aerophonic and chordophonic) originated in India.

It was not only in respect of music, or of religion and sciences, that Indian influence on Asia, and thereby on the rest of the world, was "like some great subterranean river following a spreading course and forming new streams on the way". This was the case in practically every field of culture. Indian sculpture and architecture spread eastwards and influenced the development of classical sculpture and architecture in the East and Southeast: the biggest temple complex in the world, the Hindu temple complex of Angkor Vat in Cambodia, is the most eloquent example.

Indian lore and literature spread eastwards and westwards, leading to the development of new genres of literature. The traditional lore and literature of Southeast Asia are suffused with the spirit, themes and vocabulary of Sanskrit epic literature, while (apart from the scientific and technical literature on every subject). Indian literary techniques and themes, like animal fables and the tale-within-a-tale technique, among others, spread out westwards, and inspired the writing of classics like *The Arabian Nights* and the Greek *Aesop's Fables*. Indian board games, like chess and ludo (*pachisi*), among others, likewise, spread out east and west. The former became the national game of Asia (with local varieties, all of them with local names derived from the

Sanskrit *chaturang*, in every country from Arabia to Korea and Vietnam), before acquiring its present international status.

Physical culture of every kind, from systems of physical exercises and martial arts, to comprehensive systems of health like Ayurveda (including, apart from its varieties of oral medicines, also the *panchakarma* techniques, theories of dietetics, etc.) and Hathayoga (including, besides *asanas*, a range of breathing techniques, concentration and meditation techniques, a wide range of internal and external cleansing techniques, etc.), also spread east and west, giving rise to similar techniques elsewhere. Greek medicine is acknowledged by many scholars to owe much to Indian medicine, and the renowned martial arts of the East acknowledge their Indian origin. Indian cuisine is generally acknowledged to be one of the great cuisines of the world, and the greatest when it comes to vegetarian cuisine, and is gaining popularity worldwide. Food culture all over the world would have been poor indeed without India's material contributions to the four tastes: sweet (sugar), sour (lemons, tamarinds, *kokam* and *amchur*), pungent (black pepper and ginger), and bitter (bitter gourds), as well as a wide variety of other spices and flavourings.

In respect of clothes and ornaments, again, India's contributions are of primary importance: cotton, the most important fabric in the world, originated in India, along with numerous important techniques, of weaving, dyeing and printing, basic to the textile industry. The use of diamonds originated in India: till the eighteenth century, India was the only source of diamonds, and the ornament and jewellery industry in India was a world pioneer in many ways. Beauty culture, the art of *shringara*, as described in great detail in the ancient texts, had developed very highly in ancient India, and India was the source of a great many kinds of clothing, ornaments, herbal cosmetics and applications, aromatic oils and beauty techniques.

Our claim that Indian culture can be considered the greatest and richest culture in the world, is not made only on the basis of past glories, — although, as a civilization with the only continuous tradition, the past is not a dead past but is an intrinsic part of our present identity. Nor only on the basis of past contributions to the world, — considerable, and even unmatchable, as they are. Indian culture is the greatest and richest culture in the world on the strength of its glorious present as well.

18.7. Cultural nationalism: the widest range

India is a complete cultural world in itself. Firstly, it represents every stage of development in culture from the most sophisticated, right from ancient times, to the most primitive, even in modern times or as late as the twentieth century. Secondly, the richness and variety of its cultural wealth, in every respect, is so great that it need never look beyond its own cultural frontiers for inspiration, innovation and development in any field of culture.

To illustrate the first point, of the widest range between extremes, consider the mathematical systems. Ancient India conceived and analyzed the mathematical concepts of zero and infinity, achieved a fundamental revolution by devising a numeral system which can represent any conceivable number with only ten symbols, and coined names for numbers of incredibly high denominations. (A Buddhist work, Lalitavistara, gives the names for base-numbers up to 10 raised to the 421th power, i.e. one followed by 421 zeroes.) And, at the same time, we have the Andamanese languages, which have not developed the concept of numbers beyond two. They have names only for "one" and "two", which is in effect "one" and "more than one", which is no numeral system at all, and represents the absolutely most primitive stage in any language in the world.

Likewise, in music, our Indian classical music has, since thousands of years, developed a detailed theory of music, and used the richest range of notes (twenty-two microtones as compared to the twelve notes of western classical music), scales (every possible combination of the basic notes), modes and rhythms (the most unimaginably wide range of melodies and rhythms, from the simplest to the most complicated and intricate, with e.g. rhythms having 11, 13, 17, 19 etc. beats per cycle, unimaginable outside India), and musical instruments (with the most intricate playing techniques in the world). And, at the same time, the absolutely most primitive form of singing in the world is found among the Veddas of Sri Lanka. Along with certain remote Patagonian tribes, they are the only people in the world who "not only do not possess any musical instrument, but do not even clap their hands or stamp the ground" (Curt Sachs: *The History of Musical Instruments*, p.26).

This is the case in almost every field of culture. On the one hand, India has the richest traditional cuisine in the world, one of the most highly developed traditions of architecture in all its aspects, and an incredibly wide range of costumes and ornaments, all of hoary antiquity. On the other hand, we have tribes who are hunter-gatherers and subsist only on wild berries, who live in caves, or who live almost in the nude.

As for the second point, of completeness, a glance at two representative fields of civilizational culture, religion and music, will suffice to make it clear. The range of Indian religion, both in respect of philosophy and doctrines, as well as customs and rituals, is quite a complete one. Every shade of thought and idea (theistic, atheistic and agnostic), from the most materialistic to the most spiritual, from the most rationalistic to the most irrational, from the most humane to the most barbaric, and from the most puritanical or orthodox to the most profane or heterodox, has been explored by the different schools of philosophy, different sects and different individual writers. Every kind and level of ritual and custom from the most primitive to the most sophisticated, from the simplest to the most elaborate, and from the most humane to the most ruthless, is found in one or the other part of India.

The only common thread is the complete absence of intolerant imperialistic tendencies: if such ever arose in the history of Hinduism, they died out just as quickly. Therefore, also, Hindu India, before the rise of modern liberalism in the west, was the only safe haven in the civilized world for the followers of religions and sects persecuted elsewhere: Jews, Zoroastrians, Syrian Christians, and in modern times, Armenian Christians, Tibetan Buddhists, Bahais and Ahmadiyas. (That this sometimes proved costly in the long run because of the failure to distinguish between religions and imperialist ideologies, is a different matter.)

In music, between the extremes of complexity and simplicity, India has also explored the scope for variety most thoroughly. Curt Sachs writes (*The Rise Of Music in the Ancient World*, p.157): "The roots of music are more exposed in India than anywhere else. The Vedda in Ceylon possess the earliest stage of singing that we know, and the subsequent strata of primitive music are represented by the numberless tribes that in valleys and jungles took shelter from the raids of northern invaders. So far as this primitive music is concerned, the records are complete or at least could easily be completed if special attention were paid to the music of the 'tribes'... hundreds of tribal styles..."

Then there is the folk music, the range and variety of which is mind-boggling. Every single part of India is rich in its own individual range of styles of folk music. The folk music of even any one state of India (say Maharashtra, Rajasthan or Karnataka, for example, or even Sind, Baluchistan, Sri Lanka or Bhutan for that matter) would merit a lifetime of study.

And, right on top, we have the great tradition of Indian classical music, which we have already referred to. Although the oldest living form of classical music in the world, and although it has evolved and developed over the centuries, losing and gaining in the process, Curt Sachs points out (*The Rise Of Music in the Ancient World*, p.157) that "there is no reason to believe that India's ancient music differed essentially from her modern music". Many western musicologists (Alain Daniélou, M.E. Cousins, Donald Lentz, etc.) have spoken about the superiority of Indian classical music over western classical music, but even without going that far, it is at least certain that Indian Classical music is one of the two main classical traditions in the world. And apart from classical music, we have the other great tradition, of Vedic chanting and singing in its many varieties, best preserved in South India, and different varieties of Sanskrit songs, preserved in temples and abbeys all over India.

In all these varieties of music (classical, folk, popular and tribal), we have the most unparalleled range of musical instruments in the world. They are unique in their range from the most primitive and simple to the most sophisticated and complicated in respect of techniques of making, artistic appearance, techniques of playing, and qualities of sound, in every type: idiophonic, membranophonic, aerophonic and chordophonic; monophonic, pressurephonic, polyphonic and multiphonic.

All this music and all these musical instruments were preserved down the ages by temple traditions, courts, courtesans, great masters and professional castes, musical institutions, and tribal, caste and community traditions. The twentieth century saw a consolidation of all this rich musical wealth due, on the one hand, to the invention of recording devices, and, on the other, to the enthusiasm natural in a modern India in the atmosphere of an independence movement. New generations of musicians and scholars, and government bodies like Films Division, Akashwani and Doordarshan, did a herculean job in studying, recording and popularizing all forms of Indian music. New trends in classical music (eg. the Gharana system, new semi-classical forms, including Marathi Natya Sangeet, etc.), new innovations (eg. the "Vadyavrind" orchestration of Indian melodic music, etc.), and new genres of popular music (e.g. new forms of devotional music, of popular music like the Bhavgeet genre in Marathi music, and film music) added to India's incomparable musical wealth.

This was about music. The same is the case in respect of India's cultural wealth in every other field. The same sources: ancient texts, temple traditions, courts, courtesans, great masters and professional castes, institutions, and tribal, caste and community traditions, have combined to preserve lore and literature, dance forms, arts and crafts, architectural forms, cuisine, games and physical systems, etc. etc. A detailed study will confirm that Indian culture is among the greatest and richest in the world in any and every individual field of culture, and the greatest and richest in the world in the sum total of culture.

18.8. Cultural nationalism: Hindu civilization under siege

Today, this greatest and richest culture in the world, which survived all kinds of challenges in the past, is being slowly and systematically wiped out or turned into a caricature of itself. And, if systematic steps are not taken on a war footing, it will soon be a faint and fading memory of the past. And not only will that be the end of Hindu society as we know it, but it will be a great tragedy for world culture as well.

It is necessary first to identify the forces and factors responsible for this. Tavleen Singh, for example, in her article already referred to, writes: "when I go to the Vishwanath Mandir in Benares and listen to the most powerful, magical *aarati*, I hear from the priests that the knowledge of it will probably die because the temple is now controlled by secular bureaucrats". To begin with, secularism is clearly one of the factors responsible for the gross indifference within Hindu society towards its cultural heritage.

But secularism, in this context, can be of three kinds. One is the goody-goody secularism of Mahatma Gandhi, which was based on an extreme and distorted understanding of certain intrinsic values in Hinduism. However, although it succeeded in blinding Hindu society to the true nature of its enemies by whitewashing them liberally, and thereby weakened Hindu resistance, it was nevertheless based on a deep pride in, and respect for, Hinduism and its culture. Two, the arrogant secularism of Jawaharlal Nehru, based on his westernized upbringing and perspectives, which combined the colonial white man's contempt for Hindus and Hinduism with the colonial white man's grudging admiration for some aspects of Indian culture. And, three, the secularism of leftist intellectuals, based on a rabid and pathological hatred for Hinduism and Hindu civilization. This third kind of secularism has gradually come to acquire a monopoly over the term, and today it dictates the definitions and the contours of what is, and what is not, secular. Many writers, myself included, therefore, generally club extremist secularists of this kind as leftists, whether or not the term would be applicable to them in respect of economic beliefs.

It is this secularism which froths at the mouth at the very idea that the Aryans could be natives of India, or that Indian civilization is basically Hindu civilization and that it contributed greatly to world civilization. It is secularists of this school who explode in anger when hearing that the Ramayana and Mahabharata are national epics to be taught to the younger generations, that the Gupta period was a golden age, that Vande Mataram is a patriotic song, that Savarkar was a great freedom fighter, etc. It is they who are intrinsically committed to defend and support any, simply any, ideas derogatory to, or ideologies or forces inimical to, Hinduism or Hindu civilization. It is this secularism which has acquired a deadly stranglehold over the education system and the media and has already produced several generations of a Hindu society largely ignorant of, indifferent to, and lacking in a sense of pride in, and attachment to, the Hindu roots of its civilization and the greatness of Indian culture. As a result, this society has become very susceptible to forces out to destroy its culture.

The very lethal role played by this peculiarly Indian brand of secularism in the Indian body politic, very like the role played by viruses in the human body or by computer viruses in computers, has to be recognized as a fundamental factor in rendering Hindu society, civilization and culture weak and defenceless against its enemies. But, at the same time, while this secularism is undoubtedly inimical to Hindu society and civilization, it will be misleading to conclude that secularism is also inimical to Indian culture as defined in this section, and to rest satisfied with this conclusion.

On the contrary. Secular governments, from day one, have done a great deal for Indian culture by establishing institutions and awards, and organizing periodic festivals and other activities, to promote different aspects of Indian culture.

A survey of eminent people active in different fields of culture — whether actual participants like dancers, musicians, etc.; or scholars engaged in studying, recording and filming different aspects of culture; or activists fighting to preserve our environment, wildlife, forests, cuisine, dances, musical styles and musical instruments, art forms, handicrafts, architectural styles and monuments, old manuscripts, etc.; or even lay people who appreciate or support all such activities — will show a very fair representation, perhaps even a preponderance, of secularist people. It is, perhaps, just such people that Sita Ram Goel, quoted at the very beginning of this section, had in mind when he talked about Hindus who are legitimately proud of different aspects of Indian culture, but who fail to realize that all this culture "will die if Hindu society which created it is no more there to preserve, protect and perpetuate it".

In some fields, indeed, it is not just vaguely secularist people, but even outright leftists, who are active in the task of preserving aspects of Indian culture, particularly when it comes to aspects of tribal, folk or regional culture. This may be simply because much of their support base comes from the more marginalized, or less westernized, strata of society. Or it may be because they see it as an ideological strategy to promote the "Lesser Traditions" of Indian culture, perceived to be in opposition, or at least intended to be propped up as such, to the "Greater Tradition" of Vedic or Classical Hindu civilization, which is perceived to be promoted by the elite classes, or upper castes, or by Hindutva organizations. Similarly, we find outright leftists engaged in fighting issues of environment, wildlife conservation and deforestation. This, again, may be merely because of the issues of socio-economic ideology involved. But, whatever the reasons, the fact is that they are doing their bit for Indian culture.

We find leftists even in the fields of classical music and dance, and in the arts. That the leftist version of secularism is bitter, rabid and vicious in its hatred of Hinduism and everything connected with it is undeniable. Yet even in the notorious TV serial *Tamas*, which exemplifies these traits so well (in numerous ways, every scene in the serial exudes ugly anti-Hinduism and false leftist propaganda), we find soul-stirring music and songs steeped in authentic traditions of Indian music. This is to be contrasted, for example, with the pedestrian pop varieties of Indian music we find in serials like Ramanand Sagar's *Ramayana*, so dear to the hearts of Hindutva organizations.

Of course, let us not get carried away by the above facts: rabid hatred for Hinduism and Hindu civilization is certainly not a factor likely to foster a love for Indian culture or a desire to preserve, protect and perpetuate it. And, there is no dearth of doyens of secularist practice who throw secular tantrums over even such perfectly innocuous Indian cultural acts such as lighting a lamp or waving an *aarati* to inaugurate a function. Moreover, the leftist concern for tribal or folk cultures, referred to above, does not, for example, prevent most of them from giving their unstinting support to the activities of the greatest enemies of these cultures, the Christian missionaries. Indian leftist secularism is an extremely sick and perverted ideology, which ever takes on newer and more sick and perverted forms, and the rule is that the sickest and most perverted form sets the standard. As rabid and unreasonable hatred knows no limits, it would be premature to presume limits to the depths to which secularism could sink, or to give any certificates to it.

Nevertheless, all said and done, if the greatest and richest culture in the world is in real and active danger of being set on the downward path towards extinction, it would be futile to be satisfied with merely laying the blame at the doors of secularism. In the particular case quoted by Tavleen Singh, for example, if the powerful aarati at the Vishwanath temple is in danger of dying out, it is not so much because the temple is controlled by "secular bureaucrats" — just "corrupt bureaucrats", "indifferent bureaucrats", or even simply "bureaucrats" would suffice.

In fact, with due respect to Tavleen Singh (whose thought-provoking articles have always inspired me with respect, even when I have sharply differed with many of them, since it is obvious that Tavleen Singh is very genuine and true to herself in whatever she writes), it is not secularism which is responsible for the aarati at the Vishwanath temple dying out along with literally millions of other cultural treasures. True, secularism very definitely prepares the ground for it. But the true culprits are the very forces that Tavleen Singh nowadays supports in her articles, this one being part of a series in defence of the BJP government and its economic policies: the forces of American "globalization".

18.9. Destruction by Proselytism

Ancient India classified all worldly priorities or activities into three categories: Dharma, Artha and Kama (a fourth category, Moksha, referred to an other-worldly priority). Kama, enjoyment of pleasures of all kinds (physical, mental, physiological, psychological and social) was the first priority of mankind. Artha, production and acquisition of wealth and possessions of all kinds, was a second priority necessary for the fulfillment of the first. And Dharma, Duty (towards any and every conceivable entity) or Righteousness (not in the sense of a holier-than-thou attitude, as the word is generally used, but in the original sense of doing what is right), was the guiding principle above both. It regulated the production and acquisition of wealth and the enjoyment of pleasures, besides setting the standards for all other actions.

American Imperialism, or "globalization", has its three arms, corresponding to the three priorities (rather like the situation in many mythologies where there is an evil counterpart corresponding to every good entity): Proselytism corresponds to Dharma, Capitalism to Artha, and Consumerism to Kama. It is these three arms of American Imperialism (backed by America's economic and military clout) which are responsible for India's cultural crisis.

Now Dharma, Duty or Righteousness, does not mean religion, which refers to a belief system. In that sense, Hinduism is not a religion, but a veritable parliament of religions or belief systems. We have already described the range and variety of belief systems that are included in the Hindu ethos. There is simply no single belief, ritual or custom, which can be cited as constituting the common factor between all Hindu groups, the absence of which places any group outside the Hindu pale. (Some people try to postulate caste as such a common factor, also because this serves to divide some particular offshoots of Hinduism from the rest. But this fails to explain many things, e.g. whether large sections of Christians in the South who, after decades or even centuries of conversion, still function as Brahmin Christians, Dalit Christians etc., are to be treated as Hindus who have never converted to Christianity, or as Christians.) This raises two questions: how, in the absence of a common factor, do we decide that some particular religion is outside the Hindu pale? And what, in the context of our discussion here, do religious conversions have to do with dharma?

Actually there is a common factor in that all Hindu groups follow religious systems originating in India. The Indian Constitution also recognizes this as the distinguishing point when for purposes of assigning segments of the population to different religion-based Civil Code regimens, it puts outside the operational definition of "Hindu", only those Indians who follow religions originating outside India. (There is a further distinction among the Indians following religions from outside India, not mentioned in the Constitution. These are the ancestral non-Hindus, e.g. Jews and Zoroastrians who were never Hindus but whose ancestors were non-Indians seeking refuge in, or migrating to, India in the past. And there are ex-Hindus, e.g. most Muslims and Christians, who were originally Hindus but whose ancestors were converted to Islam and Christianity in the past.)

And religious conversions have everything to do with Dharma. Whatever the meaning of the word *dharma* in other contexts, it means "religion" when used in phrases like *Hindu dharma* ("Hindu religion") and *dharma parivartan* ("religious conversion"). Moreover, even in the regular sense of Duty or Righteousness, a conversion from any Indian religion to Islam or Christianity represents a change in Dharma. The reason is that in every case it represents a change to the world-view of an intolerant, imperialist religion, and amounts to abandonment of basic concepts of Duty (towards ancestral traditions, religion and culture, etc.).

Conversion to Islam or Christianity inevitably leads to a process of total cultural de-Indianization, which I have described in detail in my book *The Aryan Invasion Theory and Indian Nationalism* (p.29-31). I will only repeat the conclusion here: this cultural de-Indianization "is not only in respect of names, languages and scripts, music, dance, and architectural styles, but even in respect of aesthetic and philosophical concepts, and social manners and styles (from styles of greeting to styles of eating). It must be remembered that ultimately every religion is rooted in the cultural and environmental ethos of its land of origin. If Hinduism uses rice, coconuts, bananas and plantain leaves, arecanuts, tulsi leaves, turmeric, etc. as the materials for its religious rituals, these are all Indian materials... This same rule applies to the entire range of customs and rituals..."

Muslim proselytizing on any significant scale is a thing of the past despite some much-publicized incidents like Meenakshipuram, since Arab money alone, in the absence of other necessary factors, can not bring about mass conversions. And conversions, if any, of stray individuals to Islam are, like the conversion of any stray individual to any belief system, a matter of personal conviction, not to be confused with organized Proselytism. But Christian Proselytism, backed by unlimited media power and finances from America, is going on at a more furious pace than ever. Large-scale conversions are going on all over the country, and not only in new tribal areas like Arunachal Pradesh, till now the only non-Christian tribal bastion in the Northeast (Christians have multiplied there from less than 0.5% in 1961 to nearly 19% in 2001, not including crypto-Christians). The missions are active in vulnerable rural and urban poor areas throughout the country, particularly in Orissa and in the South, and even in Kashmir. The *Indian Express* has carried a detailed news report about the large-scale conversions of Kashmiri Muslim youths to Christianity by American evangelists. It is clear that Christian Proselytism is not just as sinister a threat as ever, but a very much more sinister threat than it ever was before.

Now, most Muslims in India belong to communities that converted centuries ago. The same is the case with Christian communities in certain, particularly coastal, areas. Their culture (de-Indianized or otherwise) is, therefore, in many ways, an intrinsic part of our modern Indian ethos, and these communities are an intrinsic part of Indian society. But the same very definitely cannot be said about the neo-convert Christian communities, springing up all over the country, who deserve absolutely no quarters. Proselytizing in this day and age is totally unacceptable and unforgivable, and deserves to be fought with the same ruthlessness with which it functions: *nothing is unfair in the war against Proselytism.* And it is for the traditional Muslim and Christian communities in India to decide whether they want to reciprocate the Hindu attitude of live and let live, or whether they want to identify themselves with, and support, the Imperialist forces of Proselytism in their offensive against Hinduism.

In this context, the *Indian Express* report (6/4/2003) mentions certain significant facts worth noting. More than 12,000 Muslims have been converted to Christianity recently, and the report tells us: "Though conversions have not encountered any resistance from Muslim organizations, it has led to tensions between Kashmir's native Christians — a miniscule community of 650 — and the enthusiastic evangelists. The native Christians are increasingly getting vocal against the outsiders. 'This type of conversions isn't good for local Christians who have shared a cordial relationship with Muslims here for centuries...', says Pastor Leslie Richards, a native protestant living in Braen, Srinagar...".

This raises certain questions. Kashmir is supposed to be in the throes of Islamic terrorist activities, and yet there is no reaction, from either Muslim organizations or the Islamic terrorists, to the large-scale conversion of Muslims to Christianity. So firstly, what does it say about the Islamic nature of the terrorists, their real target, and the identity of the real bosses who control and finance both the missionaries and the terrorists? Secondly, when will Christian communities and organizations in the rest of the country learn to emulate the reactions and attitude of the native Kashmiri Christians? And thirdly, when will Hindus learn, from the above situation, to appreciate the sinister threat posed by Proselytism in this country, and the need for Hindus to cultivate an image of themselves which will motivate these communities and organizations to do so?

18.10 Destruction by Capitalism

Conversion is one of the main destroyers of native culture: it automatically cuts off sections of Indians from their cultural roots. In the case of Christianity (and Islam), there are specific ideological doctrines which demonize the cultural ethos of the converts' former state, and require that they be systematically abandoned or drastically modified. But all this applies only to the converts, not to Indian society in general. The other two ideological arms of American Imperialism, however, strike at the whole of Indian society.

Ancient India recognized Artha (pursuit of wealth) and Kama (pursuit of pleasures) as two of the three priorities in life, but only when regulated by the third priority: Dharma. The American ideologies of Capitalism and Consumerism, however, represent the unbridled pursuit of wealth and pleasure respectively. Dharma, by any definition, is passé: neither morals, principles or ethics, nor sentiment, respect for ancestral traditions, consideration for contemporary mankind in general, or concern for the heritage of the future, has any value whatsoever. All are "outdated" concepts that can not be allowed to stand as obstacles in the path of the acquisition of wealth or the enjoyment of pleasures.

Capitalism, or the ideology of the unbridled pursuit of wealth, is destroying culture on an unbridled scale, on three fronts: at the level of cultural activity, at the level of actual commercial activity, and at the level of Authority.

At the level of cultural activity, to begin with, countless cultural activities, seen to be non-lucrative or less lucrative, are being abandoned all over the country. Others are being severely compromised in order to keep or make them lucrative: compromise in materials or techniques used, shoddiness in workmanship or performance, short-cut methods, etc. These are resulting in loss of natural spontaneity, cultural authenticity, technological expertise and performance satisfaction, which, in turn, gradually leads to the degeneration and further abandonment of cultural activities. All this is affecting various fields of culture: musical forms and styles, musical instruments, dance forms, architectural styles, art forms, handicrafts, traditional crops, culinary items, etc.

At the level of actual commercial activity — businessmen, industrialists, traders, etc. at all scales and levels — the destruction of culture for profit is more to be expected. On a large scale, forests are exploited and destroyed, rivers are polluted, etc. India's faunal species are driven to extinction by the destruction of their natural habitats as well as by poaching and killing for commercial gain. Beaches are destroyed for sand quarrying and mountain systems for stone quarrying. Architecturally important heritage structures, sites and areas are destroyed for commercial construction, etc.

But it is at the level of Authority (i.e. the elected representatives of the people from local to national level, the bureaucrats from top to bottom, the police, the judiciary, etc.), where major decisions, and action, can be taken both for the preservation and development of culture as well as for the prevention of its destruction, that the evils of capitalism — or Money as God — have taken on the most destructive forms. Today, if big business, industrialists and traders, can lay the country to waste for profit, it is because those in authority, at every single level, have become completely purchasable. For the appropriate price, not only are blatantly destructive illegal activities winked at, but laws are even changed to accommodate these activities. Reserved forest areas are de-reserved, restrictions on construction activities in specific areas (coastal areas, wooded areas, ecologically sensitive areas, urban areas reserved for cultural activities, urban heritage areas, etc.) are officially withdrawn, and so on.

In fact, governments also function as big business, in the name of Development, or in the name of increasing government revenues. They organize big hydro-electric or other projects like the Tehri and Narmada projects at the moment, or the much publicized but fortunately aborted Silent Valley project in Kerala in the past. They even start outright commercial activities like Mayavati's aborted Taj Corridor project, or the Mufti government's amusement park project in Pahalgam. As a result, India's flora, fauna, ecological and environmental ethos, and architectural heritage, continue to be wiped out with (in the words of the *Times of India* report, 10/10/2003, on the amusement park in Pahalgam) "Terminator-like efficiency".

Moreover, those in authority have always been responsible for the protection and preservation of culture: this was the role played by kings and rulers in ancient India, who patronised and encouraged cultural activities of all kinds. Even after the advent of Islam, and all that it entailed in matters of the ruthless destruction of infidel cultures, many Muslim rulers, including most of the Moghuls, did a great deal in preserving and perpetuating many aspects of Indian culture, for which they often incurred the flak of Islamic theologians. In many cases, in fact, they developed such a deep respect and attachment for some aspects, that they even tried to appropriate credit for them. In respect of Indian music, for example, Alain Daniélou (*The Ragas of North Indian Music*, p.5) points out that "Amir Khusrau (AD 1253-1319)... wrote that Indian music was so difficult and so refined that no foreigner could totally master it even after twenty years of practice". The Muslim attachment to Indian music grew to such an extent that it led to the invention of stories about "how the various styles of Northern Indian music were developed by musicians of the Mohammedan period... Under Moslem rule, age-old stories were retold as if they had happened at the court of Akbar... Such transfer of legends is frequent everywhere. We... find ancient musical forms and musical instruments being given Persian-sounding names and starting a new career as the innovations of the Moghul court" (*ibid.*). The sum of it is that many Muslim rulers also contributed in the preservation and perpetuation, and even the enriching, of many aspects of Indian culture.

British rule in India did introduce many negative factors, such as a system of education, which, in the words of A.C. Scott (*The Theatre in Asia*, p.51), led to "the rise of a class of young prigs for whom it became the done thing to denigrate everything Indian in an attempt at blind imitation of the customs and attitudes of western people", whose effects on Indian society have only deepened and multiplied with the passage of time. Yet it also consciously did a great deal in preserving arts and crafts, monuments, old manuscripts, etc., and encouraging scholars engaged in the detailed study and meticulous recording of different aspects of Indian culture. Official British records and the works of western scholars from the colonial period are even today an incredible source of information in diverse fields.

The dawning of independence from British rule in 1947, and the accession to power of "secular" rulers eager to demonstrate their distance from anything "communal" (i.e. Hindu) did not change the picture very greatly. Many of these rulers did have some pride in Indian culture, or at least those aspects of Indian culture which were perceived as not likely to attract the "communal" label. Consequently, they did quite a bit for those aspects of Indian culture, e.g. they established institutions and academies for the study, recording, preservation and popularization of those aspects, they instituted awards to honour eminent people and scholars in different fields, they organized festivals to encourage and popularize those aspects, etc. That many of these facilities became the preserve of leftists, and became hotbeds of politics rather than of cultural activity, is a different matter; but institutions such as Akashwani, Doordarshan and Films Division did a truly wonderful, Herculean job in recording and popularizing India's immeasurable wealth of music, dance, etc.

However, the concept of Money as God has now changed all this. For perhaps the first time in India's long history, there is now no real official support for Indian culture. In the last decade or so, apparently coinciding with the advocacy and adoption of new policies of economic "reforms", it is now passÈ for governments to do anything concrete to protect, preserve, record or perpetuate India's traditional culture, or even to aid and encourage individuals or organizations doing so. Institutions established in the post-Independence era are being literally starved for funds, or funds are being used for any purpose but to achieve the original aims and objectives, or, simply, the very aims and objectives of these institutions are being changed. In any case no new activities, except occasional pedestrian "cultural" projects of a political nature, are being undertaken: the institutions are being slowly transformed from cultural to commercial institutions, in line with the "changing times".

Infinitely worse is what is happening to the detailed records of the research, documentation and collection undertaken by these institutions, in the not so distant past, to preserve, popularize and perpetuate different aspects of Indian culture. These archival records — print, tape, film or actual physical objects — are suddenly becoming an eyesore or an embarrassment, or simply a financial burden, to a cash-conscious leadership with a "reformist" eye on the "globe". A standard sequence now is as follows: state-funded museums, libraries and archives — or at least the records in them — slowly become rare or inaccessible, in different ways, to the (lay or scholarly) public eye. Often "constraints of space" force the authorities to remove these records from their protected environments and dump them in ill-maintained godowns, to rot and decay, unseen and forgotten. And, occasionally, mysterious fires break out in the places which house these archives, destroying invaluable and irreplaceable records (including those pertaining to the golden age of Indian movies), then to be forgotten forever. All these events, coincidentally, make available valuable land and funds for more lucrative commercial purposes. The persons in authority are too busy saving or making money — for themselves, or, if they are to be believed, for the public coffers — to care.

18.11. Destruction by Consumerism

In destroying Indian culture down to its roots, Capitalism, or the ideology of the unbridled pursuit of wealth, would be only half as effective without its sister ideology, Consumerism, or the ideology of the unbridled pursuit of pleasure.

Consumerism is, in a sense, an anti-ideological ideology. The very essence of this ideology is that ideologies, principles, morals, ethics, sentiments, etc. don't matter: pleasure is the only thing that matters. But pleasure can mean many things. The Bhagavad Gita classifies most things into three basic categories: *sattvik*, *rajasik* and *tamasik*. Sattvik pleasure is the pleasure a person gets by doing good things which give pleasure to, or relieve the pain of other people, or which are for the general betterment of the world. Rajasik pleasure is the pleasure a person gets by doing things, good or bad, which give him pleasure or relieve his pain, without reference to its effect on other people or on the world in general. And tamasik pleasure is the pleasure a person gets by doing bad things which give pain to, or destroy the pleasure of, other people, or which are to the general detriment of the world.

Here, at the moment, we are concerned with the effects of the pursuit of pleasure on culture. There appears to be no particular way in which the pursuit of sattvik pleasure can pose a threat to Indian culture. The pursuit of tamasik pleasure can pose a threat to anything and everything. In respect of culture, it takes the form of vandalism, of any kind or description, on monuments, heritage sites, the environment, manuscripts or other records, or deliberate sabotage of cultural activities, or of attempts to protect those cultural activities, purely for the perverted pleasure it gives. This is clearly perverted or criminal activity, and has little to do directly with the ideology of Consumerism.

Consumerism is the unbridled pursuit of rajasik pleasure. The ideology closest to it, in the annals of Indian history, is the philosophy or ideology of Charvaka, the ancient Indian sage, which can be summed up in his principle: *Rinam kritva ghritam pibeta*, "Borrow money and drink ghee". This is somewhat similar in sense to the English saying: "Eat, drink, and be merry, for tomorrow you die." He believed that the main purpose in life should be to maximize pleasure and minimize pain (a view shared by the mainstream philosophies, which considered Kama to be one of the main priorities in life), but without the constraints of Dharma, which were required by the other philosophies. He rejected the idea of any afterlife, heaven and hell, or rebirth, and held that existence began and ended with this one single life on earth. (Of course, it is possible to reject the idea of any kind of afterlife, and yet to believe in the need for some kind of constraints, if for no other reason than for the smooth working of the material world.)

Consumerism is even more of an opium of the people than religion. And it is much more powerful than Charvaka's philosophy could ever have been, since it is being propagated by media, more immensely powerful than anyone could ever possibly have imagined in the past. These can enter right into the homes of people in the most remote corner of the world (shades of George Orwell's *Nineteen Eighty-four*), and dazzle them with visions of pleasures to be enjoyed in the form of sensual entertainment and material possessions of every possible kind. The brainwashing potential of this psychological bombardment is total. Today, increasing numbers of Indians, in their millions, are becoming so increasingly obsessed with the pursuit of — and addicted to the unceasing enjoyment of — forms of sensual entertainment and material possessions which (their minds have been conditioned to believe) provide pleasure, that they are as likely to have the time, energy and inclination to bother about what is going on all around them, as a drug-addict would. Consumerism, in the first instance, is therefore a powerful tool of Capitalism in the destruction of culture: while money can only buy outward allegiance, psychological brainwashing can sap resistance and demotivate opposition more fundamentally and effectively.

But, Consumerism is not merely a neutralizer of resistance and opposition to the Capitalist destruction of culture. As an arm of American Imperialism, Consumerism in its own right is as powerful as, or perhaps even more powerful than, Capitalism, as a destroyer of culture: the forms of entertainment to which Indians, from the most tender and impressionable age, are becoming addicted, and the material possessions which are becoming objects of obsession, are not just characterized by their sensual and material nature or their ability to obsess, they are characterized by the fact that they represent American culture and ideas of culture.

Today, American music and dance; American clothes, styles and fashions; American food and food culture; American lifestyles and work-culture; American ideas of art, humour, morals, etiquette and entertainment; and all things American (or Indian clones of all these aspects of American culture, or Americanized caricatures of aspects of Indian culture), are being marketed, or brainwashed into the brains of Indians, all over India. And this not just among elite sections of urban society, as in the past, but among all classes of people in every remote corner of India, due to the ever-increasing reach of the all-pervasive media. American culture here means western in general, but American in particular; and includes anything and everything, whatever its origin, which is accepted as an approved part of American culture, or becomes the fashion there: whether African musical instruments and styles; Chinese, Mexican or Lebanese cuisine; or Spanish pop songs. Even Indian personalities, ideas or things become respectable when they acquire the stamp of approval of America. As Tavleen Singh puts it in her oft-quoted article: "Young Indians have taken to yoga because it has come back to us from the West and because Madonna swears by it."

18.12. Replacement of cultures

The lethal effects of this brain-washing are evident everywhere. To take the popular and influential field of Indian film music: films in Hindi, as well as in regional languages, at least till the late sixties (though very rarely after that), produced great and immortal music directors, singers, and poets, who did great work in tapping all kinds of musical sources to produce a beautiful and vibrant new genre of Indian music. However, there has literally been a Dr.-Jekyll-to-Mr.-Hyde transformation in this field. Now, not only are poetry and melody a thing of the past, and vulgarity, hype and noise the order of the day, but there is a determined trend of westernization in every respect. Western tunes are lifted or copied almost note for note. Western, and electronic, musical instruments have almost edged out the Indian instruments from the race. Western forms and styles of music, and methods of voice production, dominate the landscape; and natural voices (and even the falsettos which had become the bane of Indian film, and light, music in earlier decades) are being replaced by voices with artificially cultivated, blatantly western accents. And even classic songs from the Golden Age of Indian Film Music are not spared: "remix albums" present versions of old hits, so grossly westernized and vulgarized as to be blasphemous.

And it is not just film music (or similar modern genres of popular music like the bhavgeet genre in Marathi music): today, the westernizing trend is evident everywhere. The literally thousands of varieties of traditional ensembles of musical instruments, all over India, used for accompanying processions and to grace festive occasions, are rapidly becoming a thing of the past, replaced by western or electronic bands. The traditional dandiya-ras programs, with which the whole of Gujarat, and Gujarati-present areas all over India, reverberated during the Navratri festival, are being replaced everywhere by "disco-dandiya" programs; and the Bhangra of the Panjab is giving way to "Bhangra-rap". Vande Mataram is known, not in the solemn Akashwani version, or the stirring version in the old Hindi film Anand Math, but in the ghastly, westernized version composed by A.R. Rahman. And we find similar ghastly westernized versions of many other national or regional patriotic songs, and even of bhajans and devotional songs (especially among elitist classes, and among the followers of the many young, westernized, modern swamis and babas mushrooming everywhere). The list is a long one.

Today, an ever-increasing number of Indian children are becoming more familiar with the latest western, or Indian "remix", hit or "album", than with their own traditional music and dance. A glance into any house, almost anywhere in the country, will very likely show the smallest child avidly watching, and imitating, the gyrations, gestures and expressions of the performers in some "remix number" or the other. The effect is depressing. To narrate a personal experience, my sister is a teacher in an English medium school in South Mumbai managed by a Gujarati trust, and with a predominance of Gujarati students. When she joined the school around eleven years ago, she was fascinated by the way in which even the smallest Gujarati children were capable of performing the most complicated and intricate group dandiya-ras performances, almost like professionals, as a matter of course and at the shortest notice. Rejoining the school again after a gap of a few years recently, she finds a sea change in the present stock of Gujarati students, who seem as unfamiliar with the art as any ordinary group of non-Gujarati students anywhere else.

And it is not just music and dance. An ever-increasing number of children and youth, all over the country, are becoming more familiar with the different aspects of American, or western, culture, than with those of the traditional culture of India, or even of their own particular communities: pizzas, Chinese food, tacos and McDonald's burgers; the latest American slang, the latest western mannerisms and expressions, styles of eating and greeting, and of expressing emotions and sentiments ("yessss" with clenched fist upraised, special "days" of the year for different categories of loved ones, bouquets and cards for every occasion, etc.); the latest western clothing, fashions and styles; the latest Barbie-dolls and western toys; the latest western trends in cars, films, TV serials, cartoons, partying, sports, hobbies, destinations, and anything else; and the latest, or even the traditional, heroes and icons of the western worlds of music, sports, films, fashion, business, history, politics, etc. If some of these aspects are current only among elite classes, they have produced Indian clones which cater to the other classes.

All this progressive westernization (or Americanization) and de-Indianization of greater and greater numbers of Indians, and particularly of the younger generations, is slowly leading to the demise of more and more aspects of India's culture. Several people, including western scholars, have repeatedly expressed their acute distress at the fatal neglect by Indians of their rich culture. For example, Dr. James O'Barnhill, retired Professor of Theatre Arts, Brown University, USA, in an interview to the *Organiser* (5/3/1989), lamented: "I am sad to note that Indians know very little about their folk arts or the artistes... Using this medium (TV) to destroy one's own originality and to spread foreign culture is dangerous... the intellectuals...should recognize the fact that their own culture is dissolving like delta in the sea". (This, it may be noted, was in the days of Doordarshan, when private and foreign TV channels had not yet arrived on the scene.) When he had visited Gujarat some years earlier, he had met a Bhavai folk drama artiste who knew 200 plays. But, this time, the oldest Bhavai artiste knew only 65 plays: "Between two generations, 135 Bhavais were lost! Nobody bothered to record them. They were lost forever." This was in 1989. What must be the fate of the traditional Bhavais today? And what will be their fate in, say, 2020? And it is not just a question of one particular form of traditional folk theatre, it is a question of literally millions of aspects of Indian culture which are being allowed to die out, or being systematically decimated, at a break-neck pace.

The question may be asked: does all this really matter? After all, change is in the nature of things, so why bother about what may be part of a natural process of change? And there are many more important things to achieve, and problems to solve, in this world; so why interfere with what may be part of the process of progress and development?

Well, the facts of the case have been set out, in short but (I hope) comprehensively, in the above pages. To sum up, we have two basic facts: one, Indian culture is the greatest and richest culture in the world, and also the culture which represents the oldest continuous civilization; and, two, this culture is being systematically decimated, or callously allowed to die out. So, the answer to the first question is: *yes, it matters. It matters very much, and it matters almost more than anything else in the world.* On a personal level, of course, it is natural, and perfectly right, for every individual to be more concerned with problems that beset him personally. But, on a larger level, this matters more than anything else.

As to the second point, it is true that change is a part of nature, and this applies to culture as well. No one lives his life, in every way, exactly in the same manner that his grandfather lived before him — and, nor must his grandfather have done so before him. But such natural changes (apart from purely technological changes) take place in the culture of a society over the course of time, during which (apart from desirable changes wrought by internal processes of evolution and refinement) the natural influences of other cultures are assimilated into the native ethos. Culture everywhere has been, and should be, a process of give and take; and even as Indian culture has contributed more to the world than any other culture, it has received a great deal from the world as well. To take just a single example, consider the extremely important position of potatoes and chillies, natives of the American continent, in Indian cuisine. But even in these natural circumstances, a conscious and self-respecting society, with a rich culture of its own, should see to it that this leads to the enrichment, and not to the replacement, abandonment or pollution, of any aspect of its culture. And where, for some reason or the other, some aspect of culture dies out, it should be recorded in detail for future reference and use. The tragedy of Indian culture is that, in spite of the fact that the aspects of its culture, which are being callously allowed to die out, are so rich and beautiful, no efforts are made to record them for posterity.

But, what we are seeing here is not a natural process of change as described above. We are seeing the most powerful forces of Imperialism that the world has ever seen, the forces of American Imperialism, out to transform the world in its own image, and in the process destroying all other cultures with the help of its powerful ideological weapons (Proselytism, Capitalism and Consumerism), and the world is too overwhelmed, by the psychological force of these weapons, to resist, or even to care. There is nothing "natural" about it.

As to the final point, there are indeed many very important (as distinct from more important) things to be achieved, and problems to be solved, in this world. But surely it cannot be anyone's contention that they will be achieved, or solved, by destroying rich cultural traditions, or allowing them to be destroyed? And why should the destruction of rich and beautiful cultural traditions be, in any possible way, a part of the process of progress and development? Or, again, why should cultural westernization, or Americanization, be equated with the process of progress and development?

18.13. A case study in "development"

In the past, much evil, injustice and damage has been done in the name of religion; but even more evil, injustice and damage has been done, and is being done even now on an ever-increasing scale, in the name of progress and development. As a result of many of the half-baked, ill-thought of, or plainly mercenary, things which take place in the name of progress and development, the world not only becomes vastly poorer of large parts of its rich heritage, which is lost forever, but it often has to pay a heavy price for it (the lethal effects of deforestation, industrial pollution and mega-urbanization, for example, are already apparent; and will become so clear in the days to come, that even the most determined opponent of social and environmental concerns will be compelled to note them; by when, of course, it will be too late, since some things become irreversible after a point of time); and the results, even otherwise, are often pathetic, tragic and depressing.

An article by Soutik Biswas, "Modern Cultural Clashes" (*Asiaweek*, 5/3/1999), details the results of a decade of efforts by governmental agencies at "improving the lot" of the Andamanese tribals by way of social and welfare policies and programmes. The government, in the initial days, had followed a more or less "hands-off" policy: regular contacts with the, till then practically isolated, tribes began in 1974, but they were sporadic and primary. After 1990, the contact expeditions became a regular affair: "In one case, Indian politician B.P. Singhal led a parliamentary committee to the tribal heartland, met some people wandering on the trunk road, offered them toffees, suggested giving them raincoats, and asked them to pose for photographs." In 1997, "officials brought a young tribe member to the capital of Port Blair for medical treatment. He spent three months convalescing in the hospital, where he was put up in a separate cabin outfitted with a TV. Doctors and authorities lavished him with attention and gifts, they took him on drives, gave him special food." This boy "carried back the tales of the good life in the city to other tribe members".

The article then describes the results: within one year, from October 1997, more than 2000 tribals had migrated out from their habitats, lured by the fairy tales. And a sordid sequence of events, described in the article, took place over the next one-and-a-half years, as the tribals stepped out from backwardness into the modern age. The article, published already more than five years ago, concludes: "Now it may be too late to ensure the tribe members live in a protected environment. Recently, those who landed in Shantanu village were wearing dirty donated clothes, eating fried snacks and rice, and singing popular Hindi ditties they had learned from watching television. On the trunk road that cuts through their heartland, others were stopping vehicles to ask for food. 'At this rate', says Acharya [head of the Port Blair-based Society for Andaman and Nicobar Ecology], 'they will turn up as beggars and servants and prostitutes.' That would surely be a sorry epitaph for one of the world's proudest hunter-gatherer tribes."

The tragedy described above is so great that no words can even begin to fathom it. It will not be an exaggeration to say that the day on which the last of the Andamanese tribals breathes his last breath will be one of the blackest days in our modern human history, in more ways than one. Indian culture will be very much the poorer, by one of its three native races and by one of its six native language families, apart from the different other aspects, most of them probably unrecorded, of Andamanese culture (although I recall seeing a Films Division documentary, "Man in Search of Man", long ago on Doordarshan, which provided some glimpses of Andamanese culture, including some strains of their music). But, apart from that, it will show how "progress and development" can be as ruthless as "religion". If the natives of the Caribbean were ruthlessly wiped out from the face of this earth, in premodern times, in the fanatical name of religion, the natives of the Andaman islands will have been ruthlessly wiped out from the face of this earth, in modern times, in the mindless name of progress and development. Moreover, it will also show how far the world has progressed since those premodern times. The world, today, is just as blissfully ignorant of, or (even if it were to be brought to their notice) callously indifferent to, the fate of the Andamanese, as it was, then, to the fate of the Caribs and Arawaks.

The tragedy in the Andaman islands is a pointer to what is happening to India's tribal and folk cultures, and even to the tributaries of the mainstream classical cultures of India. Even if the analogy may not be an exact one for many reasons, the sight of millions of Indians abandoning their glorious culture, and striving to become pathetic clones of the west, is not very different, in principle and substance, from the pathetic sight of the Andamanese tribals "wearing dirty donated clothes, eating fried snacks and rice, and singing popular Hindi ditties they had learned from watching television".

18.14. Saving India's culture

If Indian culture faces the same fate as the culture of the Andamanese tribes, it will be a historical tragedy of indescribable proportions. The only thing which can avert this tragedy is Indian society in general waking up to a consciousness of its roots, and deciding that the survival of Indian culture, in all its richness, really matters more than anything else. Even the survival of Indian society as Hindu society, in my opinion, is incidental to the survival of Indian culture in all its richness. *If Hindu society is willing to let it die out, or be polluted or decimated, and prefers to itself survive, howsoever richly and prosperously, as a cultural clone, even a "proudly Hindu" one (whatever that may mean under those circumstances), of whichever society (currently it is western society in general, and American in particular) is dominating the world at the moment, then Hindu society itself deserves to perish "unwept, unhonoured and unsung".*

What India requires is a Nationalist ideology in which the need to protect, preserve and perpetuate Indian culture, in all its richness, is a central point of faith and action. As pointed out in the very beginning of this section, Hindutva without Indian culture as its very basis is a meaningless exercise. As I pointed out even earlier, in the Voice of India volume *Time for Stock-Taking* (1997, pp.227-8), a true Hindutvavadi should feel deep pain and should feel impelled to take strong action, not only when he hears of issues of conventional Hindutva discourse, but also "when he hears that the Andamanese races and languages are becoming extinct; that vast tracts of forests, millions of years old, are being wiped out forever; that ancient and mediaeval Hindu architectural monuments are being vandalized, looted or fatally neglected; that priceless ancient documents are being destroyed or left to rot and decay; that innumerable forms of arts and handicrafts, architectural styles, plant and animal species, musical forms and musical instruments etc. are becoming extinct; that our sacred rivers and environment are being irreversibly polluted and destroyed". (Incidentally, even as I was typing this out, I noticed a truly macabre coincidence: the above volume was published in October 1997; the introduction is dated 16 October 1997. The *Asiaweek* article dd. 5 March 1999, quoted earlier, relates that the very first incident in which the Andamanese tribals started migrating out of their isolated habitats, to their eternal doom, took place on 21 October 1997.)

Hindutva is not a narrow ideology. As I clarified in an interview to the *Free Press Journal*, 5/5/2002: "Indian culture being the greatest and richest is not a narrow or chauvinistic idea; it is a demonstrable fact. It would be chauvinistic if it acquired an imperialist tinge: that other cultures are inferior and Indian culture must dominate over or replace them. In fact, I am opposed to even internal cultural imperialism. The idea that Vedic or Sanskrit culture represents Indian culture and that other cultures within India are its subcultures and must be incorporated into it, is wrong... All other cultures native to this land: the culture of the Andaman islanders, the Nagas, the Mundas, the tribes of Arunachal Pradesh, etc. are all Indian in their own right. They don't have to be — and should not be — Sanskritized to make them Indian."

Vedic and Classical Sanskrit culture, is, of course, the pan-Indian representative face of India's ancient civilization, and that fact is not negated by the equally valid fact that all other native Indian cultures must be given their due. (I will go further here. In my 1993 book, *Aryan Invasion Theory and Indian Nationalism*, p.33, I have, rightly in that context, criticized the secularist media for the "calculated glorification of Urdu, of Lucknowi tehzib, of the Moghuls, of gazals and qawwalis, etc." But the truth is that all this is also a part, and a rich part, of our modern Indian ethos. In fact, it is old classics, which depict this culture, that I most look forward to when old Hindi film classics are shown on TV.)

And it is not only in the negative sense — of not being cultural imperialist — that Hindutva stands out against cultural imperialism. In the above volume (*Time for Stock Taking*, p.227), I put it as follows: "Hinduism is the name for the Indian territorial form of worldwide Sanatanism (call it Paganism in English). The ideology of Hindutva should therefore be a Universal ideology: [it] should spearhead a worldwide revival, rejuvenation and resurgence of spiritualism, and of all the religions and cultures which existed all over the world before the advent of imperialist ideologies". Perhaps a rather ambitious idea, when the going is increasingly getting tougher, by the day, in India itself — but, nevertheless, that must be the ultimate dream of Hindutva.

Finally, Hindutva is not opposed to any other particular culture as such: it is opposed to cultural imperialism which leads to the imposition of one culture to the detriment of others. It is opposed to the destruction and extinction of rich, diverse and beautiful aspects of the rich cultural heritage of mankind. Western, or even American, culture, are not, in themselves, enemies of Hindutva. They have assumed that position today because (religious and cultural) Proselytism, Capitalism and Consumerism are, today, the weapons of American Imperialism; and the havoc and the destruction they are causing, to the cultural heritage of India and the rest of the world, is lethal and irreversible.

The true cultural spirit of Hinduism is encapsulated in the following words of Mahatma Gandhi: "I don't want my house to be walled in on all sides and my windows to be stuffed. I want the cultures of all lands to be blown about my house as freely as possible. But I refuse to be blown off my feet by any." The tragedy today is that the culture of only one land is being allowed to blow about; and it is not a wind, but a whirlwind; and it is being allowed to blow everyone off their feet, never to stand up again. The aim of Hindutva should, therefore, be to see to it that India remains firmly and proudly rooted in its own richly diverse culture, even as the cultures of all lands (including America as much as every other) blow freely about in the true Hindu spirit.

Hindu individuals, thinkers and activists, should: (1) take up the task of identifying the different fields of culture, and (2) set up well-funded and systematically organized apex institutions, one in every single field (e.g. music, dance, cuisine, architecture, wildlife, environment, games, etc.), (3) which will draw up detailed action-plans to gather, classify, record, and document in detail everything concerning that particular field of culture, from every part of India and every possible period, (4) take measures, and conduct campaigns to arouse the conscience, and culture-consciousness, of Indians everywhere, (5) and take steps to see to it that every single aspect of the culture of every single part of India is protected, preserved, popularized and perpetuated as part of a living heritage (and where that is not possible, at least documented and recorded in detail, and kept alive in the national memory), and that, in every field of culture, ample scope is made available for inspiration and further development from within India's diverse sources.

But, while the inspiration and ideology behind the above exercise should be Hindutva, the apex institutions should function not on the basis of vote-bank politics or pedestrian jingoism, but on the basis of a purely objective and academic outlook. For example, in all the activities connected with the field of music, politicians and political considerations of any kind, should be severely kept at arms length, and only musicians, musicologists, passionate music lovers, and considerations of Music as an end in itself, should have the first as well as the final say in every matter.

As pointed out earlier, there are countless committed activists in the fields of ecology and environment, wildlife preservation, folk or tribal culture, music and dance, handicrafts etc., who may be ideologically indifferent, or even hostile, to Hindutva. There are also numerous scholars, Indian and foreign, who do serious academic research, or film-makers who make documentary films, on different aspects of Indian culture (in their personal capacity, or for different organizations, or for Films Division, or even for foreign TV channels like Discovery or National Geographic). There are many people, in their individual capacity, doing wonderful work in diverse fields: e.g. Sunderlal Bahuguna, who initiated the Chipko movement; Avinash Patwardhan, who has invented a flute which plays the 22 shrutis of ancient Indian music (*Indian Express*, 16/5/1999); Pandit Nikhil Ghosh, who has taken up the mammoth project of preparing a complete encyclopaedia of Indian classical music (*Times of India*, 18/12/1990); Dr. Jayant Narlikar, the well-known scientist, who has taken initiatives in encouraging scientific studies on the engineering marvels incorporated in Indian architecture, et al.

Any person, who, in effect, does anything to genuinely protect, preserve or perpetuate any aspect of Indian culture, deserves respect and gratitude for it (at least to the extent called for by the extent of his contribution). And, at least to that extent, that person must be regarded as a benefactor of Hinduism and Indian culture, and therefore also of Hindutva — regardless of his ideological leanings, or his attitude towards aspects of culture other than the one he is interested in, or his attitude towards Hinduism or the Indian ethos as a whole; and even if he is a bitter opponent of Hindutva — more than any avowed supporter of Hindutva whose ideas of Hindutva are restricted to the world of vote-bank politics.

But it is time for genuine Indians, who are proud to call themselves Indian, to take up the task. And it is even more imperative for genuine Hindus, who are proud to call themselves Hindus, to take up the task on a war footing.

18.15. Socio-economic nationalism

It is absolutely necessary that Hindutva must have a socio-economic ideological agenda for the nation. Apart from the obvious point that Hindutva would be only half a nationalist ideology if it has nothing to say on national socio-economic issues, there are three compelling reasons why it is imperative to have a clear-cut Hindu Nationalist socio-economic ideology.

One: today, after the demise of the Soviet Union, the USA is the sole super-power in a "uni-polar" world. We have already, in the previous section, referred to American Imperialism, with its three ideological weapons (Proselytism, Capitalism, and Consumerism) backed by the military and economic clout of the USA, and the destruction being wrought by it all over the world. The destruction described was in the fields of the cultural heritage of India, as of the rest of the world. But, it must be realized that the motive behind this destruction is not cultural vandalism: the destruction is merely an incidental, if inevitable, result of the spread of the ideologies of Christian fundamentalism, Capitalism and Consumerism. And if the USA is propagating these ideologies all over the world, it is not because the thinkers and philosophers in America sat together and concluded that this was the ideal way to spread peace and happiness all over the world, but because the overall effect of the spread of these ideologies is the tightening of the political and economic stranglehold of the USA over the rest of the world. In short, the ultimate motive is Profit: all imperialisms ultimately boil down to Economic Imperialism. In these circumstances, a Nationalist socio-economic ideology is necessary to safeguard India's economic interests from economic imperialism from any quarters, and to realize the dream of a rich, prosperous, peaceful and happy India. And to protect Indian culture, as well.

Two: in the present world, which is getting more and more ruthless and cynical, idealism of any kind is becoming a rare commodity. People usually become concerned with the larger issues that affect the greater good, or future, of humanity (or the nation), or which pertain to matters of high ethics or ideals, in only any one of two circumstances: either when they are personally affected, and stand to gain or lose personally from them (even perhaps have a personal axe to grind in the matter), or when they are genuinely motivated by noble intentions, compelling ideals or passionate dreams, or consumed (to whatever degree) by a passion for Truth and Justice. But, even in the latter case, physical, mental, emotional, financial or social tensions or injustice are factors which can seriously affect the enthusiasm, commitment and outlook of even the most enthusiastic idealist. The erstwhile idealist can become an anarchist; or he can lose all his enthusiasm and idealism and become a cynical "realist", either losing all interest in his former ideals and "outgrowing" idealism as such, or learning to use his erstwhile ideological platform for personal gain. For the sake of idealism — any idealism, not just Hindu nationalist idealism — an equitable and just socio-economic order is imperative. Every Indian must feel free to dream of a better world, and to strive hard for it, with his mind free of oppressive tensions, and his head held high.

Three: the ultimate basis of any ideology must be Truth, and the ultimate aim Justice. And, all issues of Justice can be broadly classified under two heads: Cultural Justice and Socio-Economic Justice. But, the fact is that vested interests, throughout history, have always conspired to place these two categories in mutually antagonistic slots. To put it in simple (even simplistic) terms, the advocates of cultural injustice have always positioned themselves as champions of socio-economic justice, and the advocates of socio-economic injustice have always positioned themselves as champions of cultural justice. The conflict, which should have been between Wrong and Right, has been converted into one between Left and Right. Forces supposedly fighting for the oppressed are motivated more by a pathological and rabid hatred for Hinduism, and forces supposedly fighting for Hindutva are motivated more by deeply entrenched vested interests and rabid antagonism to ideas of socio-economic egalitarianism. There is always an unspoken agreement between the two sides to maintain this state of affairs; and genuine thinkers, idealists and activists have to ultimately fall in line, on this side or that. It is time for Hindutva to break out of this vicious circle, and to start representing Right against Wrong, rather than Right against Left.

In short, it is time to evolve a Hindu Nationalist socio-economic ideology which will try to be a model and inspiration to the rest of the world, and to future generations of the human race; and which will take mankind as a whole further on the path "from untruth to truth, from darkness to light, from death to immortality" and from animalism to divinity. True evolution is to be measured, not in terms of technological and material progress and development, which are taking place at a break-neck and continually accelerating pace, but are only converting humans into a more and more organized, powerful, sophisticated, technologically advanced and materially evolved species of ruthless, selfish, self-centred, cold-blooded and mechanical animal; but in terms of spiritual progress which will make humans more and more humane, considerate, thoughtful and compassionate divine beings.

To put it in a different way: tomorrow, if a race of aliens, infinitely superior in comparison to the most advanced section of earthlings of that time — as proportionately superior, in the sense of technologically advanced, materially rich and militarily powerful, as, say, the present-day Americans are in comparison to the present-day Andamanese people — were to arrive on earth, how would we expect to be treated by them? Would we respect them as genuinely superior and advanced beings only on the strength of their technology, material wealth and power, if it were accompanied by their treatment of us with the same ruthlessness with which man treats other animals, conquering humans treat conquered peoples, masters treat slaves, the pigs on Orwell's "Animal Farm" treated the other animals, Big Brother's System treated the citizens in Orwell's *Nineteen Eighty-Four*, or, indeed, Jehovah of the Old Testament treated mankind in general and the Jews in particular? Or would we respect them if they also proved to be spiritually advanced: infinitely more humane, considerate, thoughtful and compassionate than human beings?

It is not my claim here that I am any authority on Economics or Sociology, or am in any other way qualified to try to provide a blueprint for a Hindu Nationalist Socio-Economic Ideology. In spite of this, I am going to express my strong views on the subject.

To begin with, what should be the model for such an ideology? To be truly Hindu, it may appear axiomatic that it should be in some way derived from some Hindu model. But, the central aim should be to formulate objective norms of Socio-Economic Justice, and not to dig out precedents in Hindu texts or Hindu history. Such precedents, if any, would obviously be most welcome, but they would not be a prerequisite.

In any case, while countless useful points can be picked up from our ancient texts — when even a text like the Bible can provide some gems, the number of useful quotations and hints that could be culled from our Sanskrit treasure-house of texts is beyond count — what do we have by way of general models that could be held up as ideal? There are firstly the models presented by the various Dharma Shastras (the most well known of which is, of course, the Manu Smriti), further illustrated in the myths and legends in the Puranas and the Mahabharata. There is the model visualized in the phrase *Ram Rajya*; and, finally, there is the model described in the Artha Shastra. But how valid are these models? An examination of these models in detail shows that all of them without fail give importance to the supremacy of Laws rather than the supremacy of Objective Justice. And, there is very little egalitarian or just, either in the laws themselves (many of which have obviously been established by deeply entrenched vested interests), or in the principle of the absolute supremacy of Law which lies behind them.

But, at the same time, in spite of all the inegalitarianism and injustice which permeates the laws and the stories which illustrate the application of these laws, there is a thread of basic humanitarianism which runs through the gamut of Indian civilization. It is this that makes India appropriately qualified to show the path to the rest of the world at this crucial juncture in human history — not on the basis of Hindu precedents, but on the basis of this basic humanitarianism developed to its full potential.

A.L. Basham, incidentally, has the following to say about the Indian ethos (*The Wonder that Was India*, pp.8-9): "At most periods of her history India, though a cultural unit, has been torn by internecine war. In statecraft, her rulers were cunning and unscrupulous. Famine, flood and plague visited her from time to time, and killed millions of her people. Inequality of birth was given religious sanction, and the lot of the humble was generally hard. Yet our overall impression is that in no other part of the ancient world were the relations of man and man, and of man and the state, so fair and humane. In no other early civilization were slaves so few in number, and in no other ancient lawbook are their rights so well protected as in the Arthasastra. No other ancient lawgiver proclaimed such noble ideals of fair play in battle as did Manu. In all her history of warfare Hindu India has few tales to tell of cities put to the sword or of the massacre of non-combatantsÖ There was sporadic cruelty and oppression no doubt, but, in comparison with conditions in other early cultures, it was mild. To us the most striking feature of ancient Indian civilization is its humanity."

18.16. Gandhian socio-economic principles

The basic foundation of this Hindu Nationalist Socio-Economic Ideology must be based on the philosophy and principles of Mahatma Gandhi, which best represent this basic humanitarianism developed to its full potential. The basic principles of this Gandhian socio-economic ideology may be summarized as follows:

1. Primacy to the spirit of (humanitarian) Justice over, or even in opposition to, the letter of the (religious/social/traditional/statutory) Law.
2. Swadeshi, or economic nationalism.
3. An administrative system which governs the least, and with the least interference; and which provides public utilities at the least cost to one and all; and which provides full protection, security and aid to every citizen — regardless of race, religion, caste, sex, profession, or any other mark of identity — from fear, terror, injustice,

insecurity, crime and oppression, from hunger and want, and from diseases and natural disasters.

4. *Simple Living*: (a) simple lifestyle; (b) curbs on wastage, extravagance and ostentation in public and personal life; (c) principle of small is beautiful. (d) proximity to nature, and conservation. And *High Thinking*: (a) idealism; (b) open, free and honest society; (c) emphasis on hygiene and cleanliness, and civic-mindedness; (d) sense of duty; (e) dignity of labour; (f) compassion towards, and love for, all living beings.
5. Primacy to the interests of the poorer and more oppressed persons in society, and to the benefit of the greatest number.

Today, every single one of the basic principles, mentioned above, is rejected outright by the intellectual and political powers that be. Or else these principles are followed only in the breach as hypocritical leaders and intellectuals continue to speak in terms of all-round progress and development, and socio-economic justice, even as they advocate and follow socio-economic principles, philosophies and policies blatantly violating those concepts.

(Incidentally, a phrase "Gandhian Socialism" was cooked up by the erstwhile Jana Sangh, when it broke away, in 1980, from the Janata Party formed in 1977, and formed the Bharatiya Janata Party. It evoked plenty of derision even among its supporters, and rightly so. The BJP is, was, and will always be, bitterly antagonistic to any and every form of socialism, and its intrinsic incompatibility with Mahatma Gandhi is an open secret. There is no doubt whatsoever that whatever things the BJP would have done in the name of Gandhian Socialism, would have been neither Gandhian nor socialist, in any sense of the terms. The phrase was clearly just one more cynical vote-catching gimmick, and was abandoned with alacrity when it failed to deliver the goods in 1984. I myself, at the time, was biased against Gandhi, and, consequently, was ill-disposed to examine his philosophy with an open mind. But, a rational and objective approach shows the perennial relevance of Gandhian principles, at least in the formulation of a just and equitable socio-economic system.)

Let us examine, as briefly as possible, the relevance of the above basic principles, or the different ways in which the present set-up and trends are moving in the direction opposite to these basic principles.

18.17. The spirit rather than the letter

The first basic principle, enumerated above, is the primacy of the spirit of Justice over the letter of the Law. This is important because Law has not always been synonymous with Justice in this world. A blind belief in the sanctity of the Law, and in the power of Authority to enforce the Law, has always been fostered by different entities (e.g. by different kings, governments, civilizations, religions, priesthoods, etc.) to establish, and maintain, their stranglehold over their followers or subjects. Every Authority, the Taliban leadership in Afghanistan as much as the democratic government in the USA, believes, or claims, that its system of Law is the best in the world. But the truth is that most laws are formulated, established and enforced by vested interests, and, throughout history, laws have, more often than not, been used more to perpetrate injustice and exploitation than to establish Truth and Justice. Even the seemingly most impartial and objective laws are susceptible to willful technical misinterpretations. The western or "modern" system of Justice, as much as any other, is notorious for its great capacity for manipulation and injustice.

There is an American serial on the Star World channel, *The Practice*, which depicts the gross injustices that take place in the American system, where heinous crimes — murder, serial killings, rape, cannibalism, to name a few — go unpunished because the judges, lawyers and juries conclude that even open-and-shut cases do not merit convictions if there are technical, sometimes incredibly trivial grounds for acquittal. Conversely, even openly innocent people are convicted on equally technical grounds. The serial, incidentally, defends and justifies such a system. Similarly, in India, rules and laws and (especially in modern contexts) "discipline" have always been, at the very least, instruments for the victimization of sincere people, for the benefit of vested interests, and for the legitimization of unjust or wasteful systems and activities.

There is no doubt that a lawless society cannot be an ideal: laws are absolutely necessary for the smooth running of society; but only when they are formulated, and administered, on the principles of Truth and Justice, and guided by logic, common sense, and principles of common humanitarianism. There should be no place for blind and unthinking dogmatism. Gandhi always believed in following the inner voice of conscience over the letter of the law. He led agitations against unjust laws (the Salt Satyagraha is a case in point) and unjust legal systems. In spite of his known conservatism, he strongly rejected accepting even the authority of scripture "if it is in conflict with sober reason or the dictates of the heart... when it supplants reason sanctified by the still, small voice within", if it is "opposed to the fundamental maxims of morality... [or] opposed to trained reason". According to him, "in Hinduism, we have got an admirable footrule to measure every Shastra and every rule of conduct, and that is Truth" (quoted by Arun Shourie in *Hinduism — Essence and Consequences*, ch.11).

The most, if not the only, objective way of judging, from the point of view of the inner voice, whether a law is just or unjust, or on any point of conflict of interests, which side is in the right, is by placing oneself in the place of the affected person, or of both the conflicting sides in turn, even when one of the two sides is one's own self, and applying the principle (often attributed to the Bible, but found in many other places, among them in the sayings of Confucius and in the Mahabharata): "Do unto others as you would have them do unto you." Of course, this principle must be applied honestly and objectively, and it must be clarified with the addition "if you were in their place", else it is perfectly possible for people to justify unjust acts while claiming that they are applying this principle.

This can be illustrated by the well-known fable about the fox and the stork: the fox calls the stork for supper, and serves the food (porridge or soup) in a flat dish, and the fox merrily laps up his food while the stork stays hungry. To pay him back, the stork then calls the fox for supper, and serves the food in a thin, long-necked pitcher, and this time it is the fox who starves while the stork enjoys his meal. In this story, however, the fox could always claim that he was following the above principle: he would have liked to be served in a flat dish, and so he also served the stork in a flat dish, and therefore he did unto the stork as he would have had the stork do unto him! This is obviously dishonest logic: the fox, if he had placed himself in the place of the stork as a stork rather than as a fox, would have realized that the stork would want his food in a thin, long-necked pitcher. The same kind of dishonest logic is demonstrated by missionaries when they strive to convert Hindus, for example, to Christianity. If asked whether they would like to see Christians being converted to Hinduism, they would naturally reply in the negative. But if asked whether they would have liked to see Hindus being converted to Christianity if they themselves had been Hindus, they would reply in the affirmative on the ground that Christianity is the only true religion, and conversion to Christianity is salvation from hell-fire!

It is inevitable that, human nature being what it is, there will always be dishonesty in the application of principles. The point here is that *the spirit of impartial and objective Justice and Truth are more important than the letter of blind Law. And this should be the most fundamental principle of any Hindu Nationalist socio-economic ideology.*

18.18. Swadeshi

The second Gandhian principle is maximum economic self-sufficiency, or *Swadeshi.* This should naturally be the cornerstone of any national socio-economic policy, leftist or rightist. But, today, this basic mantra of our pre-Independence era has been thrown to the dogs. An article by Jay Dubashi, entitled "Into Foreign Hands" (*Times of India*, 17/1/2002), puts it in a nutshell: "For India, independence meant transfer of power from an alien to the local political class... But things are different now. The state is in retreat everywhere, and power is being transferred from the political class to the business class, ... first to the Indian business class and through it, to foreign business led by multinationals. The transfer of power to the foreign business class has been going on for the last ten years. I call this reverse transfer of power. Power, which was wrested from foreigners 50-odd years ago, is passing back into the hands of foreigners once again, with the active collaboration of our new political class... Ten years from now, maybe five, almost everything that is currently in the name of the Indian state will pass into the clutches of the international business class, through their intermediaries in India... Everything that is Indian will cease to be Indian. Indians will serve their new foreign masters as diligently as their fathers and grandfathers served the British... The real story is that India and Indians are being betrayed by this new class just as they were betrayed by another new class fathered by Thomas Babington Macaulay two centuries ago. This time the new class is being fathered by multinationals and their agents, the World Bank, IMF and WTO, the new tribal leaders of Globalization. India is being colonized once again with the help of our new political class and history is repeating itself with a reverse transfer of power, first as national betrayal, and then as a colossal national tragedy in the making."

Dubashi names banks, insurance, steel, power, petroleum, airports, ports and harbours, railways, highways, "and finally defence industries", as some of the major areas which will pass into the hands of foreigners. But the virus has spread even further: the media and education system, retail trade, the fishing industry... foreigners and foreign firms are even sought to be appointed on the Planning Commission, and (as per reports in the *Times of India*, 28/9/2004) islands in Lakshadweep and the Andamans are to be leased to "private and international operators". The country and its people are being sold into economic slavery with a thoroughness and a completeness which would have shamed the proverbial Jaichand, Mir Jafar or Quisling.

The other aspect of this anti-*swadeṣhi* trend is that import duties and restrictions are being increasingly reduced or eliminated, and foreign goods are flooding the market. The general effect of this trend is that Indian industries are having to face a situation not unlike the one they faced during the days of British colonial rule, when goods from the British manufacturers were allowed to flood the markets while the ruling (then British, now "Indian") administration did its best to maim and cripple the local industries to eliminate competition for the imported goods. Indian industries are slowly but surely being wiped out. As Dubashi points out in another article, the common people, and particularly the middle classes, dazzled by the vistas of imported goods flooding the market, and consumed by the consumerist frenzy, see no reason to oppose this new colonization. It is only when the effects of this flood start taking a toll on their own particular jobs and means of livelihood, and render them unable to enjoy the consumerist goodies, that they wake up, at least to their own plight if not to the larger issues involved. But by then it is obviously too late.

The increasing foreign invasion, in the name of "liberalization" and "reforms", is also taking a toll on public utilities and services that are enjoyed by the common man. To take an example, the nationalization of banks in India was an important step in opening up the services of banking to the poorer and common public. Savings were encouraged, and banking came within the reach of the common man. By allowing foreign and private banks full entry into the market, and allowing them to pull off the cream of the deposits and business, fully free of any social obligations, the task of public sector banks has been made doubly unenviable. Today the totally unencumbered foreign and private banks are cornering all the profitable and elite business, making it indispensable for public sector banks to shed their social obligations and become elitist in their own turn, in every way, if they want to stay alive without conking out, even while they continue to be handicapped by crippling political chains which they are never likely to be allowed to shed: political interference, caste-based reservations, etc.

The results: firstly, banking is becoming an increasingly complicated and elitist activity. Even opening a bank account (earlier, all that was required was an introducer and the minimum amount) is becoming more and more complicated and expensive. The number of charges and costs, and red-tape and rules, that a bank is increasingly having to impose on account-holders, is making the holding of a bank account ever more difficult for the common man. Secondly, banks have long since ceased to be a source of employment. And thirdly, poorer and lower-middle-class customers are increasingly being driven into the arms of co-operative banks, and the security of their bank deposits is no more a matter of certainty. This is the case not only with banks, but with all public activities, where the entry of foreign, and elitist private, entities is taking many services out of reach of the common man, closing down employment avenues, and generally making life more and more complicated and insecure for him.

Dubashi, in the above article, writes: "Surprisingly, very few Indians are aware that a transfer of power on this scale is taking place. They think that the economy is only being liberalized, without realizing that it is being globalized too, for the two go together..." However, Dubashi is wrong here. Actually, the economy is only being globalized on a war footing, it is not being liberalized; and the two, liberalization and globalization, do not necessarily go together. It is time, first of all, to stop the blatant misuse of certain words. Just as everything cultural originating in, or accepted by, America is treated as representative of "the times" (and automatically makes other things "outdated"), so also everything economic dictated by America through its puppet world bodies is treated as representative of "liberalization", and every kowtowing to these dictates is treated as representative of economic "reform". But "liberal" means "free", and "reform" means "make better". Is it axiomatic that the things that are happening today, in the name of liberalization and reform, are making society, or the people who constitute that society, economically freer or better off?

What is happening, as already pointed out, is that the economy is being made liberal in India only for foreigners. Foreign business interests, backed by massive resources, unencumbered by political chains and crippling bureaucratic procedures, and with the active collaboration of the political classes, are eating up their local "competition", killing or taking over local industries, and creating more and more unemployment. This is certainly not making Indians economically freer or better off.

Apologists of the system in the media, and there is no dearth of them, often provide examples, such as the recent hue and cry in the USA and the West in general over the issue of out-sourcing of IT jobs to India, to show how this globalization can be made to turn to our advantage if pursued in the right manner. But this, in fact, illustrates the point being made here. The industrialists and big businesses in the West, which are outsourcing jobs to India, are not doing it out of love for India or Indians — they are doing it to improve profits. The losers are the common people among the western population, and the gainers are the more elitist and "upwardly mobile" sections among the Indian population. In essence, it is simply an illustration of the capitalist maxim: "Elites of the world, unite! You have everything to gain." The common people among the western populations, moreover, have less to lose, when the law of the jungle is made universally applicable, than the common people among the Indian population.

Indians fail to realize the dangers of what is taking place because they are hypnotized by the American economic model. But the American economic model is based on the principle of the law of the jungle as expressed in phrases like "the survival of the fittest", "might is right", "the winner takes all", "history is written by the victor", "big fish eats small fish", "it's a rat-race", "someone has to sacrifice", etc. It represents an economic lifestyle which is possible only in a grossly unequal and inequitable world, where an overwhelming proportion of the limited wealth and resources of the world is necessarily enjoyed by a small minority of people, and which, therefore, actually rationalizes, ideologizes and glorifies gross inequality and inequity. The vast majority of the population is kept drugged and brain-washed with the opiums of religion, politics, entertainment, and traditional vices; or kept in check by the power of establishmentarian intimidation, by "the rule of Law", or by plain selfish greed. The ultimate dream of any individual in this controlled and thought-controlling world becomes, not to work for a just and equitable world, but to work to be on "the right side" of the dividing lines of an unjust society and world — to join, gate-crash into, or be co-opted into, the ranks of the privileged few. The "upwardly mobile" sections among the middle classes have few objections to the developing scenarios within India, since, apart from sharing in the general capitalist dream of themselves being part of the privileged few in an unjust and unequal world, "the ultimate aim of this greedy new class is", as Dubashi puts it, "a job in New York or London".

A Swadeshi ideology which places the economic interests of India and the common Indian at the top of its agenda has to be the basic cornerstone of any Hindu Nationalist economic agenda.

18.19. The limited yet dutiful state

For our third principle, consider how the issue of what is truly "liberal" goes deeper. *To be truly liberal or free, the state should allow every citizen to live his life as he wants; and all economic activity (within the country) to take place freely, and wealth to be created without hindrance or bureaucratic controls, red tape and interference.* This should be subject to only the following conditions: that nothing criminal takes place, that there is no injustice done to anyone (i.e. that everyone's rights are protected, and no one's rights are violated, whether of the individual or of the society or nation in general) in the process, and, of course, that the state gets its reasonable share in the wealth that is created, in the form of increased revenues. At the same time, the state should concentrate on providing efficient public utilities and facilities to one and all at the least cost, and to make life as free, smooth, easy and simple as possible.

Today, we are witnessing just the opposite tendency. The economically "reformist" state is actually becoming more and more illiberal and totalitarian, more and more like the Big Brother state in Orwell's "Nineteen Eighty-four", where every single citizen is identified, numbered and classified, and a sharp watch and surveillance, and control, is kept on every action and activity. No individual can start out on any economic activity, even the most simple activity for the basic purpose of earning his livelihood, without the express permission of the state in the form of licences, registrations and permits. And this is followed by a permanent process of meaningless, endless and mandatory paperwork, red tape and procedures, with all the attendant bureaucratic hassles, harassment and corruption, even as the state tightens its vice-like grip over every aspect of his life. At the same time, the state increasingly shrugs off its responsibilities in respect of providing public utilities and facilities to the common citizen, on the ground that "it is not the business of the government to do business".

As already pointed out, one way for totalitarian forces to keep the general populace in a state of submission is to keep them drugged and brain-washed with the opiums of religion, politics, entertainment, and traditional vices. But that is only one half of the strategy. The other half is to keep them in a permanent state of harassment, which will leave them too tired to care about anything except getting back to their opiums. Hence, for example, the emphasis is not on increasing tax collections, but on creating newer and newer taxes (the latest is service tax, an earlier one was TDS, and the next one in line is MODVAT) — with more and more complicated rules, formalities, forms and procedures; complicated calculations to be made; official red tape to be gone through; books, records and files to be maintained; official deadlines to be met, professionals to be paid and officials to be appeased, etc. — and on bringing more and more people into the "tax net". Hence also the emphasis on having everyone acquire a PAN (a permanent Income Tax account number) and file returns, even if they are salary earners whose tax gets deducted at source, or if they are people whose income is so far below the taxable limit as to be negligible.

Apart from the Big Brother angle, the other motive behind making procedures more and more complicated, and the reach of the state more and more intrusive and all-pervading, is to increase the scope for unlimited corruption. Corruption is a worldwide phenomenon, but India is among the nations where blatant corruption has become an accepted part of life. Any position in any government office is a passport to wealth: not just in revenue departments (income tax, sales tax, customs, octroi, excise, land revenue etc.), but in any office connected with any central- or state-government or municipal or village-level administrative activity. In any of these offices, there is a long line of people to be paid before the smallest and most trivial job can be done. And the whole thing is so open as to practically be the official procedure. Positions, postings and transfers in the more lucrative departments and areas are, therefore, purchased and sold for prices which can, in many cases, go as high as crores of rupees.

Needless to say, no criminal activity, however heinous, is out of bounds in a society where corruption is so blatant, and governmental agencies are so all-powerful and purchasable. Far from providing freedom, security and aid to one and all, the administration is itself the biggest source of fear and terror to the common man. A common piece of wisdom is that it is better to climb the steps of a funeral pyre than to climb the steps of a police station, a court or a government office. Nothing strikes terror in the common or middle-class man so much as the sight of a policeman or other law-enforcing official approaching him, or the receipt of an official letter or notice from any government agency. These are recognized as greater extortionists and terrorists than the actual criminal classes who go by those names. (The rare incorruptible or honest person has to either change himself, or learn to keep his eyes and mouth shut; or else be victimized or hounded out.) Apart from that, they are instruments of terror in the hands of equally corrupt and all-powerful politicians, to be used not so much against their political opponents as against the common man, or against anyone else, who rebels against or exposes the system.

Even otherwise, the common man who crosses a railway

track, or who transgresses some minor rule, is more likely to be caught and looted or punished by the guardians of the law, than the gangster or mafia don, the trafficker in drugs or women, the adulterator of food, medicines or other materials, or any other genuine criminal, who, more often than not, would enjoy their protection. In such an atmosphere, in a society where administrative corruption is accepted by one and all as "natural" and inevitable, any kind of crime is not only possible but natural and inevitable. And, today, crime of any and every kind flourishes in every part of the country.

This is hardly surprising when we consider that the rot starts from the very top. When some top leaders in the last BJP-led government were caught on camera accepting bribes, the entire force of the law-enforcing agencies was unleashed on the Tehelka news agency which carried out the exposure; and in the present Congress-led government, out-and-out criminals occupy ministerial posts. The commonest politician is, at the least, a *crorepati* (multimillionaire), though more often than not, he is not even a taxpayer. And the more criminal the leaders and rulers, the more draconian and illiberal the powers they give themselves, and their government agencies, to victimize, loot and terrorize the common man. Writing on one such new finance ministry circular which authorizes income tax officials to confiscate property of anyone suspected of evading taxes, Tavleen Singh ("His right to attach property", *Sunday Express*, 10/10/2004), makes some sharp observations:

"What the finance minister has done is give petty, and usually corrupt, officials the right to march into your home or mine and take it over if according to his assessment, we haven't paid enough taxes... We never before had a Finance Minister who believes he has the fundamental right to trample upon our rights in the name of tax collection. The most they did in the past was 'raid' those they suspected of evading taxes. A barbaric enough practice in a country that fancies itself as civilized, but baby stuff compared to what

Chidambaram now orders his goons to do... The Finance Minister has also decided that tax inspectors will be held responsible if they fail to 'attach' in advance the property of a possible defaulter. Draconian is too mild a word for what the Finance Minister is up to, but we must remember that this is the man who once gave us TADA and the Defamation Bill.

"There are other reasons to fight for our right to property, and they concern the poorest of the poor. Because Indians do not have the right to own property, policemen and municipal officials routinely confiscate and destroy property belonging to pavement hawkers, rickshawallahs and street children. These are people who constitute what our politicians like to call the 'weakest sections' of the society, so let us have no qualms in acknowledging that the Prime Minister's move to introduce reservations for 'weaker sections' in private companies is for political and not compassionate reasons. Had any Prime Minister one ounce of compassion for the 'weaker sections', he would have arrested officials and policemen who steal from pavement hawkers and rickshawallahs...

"Meanwhile, I have a proposition for P. Chidambaram. If he insists on going ahead with the mad idea, then let us begin in Parliament. Let every Member of Parliament's declaration of assets be scrutinized not just by the Finance Ministry's unreliable policemen but us. Let us find out how men who began their career in politics with a few hundred rupees to their name became owners of lakhs and crores worth of assets. I am willing to bet that men who have declared themselves worth only a couple of lakhs will be wearing watches that cost more than that. Let us set up a citizen's tribunal before which the MPs can appear and have their assets publicly scrutinized. Let us ask them the sort of questions tax inspectors ask when they barge into people's homes: How much is that shawl, that pair of shoes, that bangle for? Who paid for these things? Where are the bills? Can you prove they were heirlooms? If not, we hereby attach your property. If our elected representatives are prepared to go through with this kind of exercise and if our ministers and wives also come forward to explain how they acquired their crores' worth of assets, then it would be fair for the Finance Minister to go ahead with the draconian new measures. Otherwise, it is time he woke up to the reality that India is no longer an economic dictatorship, and can never be. All he will achieve through his madcap schemes is to widen the roads of corruption. The only people who must be thrilled by his new measures are the tax inspectors. Does P Chidambaram not understand this?"

(An article in the *Sunday Times*, 17/10/2004, "Is the raid-raj back to hound the taxpayers? The FM has provided corrupt IT officials an opportunity to unleash terror", lists four other new measures by the Finance Minister — an amended section 285BA to the Income Tax act, changes in the TDS reporting techniques, a new section 277A, and changes relating to the Gift Tax, and corollaries — which can promote a reign of terror and corruption.)

It is very clear, Tavleen Singh's expressions of hope or wishful thinking ("India is no longer an economic dictatorship, and can never be") notwithstanding, that P. Chidambaram understands very well what he is doing and what it will entail. In the name of "liberalization" and "reforms", India is steadily marching towards Orwell's *Nineteen Eighty-Four*. While the ones who will suffer the most are definitely the "poorest of the poor" and the "weaker sections of society", every other citizen who desires to work, earn and live in peace will become a victim of perpetual state-sponsored terrorism, especially the independent-minded citizen who has a conscience.

Can a state that promotes perpetual terrorism against its citizens protect those citizens from other terrorists? Not from the "Islamic" or "Pak-sponsored" terrorists, so dear to the discourse of our politicians, but from the terrorists who more directly affect the common man and make his life perpetually miserable. For example, lower-caste people in remote villages from the dominant castes in their areas (cfr. Nalini Singh: "*Aankhon Dekhi* — Booth-capturing viewed from a BSP field office", *Times of India*, 18/4/2004). Or any linguistic, religious, caste, or other minority in any area from the majority in that area. Or women from predator men, children from predator adults, aged people from ruthless youth, and physically or mentally handicapped people from other, "normal" people. Or inmates of prisons, orphanages, old-age homes, mental asylums and boarding schools, workers in factories and offices, or even residents of ordinary homes, localities or villages, from their various tormentors. And can such a state protect the common man from injustice and insecurity, crime and oppression, hunger and want, diseases and natural disasters, ignorance and illiteracy, superstitions and oppressive traditions?

Providing protection, security and aid, to one and all, from all these things, is not a part of any "liberalization" or "reform" agenda or program. But, it should be a very important and basic part of any Hindu Nationalist socio-economic agenda.

18.20. Simple living, high thinking

Simple living and high thinking, our fourth principle, is the key to the successful management of any economy, domestic or national. But, in the consumerist and capitalist atmosphere prevailing in India today, what we actually find is a prevalence of extravagant living and low thinking. The emphasis is on mega-economics, on wastage, extravagance and ostentation in public and personal spending, and on a self-centred way of life in which morals, ethics, and civic sense have no place whatsoever.

The ideal way of life, as propagated through the media and brainwashed into the receptive minds even of mature adults and old people, not to speak of the impressionable children and youth primarily targeted, is the consumerist way of life, characterized by an insatiable greed for material possessions and a "neighbour's envy, owner's pride" philosophy. The enjoyment of pleasures, even the occasional splurge or extravagance, is an absolutely essential part of life — after all, Kama is one of the three priorities in life. But, apart from the fact that, beyond a point, the law of diminishing returns applies even to the enjoyment of pleasures, the fact today is that the very definition of "pleasures", and the things which are supposed to provide those pleasures, is dictated by the media and the capitalist forces controlling the media. The use-and-throw culture of western consumerism, with all the accompanying wholesale depletion of natural resources, wastage and extravagance, and pollution of every aspect of the environment, is becoming prevalent everywhere. *Life, for the average Indian, has become a feverish, competitive, acquisitive, exhibitionistic and expensive activity, and Indian society is beginning to feel all the lethal ill-effects — social, economic and psychological — of consumerist life, too many and too complicated to be detailed here.*

So far as the national economy is concerned, India today combines the worst features of the erstwhile socialist economy with the worst features of the present capitalist-consumerist economy. The central characteristic is financial inefficiency, mismanagement, wastage and corruption on a massive and gigantic scale. To begin with, the very structure of the administration, at every level, central, state, district and local, is unwieldy and uneconomical. A very large proportion of the revenues received by the administration from every source goes in paying the salaries, perks and other expenses of the elected representatives of the people, the bureaucrats, and the employees. Periodic wage revisions — at the central and state government levels, the periodic Pay Commission reports; at the level of local bodies and public sector undertakings, periodic bipartite agreements between the bodies or managements and trade unions; and at the level of the elected representatives, periodic legislations and bills passed by themselves — add to the spiraling costs.

Secondly, inefficient and senseless procedures, and endless red tape, cause incredibly massive wastage of funds. There is the endless paperwork, which seems to serve no purpose except to cause wastage of time, energy, money and space. (Orwell, in *Animal Farm*, parodies this very well: "There was, as Squealer was never tired of explaining, endless work in the supervision and organization of the farm. Much of this work was of a kind that the other animals were too ignorant to understand. For example, Squealer told them that the pigs had to expend enormous labours every day upon mysterious things called 'files', 'reports', 'minutes', and 'memoranda'. These were large sheets of paper which had to be closely covered with writing, and as soon as they were so covered, they were burnt in the furnace. This was of the highest importance for the welfare of the farm, Squealer said".) An entire book could be written only on the subject of bureaucratic paperwork. The endless costs — in salaries for the paperworkers; costs of endless files, paper and printing; expenses of maintaining premises and godowns for the endless papers; postal costs in sending endless correspondence back and forth etc. — are incalculable.

Then there are the expenses incurred in the continuous transfers of staff from one department to another, and one place to another — the costs of travel, the disruptions in smooth working, the costs in transfer of records, etc. — usually on the basis of the whims, vested interests or political agendas of the authorities, or on the basis of trade-union rivalries or dictates. Then there are countless committees and commissions, appointed to study or inquire into various issues, which only end up draining public funds. And there are the endless red tape activities, which result in massive expenses and losses, for which there can be no logical explanation. To give just one example, anyone familiar with the taxation scene in India will be aware of statutory compulsions resulting in people having to pay taxes of nominal sums like one rupee. In the last few months, literally lakhs of tax-payers have either received communications from the Income tax department, asking them to pay tax differences of one rupee, or else have received tax refund orders of one rupee. The costs and expenses (printing, paper, procedural, postal) incurred in each of these one-rupee transactions must be at least between fifty to a hundred rupees!

Thirdly, the political games played by politicians to create or consolidate their vote-banks cause massive wastages, losses or expenditure of public funds. This includes the expenditures on wasteful public functions, including stone-laying and ribbon-cutting functions, road renaming ceremonies, "symposiums" and "conferences" (usually just extravagant jamborees) etc. Endless public expenditures result from complicated political games involving caste-based reservations and facilities. Massive losses are incurred by government bodies in the cause of political gimmicks of various kinds, e.g. the loan *melas* organized in the aftermath of the nationalization of banks, the continuous formation of new districts (or renaming of old districts) or administrative offices, the declaration of free power and water for "farmers" in various states, and so on.

Finally, there is the single biggest factor: corruption in public life. Corruption has become practically a religion in India. The amount of corruption that goes on in India, at every level of the elected representatives of the people, and at every level of bureaucrats and government servants, is mind-boggling. The avenues for corruption are endless. The elected representatives of the people, and bureaucrats, make full use of public funds in their official capacities, to enjoy (along with their families and friends) every possible perquisite, luxury and enjoyment in keeping with their exalted positions. In addition, they govern the inflow and outflow of public funds in many ways. Thousands of crores of rupees are awarded for contracts with the appropriate kickbacks, or are spent every year on public amenities and projects which exist only on paper. Thousands of crores of rupees are allowed to be drained off from the public funds by criminals (the fake stamps case which rocked Maharashtra in the recent past is one prominent example), or are excused, adjusted or written off (e.g. taxes, bank loans, pending power bills, etc.) for the appropriate considerations, etc. Big projects are taken up, and laws, systems, and procedures, are devised, solely to facilitate all these activities. Everything is more or less clear and open and "natural".

This all-round corruption, which has percolated to every level of society, and the stoic acceptance of it, by one and all, as "natural" and inevitable (anyone who fails to conform to the pattern is considered somewhat abnormal), has yet another fall-out. It makes the common man more and more cynical, self-centred, selfish, and indifferent to, or wary of, anything and everything going on around him which does not directly benefit or affect him. There is total civic apathy, particularly, but not exclusively, in urban areas. As a piece by Jug Suraiya, not one of my favourite journalists, puts it (*Times of India*, 3/10/2004): "Our mofussil towns are open cesspits. Despite their glitzy malls and five star hotels, our metros look like a bombed-out no man's land. Rubble, garbage, scavenging dogs and cows, humans spitting, defecating and peeing everywhere — people reduced to biological functions, primal anatomy. Buildings, even new buildings, are in a state of pro-active decrepitude, in terminal decay before they are complete. Roads and pavements forever dug up, like a perpetual grave the city digs for itself. Nothing works — traffic lights, bijli, water, transport, public toilets. There is an air of irremediable squalor, an entrenched inertia, as unremovable as the 'paan thook' that stains every conceivable surface like self-generative stigmata."

Suraiya continues: "We add to this ugliness in our normal responses to each other. When was the last time you smiled at a stranger you passed in the street, or he at you? ... What's to smile about, anyway? Or say 'Thank you', or 'Please'. Only sissies and sycophants do that... We are even more beastly to animals than we are to each other. Visit any zoo and try to figure out who should be behind bars — the animals or the crowds who cruelly torment them? ... We push and shove and dhak and queue-jump... our ugliness has nothing to do with real or imagined poverty. It has to do with a deep-rooted insensitivity to our surroundings, which includes other people." The deafening noise pollution in urban areas, especially during festival seasons, when it goes on into the early hours of the morning, is another feature of this civic apathy.

There is a general atmosphere of cynicism, hypocrisy, corruption, civic apathy, selfishness, ruthlessness, and disdain for any kind of idealism, morals, ethics, decency and sensitivity. *The primary task of any genuine Hindu Nationalist ideology should be to change this picture, and to make Simple Living and High Thinking, in every sense of the terms, the guiding principles of public as well as personal life in India.*

18.21. Right against Wrong

Finally, as emphasized earlier, the primary aim of Hindu Nationalist socio-economic ideology should be to represent Right against Wrong, and not to represent Right against Left. In opposition to Capitalist ideology, and in keeping with Gandhian philosophy, the aim should be to give primacy to the interests of the poorer and more oppressed sections of society, and to the benefit of the greatest number.

In the last few years, in the name of globalization, liberalization and economic "reforms", the economic policies followed in India have moved in the opposite direction: primacy is given, in every respect, to the interests of the richer sections of society, and to the benefit of the privileged few. Under the "reform" regimes, whether of the BJP or the Congress, or even of the erstwhile "third front" which occupied the centre-stage for a few years, the rich are becoming richer and richer, and the poor are becoming poorer and poorer, in leaps and bounds. The economic chasm between the rich and the poor is widening by the day.

The point is not that people should not have the right to earn money and become rich. In fact, any society or nation can truly progress and prosper only when every person has full freedom and incentive to earn as much as he can, without interference or hindrance from the state, so long as he does not indulge in criminal acts, or destructive or anti-national activities, and does not infringe on the legitimate rights of any other person. But, even when all these conditions are fulfilled — i.e. even when we are talking about legitimate earnings, and not about the illegitimate earnings of gangsters, scamsters, corrupt politicians, corrupt bureaucrats, and criminals of every possible kind — there is something ugly, indecent, and unethical about the kind of disparity in earnings that we see around us today. On the one hand, we see high profile personalities like an Amitabh Bachchan or a Sachin Tendulkar earning in crores for an advertising assignment, or an M.F. Hussain earning crores of rupees for a painting. Passing through different levels of earnings — those earning crores of rupees per month, those earning lakhs, those earning ten thousands, and those earning thousands of rupees per month — we come right down to the millions of workers who work themselves down to the bone, many for as long as ten to twelve hours per day, or more, and earn only enough to keep their body and soul together. There are people, even small children, working in such conditions in factories and manufacturing units of all kinds, in fields, or as domestics in houses, all over the country, for as little as a few hundred rupees per month, or less!

While the above situation is undoubtedly unfair, it is

not being suggested here that there should be a French, or Bolshevik kind of Revolution in India where the rich are caught and slaughtered in the streets, or hung from every tree; or at least divested of their personal properties and everyone brought down to one and the same level. But it is at least legitimate to expect that government policies, or policies of the state, should not be formulated for their special benefit, but for the benefit of the poorer sections of society — the poorer the section, the more slanted in their favour, and the richer the section, the less slanted in their favour.

But, in the name of liberalization and "reforms", the policies of the government are only becoming more and more pro-rich and anti-poor by the day. Now, every budget sees duties and taxes being reduced sharply on elitist goods and activities: luxury cars, air conditioners, foreign liquor, luxury consumer goods (posh fridges, TVs, etc.), laptops, high-tech goods, foreign trips and foreign education, air travel, etc., even as items of daily necessity for the poor and the genuine middle classes become costlier by the day, and the common people are told by each successive finance minister that they must be prepared to make sacrifices in the interests of the nation and the national economy. One example of the trend is the continuous fall in the rates of international and long-distance phone calls in the last few years, even as local calls become costlier all the time.

Arguing in defence of the liberalization and "reform" policies, and in giving an illustration of how things are becoming cheaper, the editor of a business journal, in a discussion on the NDTV news channel in the immediate aftermath of the defeat of the BJP in the 2004 Lok Sabha elections, pointed out that, if he wanted to speak to his cousin in London, a call which would earlier have cost him eighty rupees would now cost him only eight rupees. But what he failed to point out was that just five years ago, a local phone call from a public call box, operable with a one-rupee coin, lasted for five minutes. Today, it lasts only for ninety seconds. So, for anyone wanting to speak to his cousin, staying in another part of the same city, for around five minutes, earlier it would have cost him one rupee, and now it would cost him four rupees. And there have been further reductions in the rates of international phone calls since the above discussion. In such matters, it cannot even be claimed that an American model is being followed: in most parts of the USA, local calls are free! This example was about phone calls, but it is illustrative of the "liberalized" official policy today: make elitist goods and services easier and cheaper, and the common man's goods and services more difficult and expensive. Shades of Marie-Antoinette: as for the common people, "if they cannot get water, let them drink coke!"

Likewise, financial policies are formulated solely with elitist industries in mind — namely, the entertainment (films, "music", fashion, cosmetics, cricket, elite journalism and media, etc.) and info-tech industries, as opposed to basic manufacturing and farming. These industries, which even otherwise are the centre of attraction for entrepreneurs and for the elitist and "upwardly mobile" youth, for their glamour value and easy earning potential, are given special tax rebates and concessions, and umpteen other facilities (all originally intended for priority sectors, i.e. for industries or areas in which investment and activity was necessary for the progress of the nation, but in which industrialists or entrepreneurs would not otherwise have been very interested in investing or working). And the politicians in power are always ready to demonstrate their sensitivity to the monetary concerns of the elites in these industries: e.g. the various special tax and duty exemptions given by the finance ministers of the late BJP government to various *crorepati* test cricketers, the special official concerns against video piracy, etc.

The stepmotherly treatment to basic manufacturing industries (which, incidentally, is going to prove very costly for the national economy in the long run), along with the foreign economic invasion already referred to earlier, is leading to the closing down of mills and factories all over the country. In combination with wholesale privatization of more and more public-sector activities and institutions, wholesale computerization, and more and more anti-worker laws and policies (contract labour, hire-and-fire, VRS and CRS schemes, etc.), there is massive loss of job security and jobs for the poor and middle classes. If all this had been accompanied by genuine freedom to work, earn and live according to their talents and capacities, that would have been some compensation, at least to the more enterprising sections among them. But as pointed out earlier, there is genuine freedom only for foreigners, and for the elite sections of society. For the rest, the official step-motherly treatment of street hawkers (perhaps the oldest and most traditional examples of self-employed people in India) and of cottage industries in urban slum areas and in villages all over the country today illustrates how "liberal" the Indian economy is becoming for the common people.

All "developmental" activities are concerned only with the rich sections of society in mind. In Mumbai, for example, the extensive mill lands are being sold, and these erstwhile centres of hectic industrial activity are being converted into posh malls and elitist clubs, hotels, departmental stores and posh residential complexes. In other parts of the city as well, middle and lower class residents are being squeezed out from their traditional areas by the powerful builders-lobby (a mafia in itself, apart from its links with actual underground gangs and with politicians). Massive public funds are spent on building flyovers and constructing parking facilities for car owners, even as public roads become increasingly car-friendly as well as hawker- and pedestrian-unfriendly. In rural areas, massive projects are undertaken, in which poor people are displaced from their traditional homes with little or no compensation.

Is it any wonder that we find, on the one hand, poor workers in urban areas committing suicide after being thrown out of long-held jobs because the big industrial houses employing them find it uneconomical to retain their services (the case of Anant Dalvi and Akhtar Khan, ex-employees of Tata Power Company, in Mumbai in October 2003, for example), and poor farmers in rural areas committing suicide after years of drought and inability to repay their debts? And on the other hand, big industrial houses and the rich and the powerful borrowing crores and crores of rupees from public sector banks, failing to pay them back, declaring their units which borrowed the money as bankrupt or otherwise getting their debts "restructured" or written off, and continuing to enjoy multi-crore rupee lifestyles as if nothing has happened? A detailed investigation by the *Indian Express* (1/12/2002) reveals that such bad debts, owed by practically all the big industrial houses, total Rs.11,00,00,00,00,000/- , which could "pay for all our defence bills for two years, an expressway in every state, a school in every village".

The primary concern of Hindu Nationalist socio-economic ideology should be to evolve an ideal model of economic development: one which benefits all sections of society, but which gives particular importance to the concerns and interests of the poorer, weaker and more vulnerable sections; and which does everything to encourage initiative and activity among all sections, but does not give unfair leeway to the rich and the powerful to loot the public, or to loot public funds.

To sum up: we must evolve a nationalist socio-economic ideology which will try to (1) make India a rich, prosperous, peaceful and happy nation; and (2) see that, basically, for every Indian, regardless of race, religion, caste, sex, profession, or any other mark of identity, India truly becomes a land "where the mind is without fear, and the head is held high". The primary guiding principle should be: *sarve bhavantu sukhinah, sarve santu niramayah, sarve bhadrani pashyantu, ma kashchid duhkha bhag bhavet,* "May all be contented and happy, may all be free of pain and disease, may all ever see auspicious times, may no one be unhappy".

In this respect also, as in the case of Indian culture, it is time for genuine Indians, who are proud to call themselves Indian, to take up the task on a war footing.

18.22. Pseudo-Hindutva

Much of what I have written in the above sections on Cultural Nationalism and Socio-Economic Nationalism may appear to represent naïve and Utopian idealism, and in the air of deep cynicism that prevails everywhere today, it may appear futile. But these are things that had to be written, for the sake of humanity and humanitarianism as much as for the true definition of Hindutva.

Also, they had to be written because I had to get them off my chest. They are ideals which I have believed in since long before I became acquainted with Voice of India (in the latter half of the eighties) or even the RSS (in the latter half of the seventies) or any other Hindutva organization or Hindu-minded individual. I studied in St. Xavier's High School, a prominent Catholic school in south Mumbai, and in most matters I consider it one of the best periods in my life, and I continue to feel a strong nostalgic and sentimental attachment to my school. However, the constant and continuous barrage of subtle and not-so-subtle brainwashing that I faced in my schooldays, and the effect of all this that I observed on other people, produced a spontaneous reaction in my mind which led to a deep Hindu consciousness.

In my college days, I became increasingly aware of the incredible greatness and richness of Indian culture, and it became my life's ambition to produce a detailed Encyclopaedia which would cover every single aspect of Indian culture, and present it in a series of volumes. To this end, most of my college days were spent in various libraries (Mumbai University, British Council, etc.) gathering details on different aspects of Indian culture in the context of world culture. However, before long, I realized that the project I had in mind was too massive and complicated for a single person with extremely limited resources. I therefore decided to concentrate on writing a book that would at least outline a blueprint for such a project.

Meanwhile, the declaration of Emergency by Indira Gandhi, her banning of the RSS, and the subsequent anti-RSS and anti-"communal" propaganda in the media, made me acutely aware of the secular-versus-communal debate in India. The book *Freedom at Midnight* by Collins and Lapierre (1976) motivated me to want to associate myself with the RSS and the Hindu Mahasabha. After the Emergency was lifted in 1977, and the ban on the RSS was subsequently lifted, I searched out the nearest RSS office, and expressed my desire to become a member of the organization. I was invited to attend the local shakha at the August Kranti Maidan. I started attending the morning shakha, and soon became acquainted with many of the members and dignitaries of the RSS in Mumbai. This particular shakha or branch was then also known as the Mumbai Mahanagar Karyalaya branch, and was often attended by visiting RSS dignitaries from outside Mumbai as well.

As I became more and more closely acquainted with the RSS, I also found myself becoming more and more disillusioned. At the same time, the political atmosphere was hotting up, with the usual allegations of "communalism" being bandied around. In this atmosphere, in 1978, I decided to write a book that would set out the whole ideological position as I saw it. The first chapter, "Communalism", would analyze the concepts of communalism and Hindu nationalism in minute detail. The next four chapters would analyze in detail the forces arraigned against Hindu nationalism. And the sixth chapter, "Blueprint", would present a blueprint for Hindu Nationalist ideology. Ultimately, only the first chapter was written out, in a 200-page notebook, still in my possession in a tattered and yellowed state. (Incidentally, this is one of the many reasons why I hold Sita Ram Goel in the very highest esteem. My tendency to set out to write detailed tomes on subjects on which I feel passionately, and then drop the projects halfway, is perhaps indicative of a basic lazy streak in my character, or of an inherent weakness that cannot stand the intense mental strain of putting deeply-felt thoughts in writing. Without the clear vision, the dynamic personality, and the moral presence of Sita Ram Goel behind me, I know that, of my two books, on the *Aryan Invasion Theory* and the *Rigveda*, the first would definitely have been abandoned half-way through, and the second never even conceived.)

The article (which is what the chapter amounts to) written in 1978 is extremely dated, since it obviously has no inkling of events to come, and is written in the rather juvenile style of a 20-year-old. Thus, it illustrates points by giving examples based on personal experiences with classmates in school; exhibits ignorance of basic Sanskrit by construing the word *Hinduriti* in Savarkar's definition of *Hindutva* to be *Hindu-riti* rather than *Hindur-iti*, taking this to mean "Hindu customs", and then extending the meaning to "Hindu culture"; and it contains some rather abusive remarks on Mahatma Gandhi which I would definitely revoke now. *But the basic ideas I held then, even if expressed naively, are the same basic ideas held by me even now, as expressed in the present article*: that Hindu nationalism is a question of cultural justice; that there is a separate question of socio-economic justice which requires equal attention; that there is a conspiracy to perpetuate socio-economic injustice by those claiming to be fighting for cultural justice, and to perpetuate cultural injustice by those claiming to be fighting for socio-economic justice; that conversion to Islam and Christianity leads to cultural de-Indianization, but also that Muslims and Christians as such are as Indian as Hindus; that internal cultural imperialism is also wrong; that Indian culture is the greatest and richest in the world, and that Hindu nationalism should involve the protection and preservation of every aspect of culture from every part of India; that the winds from all the cultures of the world should blow freely about the country; that social evils within Hinduism should be rejected outright; etc., etc.

This is why I have taken the opportunity of this commemorative volume to set out in brief my long-held ideas about the basic ideology of true Hindutva that I had set out to define way back in 1978 — which I feel was also the basic ideology behind Sita Ram Goel's writings, and which I also feel is even more relevant today than it was in 1978 — as a kind of ideological offering to the memory of Sita Ram Goel.

What is relevant to this section of my present article is that already in 1978, I judged the RSS and its political wing, the Jan Sangh, and found them not only severely wanting in every respect, but positively dangerous to Hinduism and true Hindutva. I noted that the Jan Sangh was the only constituent of the then ruling Janata Party that completely abandoned all its ideological trappings without blinking an eyelid. It became Secular with a vengeance. It entered into an alliance with a faction of the Muslim League in Kerala and with small separatist parties in Kashmir, even as its leader Nanaji Deshmukh declared that "communal" parties like the Hindu Mahasabha had no place in a democratic India. Its leaders in the government defended Secularism on every platform and agreed when the Minority Commission was established. They sidelined their own MP Om Prakash Tyagi, a non-RSS Arya Samaji who tried to introduce a Freedom of Religion bill to ban conversions. (To date, such bills have been passed only by the Congress state Governments of Orissa, Madhya Pradesh and Arunachal Pradesh, never by any BJP government.)

More importantly, I noted that the Jan Sangh in reality was "a capitalist, vested-interest-protecting political party", or "a party of big businessmen, industrialists and maharajahs, and other vested interests". In the Jan Sangh as I saw it, "all the forces of capitalism and economic injustice have grouped together claiming to stand for Indian culture, using the support thus gained for fighting [against] economic justice". Even worse, the Jan Sangh functioned almost as "a stooge of America", and the "Jan Sanghis are more prone to lean towards the USA than [towards] India itself".

About the RSS, I noted that it was anything but the "cultural organization" it claimed to be: "The RSS is not really a cultural organization since it does not appear to show itself to be wanting to have anything to do with any cultural aspect of India." The uniform as well as the marching-band music of the RSS were western. Discussions with members and leaders showed that "to the RSS, costumes, wildlife and plant life, music, habits of eating, all are unimportant and inessential" to their definition of Hindutva. Of all the organizations spawned by the RSS, "nowhere is there any organization which has anything to do with any aspect of Indian culture... no organization which has anything to do with Indian music or dance, art or architecture, handicrafts or costumes, wildlife or plant life".

The RSS, in fact, has a basic contempt for aspects of culture such as music and dance, which are contemptuously referred to as "nach-gana" and dismissed as irrelevant in matters of nationalism. I have heard this phrase used on umpteen occasions in this manner, notably, in 1978 whenever I discussed the uniform-and-marching-music issue with RSS members and functionaries; later during the days of Rajiv Gandhi's Festivals of India; still later when the Sena-BJP government in Maharashtra proudly organized a tax-free "Michael Jackson show" in Mumbai; and more recently, in discussing the cultural effects of the foreign media which the BJP government has allowed to flood India and influence her youth. Likewise, costumes: in fact, today, the RSS is actually considering changing its uniform to jeans and T-shirts in order to attract the youth! Cultural Nationalism, as described in this article, is anathema to the RSS.

All the prominent organizations branching out from the RSS — the Jan Sangh, ABVP, BMS, VHP, etc. — are concerned only with "the creation of a mass base... the intention is to create a political base, [which] is in itself the ultimate aim". And "the RSS, far from creating nationalist Indians, actually works as a sort of nationalism neutralizer. It tries to convert nationalist spirit into RSS spirit, and brainwashes its members into believing that 'the RSS is India, and India is the RSS'... the only traditions that a 'swayamsevak' need know in order to be a nationalist are the traditions and culture of the RSS. The only spirit of patriotism that he need imbibe is an absolute, unshakeable faith in the RSS." I concluded that "the RSS is an organization for building up a political base, without any ideals of nationalism behind it whatsoever. The only intention [behind] building this political base seems to be to further the interests of certain vested interests represented by certain groups, and not the promotion of nationalism."

I soon drifted away from the RSS, although I continued to keep up my acquaintance with my RSS friends. In the 1984 Lok Sabha elections, I chose to vote for an independent candidate supported by the Hindu Mahasabha, who clearly had no chance of winning, rather than for the desperately Secularist BJP. Subsequently, I would have remained aloof from the Sangh Parivar and its "Hindutva" political shenanigans, were it not for certain new developments which led me down the slippery path once more: the Gangajal-Bharatmata rathyatra which criss-crossed the country with great fanfare; the seeming metamorphosis of the Shiv Sena from a Marathi regionalist party into a "Hindutva" one; the Assam anti-infiltration agitation supported by the ABVP; the Shah Bano case and subsequent developments; and, finally, the Ayodhya movement which swept away everything in its path. I again started attending the functions and rallies of

"Hindutva" parties and organizations, getting agitated and excited over "Hindutva" issues, poring over articles and news reports pertaining to such issues, and spending time, money and energy in the pursuit of the RSS brand of "Hindutva".

It took me a few years this time to get disillusioned once more, or rather, to open my eyes fully once more to what the so-called "saffron brigade" really represented. But, in the face of the pathological virulence and rabidity of the incessant anti-Hindu rhetoric and activities of the secularist brigade in India, which is the best insurance policy that the "saffron brigade" could ask for to keep its flock in line and to add to their numbers, the whole thing seemed to become a question of having to choose between the devil and the deep sea. As I rather euphemistically put it (in *Time for Stock-Taking*, pp.223-4), "...the Hindu plank on the national level has been totally appropriated by the Sangh Parivar... when the Sangh Parivar starts taking Hindus down the garden path, conscious Hindus are caught in a real trap. Supporting, or going along with, this suicidal course is a travesty of all that they believe in, and opposing it would constitute the dreaded sin of playing into the enemy's hands. Either way, they are, in a sense, stabbing Hinduism and Hindutva in the back."

Sita Ram Goel, when I sent him my above contribution to the volume, expressed his full agreement with this view. It was true, he told me on the phone, that the Sangh Parivar's political games were exactly calculated to put all thinking Hindus in a dharma-sankat (moral quandary), and it was certainly difficult to decide what to do. In the 1998 Lok Sabha elections, in any case, I decided not to vote at all. But, one year of BJP rule, and I knew what I had to do: I voted for the Congress in the 1999 Lok Sabha elections, as definitely the lesser of the two evils. The subsequent five years of BJP rule, from 1999-2004, has proved beyond the shadow of any doubt that the "Hindutva" of the BJP and its front organizations (including the RSS, which was originally its parent but has, since a long time now, become a full-fledged front of the BJP) is nothing but Pseudo-Hindutva, and *this Pseudo-Hindutva is an anti-Hindu force far more dangerous to Hinduism, Indian culture and true Hindutva than the forces of Islam, Christianity and Marxism.*

18.23. Anti-national policies in the name of Hindutva

As I wrote in the preface to the 2003 reprint of my 1993 book *Aryan Invasion Theory and Indian Nationalism*, BJP rule was proving that "more foreign agency, anti-nationalism and injustice are possible in India in the name of Hinduism and Hindutva than in the name of Islam and Christianity or Secularism and Leftism. And more dangerous since it is cloaked in the garb of Nationalism". I was apprehensive Sita Ram Goel would disapprove; but, in a phone conversation soon after, he expressed his full agreement with, and approval of, everything I had written in this preface.

I had originally intended to give a long and detailed inventory of the anti-Hindu, anti-national, anti-democratic and anti-poor acts of omission and commission of the BJP-led government during its six years of misrule at the centre. However, I will not do so here because, like the subject of Indian culture, it is a vast subject, which will require not just a separate book but a separate encyclopaedia devoted to it. The 2003 preface just quoted makes some brief remarks on the subject. I will only point out the general implications here.

It goes without saying that the BJP and the Parivar that it leads by the nose, are fundamentally incapable — not just politically, but intellectually — of comprehending the deeper aspects of conventional Hindutva as represented in the detailed books published by Voice of India. This fundamental incapacity is also analyzed in detail in various books by Sita Ram Goel and Koenraad Elst. Therefore, clearly, no one could have seriously expected them to do anything which would show any consciousness or awareness of the deeper issues involved. But, people certainly did expect them to do something about the more pedestrian, if not always less important, issues of conventional Hindutva which have always been the subject of discourse of the Parivar, its leaders and its publications. At the very least, it was expected that the BJP, as a nationalist or patriotic party, would at least represent, and try to protect, the best interests of India as a nation.

On the contrary, the BJP, in these six years, consciously, and with missionary zeal, set out to outdo all the previous secular governments in acts of what it had always termed "pseudo-secularism". The 1997 (i.e. before the BJP came to power at the centre), Voice of India publication *Time for Stock-Taking* contains a section entitled "Some Revealing Press Reports", which exposed the BJP's tendencies in this regard, but this was merely the bare tip of the iceberg. *In its six years of rule, the BJP succeeded beyond the shadow of any doubt, and in every single respect (M.M. Joshi's minor "saffronization" antics notwithstanding), in beating all the previous secular governments hollow in "appeasement of minorities" and "discrimination against Hindus".* As I said earlier, I will not bother to give a single example here because the subject requires an encyclopaedia to itself, especially if it is also going to cover the BJP's record in this respect in all its previous avatars: in the Jan Sangh days, the Janata Party days, the pre-Ayodhya BJP days, the pre-demolition Ayodhya days, and the post-demolition-pre-power days.

The result is a deep disenchantment, disillusionment, cynicism, and sense of betrayal, in the minds of all genuine, thinking Hindus. Today, with the return of the original secularists to power, we again see issues cropping up which could re-ignite a brief flicker in the Hindu psyche. Already we have the issue of 5% reservations for Muslims proposed by the new Protestant Chief Minister of Andhra Pradesh, besides the venomous secularist antics of Arjun Singh and Mani Shankar Aiyar, among others. But only a brief flicker, because, one, the BJP has succeeded completely in converting Hindutva issues into a sick joke, and two, there is little doubt (none whatsoever in my own mind) that if the BJP, God forbid, had won the recent Lok Sabha elections, they would have introduced these reservations themselves on an all-India level. The BJP has very conclusively proved that whatever the secularists can do, they can do better.

The first dimension of the case is that even if the BJP in power had been half as "pseudo-secular" as the earlier secularists, it would have been twice as bad, since the BJP had wormed its way into power (rising from 2 Lok Sabha seats in 1984) on Hindutva issues. And in actual fact, the BJP in power was at least twice as "pseudo-secular" as the secularists.

The second dimension is that its "pseudo-secularism" is infinitely more dangerous than that of the Secularists in another sense: even minor "pseudo-secular" acts of the secularists produced sharp reactions from the Sangh Parivar organizations and other thinking Hindus. But even major "pseudo-secular" acts of the BJP government met with stony silence. Worse, not just silence, but the opposite: *all the "Hindutva" energies of the Sangh Parivar organizations and publications were channeled into the task of, by turn, downplaying, defending, justifying, and finally zealously promoting, the "pseudo-secular" acts and the rationale behind these acts.*

It would seem that such a situation would have its drawbacks, in the sense that it would place serious doubts on the integrity and credibility of these organizations. But the Sangh Parivar organizations have two master-techniques at hand, which are expected to calm down or rein in any disgruntlement among the ranks of their cadres and supporters, and preserve their reputation. The first technique is for its leaders to periodically abuse the BJP leadership in public, whenever its particular acts go too blatantly against the particular ideological aspects supposedly represented by the particular organization (the RSS-VHP, Bharatiya Mazdoor Sangh, Swadeshi Jagaran Manch, or whatever, as the case may be). Occasionally they even go so far as to accuse them of being worse than the secularists. Meanwhile, in private, they resort to their favourite justification: Strategy. Or they downplay the relevance of the "pseudo-secular" acts as something to be expected from politicians, with the sage advice: "We should not depend on them." But, when push comes to shove — in short, when it's Election Time — the leaders swiftly tone down their voices, and get down to the task of mobilizing the cadres and supporters to work for the BJP on the basis of the TINA (There Is No Alternative) argument. The second technique is: if the BJP loses *despite* their best efforts, to loudly proclaim, or spread the word, that the BJP lost *because* they worked against it, or failed to work for it. The BJP defeat is, therefore, not a defeat for these organizations; and they are free to continue the pursuit of their activities, aimed at the sole objective of slowly leading their cadres and supporters back to the Only Alternative.

Leave alone "pseudo-secularism", the record of the BJP in power has been more dangerous even in respect of plain and simple nationalism or patriotism. The BJP is not only not Hindu Nationalist, it is not even plain Nationalist or Patriotic. To put it plainly, the BJP represents the USA, or at least the International Capitalist class with its base in the USA, more than it represents India. If it was said of the CPI that its leaders "open out their umbrellas in Delhi when it rains in Moscow", it could be said of the BJP that its leaders "pull out their snow-shovels in Mumbai when it snows in New York". Jay Dubashi, in his article dd. 17/1/2002, quoted earlier, where he describes how the Indian political class is selling off the country to the foreign business class, notes that "all this is happening under the auspices of an administration whose leaders swore by swadeshi until recently, that is, before they came to power". In my 2003 preface already referred to, I wrote: "today (at this time of writing), India is in the control of a regime which is umbilically affiliated to a foreign country: the USA. All its socio-economic policies are devised solely for the benefit of that country, and all its political policies are harmonized with those of that country, as surely the colonialist policies of the British East India Company were devised for the benefit of Great Britain and to the detriment of India and Indians."

It is not just in respect of the economy (although the economy does control almost everything else); it has been an all-round sell-out to the USA. Consider some specific examples. India's official reaction to the September 11 event included minutes of silence in Parliament, the PM's presence at the ceremony in New York, and fervent official statements of sympathy and support to the US. But remember that that country was the real patron of the Punjab-JK terrorists and of separatist movements in the Northeast, not to mention the missionary network all over India. And that a US company was responsible for the Bhopal tragedy which caused the death of tens of thousands of Indians but did not evoke even a cursory reaction from the US. India started a "military cooperation" with the US which, according to newspaper reports, enabled the US army to acquire certain specialized techniques of desert and mountain combat, and certain other information zealously guarded by earlier governments. India's plans to send troops to Iraq were prevented only by apprehensions about the fall-out on the approaching Lok Sabha elections.

The sudden newfound love for Peace with Pakistan burst out suddenly on a certain day in 2003 when the US, as reported on the front page of the *Times of India*, in the name of its "war against terror", issued an ultimatum to both India and Pakistan to immediately mend their fences, or else... The Peace fever that instantly had the Indian government in its throes percolated down to every level, and the effect was ludicrous. A TV serial on the Star Plus channel, *Sara Akash*, transformed overnight a story-line of Pak-sponsored terrorism into a story-line of India and Pakistan as brotherly comrades-in-arms against stateless terrorists. (After the Lok Sabha elections, the serial reverted to its original story line.) The glee on the faces of India's cabinet ministers every time the Indian government received a pat on the back from some minor US functionary spoke volumes. All this contrasts sharply with the actions of Indira Gandhi who defied the USA to do its worst when it sent its Seventh Fleet to the Indian Ocean to intimidate India at the height of the 1971 Indo-Pak war.

In short, BJP rule has proved to be neither Hindu-nationalistic, nor even plain nationalistic or patriotic. The most dangerous part of the whole thing is that, since this anti-Hindu and anti-nationalist regime functioned in the name of Nationalism (and, in whispers, Hindu Nationalism), Hindutva stands indicted for its crimes, and its sins of omission and commission. BJP rule did everything to blacken the name of Hindutva: under the BJP, casteist politics, corruption, bureaucratic interference, vindictive politics (e.g. Tehelka), politics of personality and sycophancy, and anti-poor and anti-middle class activities (many detailed in the previous section on socio-economic nationalism), reached new heights and unmatched proportions. Moreover — and this is where I break ranks with most other Hindu-minded writers — we had Gujarat.

In my 1993 book, I had written that the leftist and secularist response to every "riot started by Muslims is the same: huge amounts of money are paid to the Muslim 'victims' of the riots; action is demanded, and often taken, against police officials for 'atrocities against Muslims'; conferences are held and reports published in which 'Hindu Communalists' are held ultimately responsible for the riots", etc. For the first time I realized that, in Gujarat, the pseudo-Hindutva forces had gone out of their way to try to prove the enemies of Hindutva right for once.

The Gujarat riots did not represent a "heroic defence of Hindu Society", as I would classify the equally widely condemned, but much less defended, activities of Dara Singh in Orissa. In my opinion, Dara Singh was a true Hindutva hero who fought against extremely powerful and dangerous forces in defence of Hindu society. Or even, to some extent, the Mumbai riots of 1992-1993, where nearly a week of one-sided riots by Muslims, in a charged atmosphere, led to a violent Hindu reaction, as I have shown in an article based on *Times of India* news reports. So what I am writing here about Gujarat is not out of any sudden conversion to Secularism. Nor were the Gujarat riots communal clashes between lumpen elements in two castes or communities (such as often occur in different parts of the country, particularly in states like UP and Bihar), where, if the two communities happen to be of different religions, discussions on the clashes take on Secularist overtones.

These riots were part of an out-and-out political strategy, worked out by a cynical and ideology-less political formation, *ever-willing, at one and the same time, to indulge in competitive appeasement policies and to target a community for electoral gain*, to capture power in Gujarat. I had privately predicted, months before — not on the basis of insider information, or of astrology, but on the basis of simple logic — that the BJP, which had been losing election after election (municipal corporations and councils, zilla parishads, panchayats) in Gujarat in the last few years, would win the assembly elections on the basis of riots. And, after the events, we had "Hindutva" leaders gleefully announcing that Gujarat could be replicated all over the country.

18.24. Where to go from pseudo-Hindutva?

Now why was it necessary for me to write all this in a Voice of India book? The answer is: it is precisely in a Voice of India book that we must distinguish between true Hindutva and the cynical world of pseudo-Hindutva politics, since Pseudo-Hindutva represents the greatest danger to true Hindutva. In the 2003 preface to the reprint of my 1993 book, I referred to the fact that the BJP, after all its "anti-poor, anti-middle class, pro-rich, pro-NRI and pro-American policies" could still bring the Hindu masses to heel at the time of every elections "by a variety of familiar and no-less-effective-because-repeated tactics: by visions of bogeys in neighbouring countries, by the timely actions (Kargil, Godhra, and many more to come) of helpful 'enemies', by Issues (temples, riots, etc.) which appear at the time of elections with as unfailing a regularity as they die out immediately afterwards... all perfectly orchestrated by the Family with a Hundred Tongues — in the name of Hinduism and Hindutva".

I even expressed distress at the fact that "the Gujarat events can take place without causing Muslims anywhere else in India (or abroad) to raise a whimper: Muslim BJP ministers (voted to power by largely Muslim electorates) continue to support and even aggressively defend everything; Muslim Mullahs and clerics continue to join the BJP in large numbers and participate in their Iftar parties and other programmes; Muslim MPs, MLAs, etc. (even those, as in UP, elected from parties which wooed the Muslim voters on 'pseudo-secularist' and anti-BJP lines) continue to prop up BJP governments without batting an eyelid; and common Muslims go about their (as for all Indians under this regime) increasingly insecure lives as though nothing has happened."

I half-suspected that Sita Ram Goel would object to all this. But I trusted his judgement. And I was right: when I contacted him on the phone after sending this preface, he told me that I was right in everything I had written, and that he would print everything without changing a word. He also told me not to bother about people who chose to misunderstand me.

It was clear that the BJP would have employed the same techniques to win the 2004 Lok Sabha elections. How far they would have succeeded, we will never know, since the Gods intervened to save India — not only from riots, but from another 5-year term of BJP rule which would have completely annihilated Hinduism, Hindutva and Indian culture once and for all. The BJP was hypnotized by its own hype and propaganda, by the massive upsurge in its support among elitist groups (NRIs; the rich classes and the upwardly mobile consumerist "middle classes"; big business and stock exchange circles; the film, cricket and fashion worlds; the English-language media, etc.), and by its open endorsement by America and the West. It suddenly decided that "Atalji's" image, its record of "economic reforms", and a sudden newfound "popularity" among Muslims (as represented by President Musharraf, Hurriyat leaders, the Shahi Imam and countless other mercenary Mullahs and Maulanas, "progressive" Muslim leaders like Arif Mohammad Khan and Najma Heptullah, and a host of Urdu poets and academics — a full hand, so to say) would sweep it back to power. The "Hindutva" front organizations were asked to lie low, which they dutifully did. And India was saved. For now.

The recent Vidhan Sabha elections in Maharashtra, in October 2004, provided an even more telling instance of Pseudo-Hindutva. Three months before the elections, the VHP launched a *"Chalo Pratapgad"* agitation, to demolish the Afzal Khan tomb in Satara district (which, incidentally, was the subject of a very intelligent article by Bhai Mahavir in the *Organiser* long ago). The agitation was very obviously aimed at the elections; but the BJP was in two minds, and ultimately decided against direct involvement in the agitation, which, in any case, turned out to be a damp squib. After the elections, which the BJP lost, VHP vice-president Acharya Giriraj Kishore, in a statement, declared: "Emotive issues are more important in elections unlike those of governance and development, which do not fetch votes... the parties have paid for giving up Hindutva issues", and cited the Afzal Khan tomb issue as one of the two Hindutva issues meant by him (*Sunday Express*, 17/10/2004). Could anything be more blatant?

(And what was this "Hindutva issue"? The *Sunday Express* (12/9/2004) explained that the tomb was "ordered to be built by Shivaji himself" as a gesture of courtesy, and was regarded by "most local saffron groups, closely associated with the history of the fortified Pratapgad... as an enduring symbol of Shivaji's courage, a symbol of his victory over a Moghul general". Further, the *Express* reports: "Collector Subhrao Patil says: 'They said, don't glorify the tomb. We have removed all decoration and chandeliers from the site. The annual fair in December every year has been banned. Even the board of the tomb from a respectful Hazrat Mohammed Afzal Khan has become Afzal Khan tomb, Maharashtra government. Where is the issue now?' The government has even passed orders against people visiting the tomb site. For the last three years, nobody has even been allowed within its 200-metre compound." The *Sunday Times*, also of 12/9/2004, adds that the Shiv Sena did not agree to the idea of an agitation as "the district administration had accepted the Sena's demand that additional construction should not be allowed at the memorial, the area should be taken over by the government, and that a museum highlighting Shivaji's military skills be established". So what was the "Hindutva issue", beyond trying to help the BJP to capture power?)

After its election defeat of 2004, the BJP has been in a state of shell shock. It does not know whether to fall back on its particular brand of "Hindutva", or to march forward on the Secularist path. There are strong arguments being made in both directions by different sections of their "well-wishers" (who are, in any case, not well-wishers of Hindutva). But the Secularists will do their best to give pseudo-Hindutva another lease of life, again and yet again. And India will continue to be tossed around like a ball between the forces of Secularism and pseudo-Hindutva.

We must acquire a proper perspective. On the one hand, we have the ideology and philosophy of true Hindutva. On the other hand, we have a Parivar that has completely usurped and monopolized the term Hindutva, but which in fact functions as an ideological black hole sucking in and annihilating all Hindutva matter and material. (In Stephen Hawking's latest definition of black holes, the matter is not annihilated; it comes out again in a mangled form.) Are the two compatible with each other? The Sangh Parivar does not function like a Hindutva organization; it functions like a Secularist organization that also has minority-bashing as an option of last resort. Is minority-bashing Hindutva?

I have always compared the Sangh Parivar to George Orwell's *Animal Farm*. Every single Hindu must read this classic in minute detail to the last word, and then ask himself a serious question. The first chapter of the book details the philosophy or ideology of Animalism in detail. In the second chapter, the Pigs take over the Manor Farm from its owner, Mr. Jones, in the name of Animalism. At the end of the book, who proves to have been the greater enemy of the (other) animals and of Animalism: Mr. Jones or the Pigs?

In his classic *How I Became a Hindu*, Sita Ram Goel relates his experiences with the Sangh Parivar. At the very end of the book, he writes: "I am reminded of a Chinese story. A landlord was in the habit of strangling his wives. Every time he strangled a wife, another woman came forward to marry him. When people told the new ones the number of women he had already strangled, every one of them replied, 'Oh! They didn't understand the old dear.' And everyone of them got strangled in her own turn."

Sita Ram Goel was referring to party after party trying to woo Muslims. But the example, particularly in view of all that he relates before, is more appropriate in respect of generation after generation, and group after group, of Hindus who get enamoured of Sangh politics, in spite of its history of repeated betrayals.

So the question now is: can we do without the Sangh Parivar if we want to bring Hindutva ideology to fruition? The answer is: the question of doing with or without the Sangh Parivar just simply does not arise. The ideal before us is that of Sita Ram Goel, who single-handedly built up a whole new vista of Hindutva literature without parallel in the whole history of Hindutva thought. In spite of his very bitter experiences with the Sangh Parivar, he never bore any ill-will or rancour, and maintained very friendly relations with the members of the Parivar. But he never wasted any time in dealing with the Sangh Parivar nor fell into their political trap. As he explained to me, in his letter of 9/10/1991: "I do not care whether the RSS succeeds or fails. Both eventualities are meaningless for me."

If a single word will describe Sita Ram Goel, it is the word *karmayogi*, very aptly used by Virendra Parekh in his contribution to this volume. *Today, India needs true karmayogis like Sita Ram Goel in every field of Indian culture and every socio-economic field. Karmayogis who will do for India, each in his particular field, what Sita Ram Goel has done for Hindutva as a whole.* And who will steer clear of the world of dirty politics even as their work lights up the future of the nation as no political formation can ever dream of doing.

(Shrikant Talageri is Bachelor of Commerce from Mumbai University, employed as a computer operator in the Central Bank of India, Mumbai. He has devoted his spare time to studies of music, linguistics and mathematics, and is the author of a monograph on the Konkani language and two books on the Aryan invasion debate.)

Index